Road Trip to Hell

Road Trip to Hell

Tabloid Tales of Saddam, Iraq and a Bloody War

Chris Hughes

MONDAY BOOKS

© Chris Hughes 2006
First published in Great Britain in 2006 by Monday Books

A CIP catalogue record for this title is available from the British Library

ISBN 0-9552854-2-9
(2007 ISBN: 978-0-9552854-2-4)

Typeset by Avon DataSet Ltd, Bidford on Avon, Warwickshire

Printed and bound by Cox and Wyman, Reading, Berkshire

www.mondaybooks.com
info@mondaybooks.com

To my late mum, and my dad

Contents

Acknowledgments, etc

I'd like to thank a few people.

Adil and Nibras: two of the bravest and best men I've ever met.

My colleagues at the *Daily Mirror*, who have all – from Richard Wallace and Conor Hanna down – encouraged me to write this book.

The staff of the *Mirror* newsdesk – I don't always paint them in the best light in this book, but they're a great bunch.

Louise Flood, our newsdesk secretary, without whose patience, good humour and calm organisation the place would grind to a halt.

The picture desk, for allowing us to use their photographs.

All of the photographers who were with me on my various trips to Iraq – Julian Andrews, particularly, John Ferguson, Ian Vogler, James Vellacott and Chris Grieve. They were all good company, and all great at what they do. They experienced most of the events that I discuss in these pages, so, in a sense, it's their book too.

The American and British troops and security personnel under whose protection I sometimes lived in Iraq, and the MoD staff who facilitated some of my trips.

My sister, Emma, for her support; Bruce McKenna, James McMillan, Stuart Halford and Jeff Pickett. And, finally, Dan Collins, who persuaded me I had a story worth telling and that, with a little help in the editing process, I could tell it in a reasonably interesting way. Let's hope he was right!

The 'etc' bit is this: There's some swearing in this book and also some horrific photographs. It's impossible to convey life as a tabloid journalist without using some of the bad language that is commonplace for us. Similarly, it's impossible – and, I think, wrong – to try to convey life in Iraq without using shocking images. The Iraqis see this stuff every day. I think we should see it, too.

One last thing: any opinions expressed in this book are mine and no-one else's.

Foreword

I wanted to call this book 'Clueless in Gaza', but – though he must be tempted – George W Bush rarely invades places with potential for witty literary allusion.

I suppose 'Between Iraq and a Hard Place' might have fit the bill too, but then Iraq *is* a hard place and, anyway, someone else must have used that title by now.

So 'Road Trip To Hell' it is.

There's a bit of truth in all three titles.

Like most Westerners who go to Iraq, I *was* clueless at first. I'm still no expert; no matter how often I return, and I've been a dozen and more times by now, I can never seem to get very far beneath the surface of this amazing country, with its bizarre combination of medieval clans, modern weapons and religious fundamentalism. Maybe that's no surprise. I started out in journalism as a showbiz hack, writing about people like Phil Collins, Wham! and Paula Abdul (whoever she was). I switched to the *Daily Mirror*'s news operation some years ago, but I don't have a deep knowledge of Middle Eastern politics, or a degree in Arabic, or a Doctorate in International Relations. How can I hope to understand these people and their culture and history on anything more than a fairly superficial level?

Then again, our leaders and their advisors *do* have those degrees and doctorates, and years and years of experience in the region, and they're no wiser than me. If they were, we wouldn't have got into this war in the first place because, in retrospect, what's happened in Iraq was all too predictable.

A lot of foreign correspondents, especially those on the broadsheets – people like Steve Farrell of *The Times*, Oliver Poole of

The Daily Telegraph, Kim Sengupta from *The Independent* – spend almost all of their time in Baghdad. They're tremendously professional, these guys, all of them living outside the safety of Green Zone, unprotected and terribly vulnerable. They know their patch inside out. I don't have their depth of knowledge about the city, or anywhere else.

But though I don't have depth, I do have breadth: I've been all over Iraq in the last few years, on a road trip through the country as it has slid into horrible, bloody turmoil – hell, in parts, by any definition.

I was one of the first Western journalists into the country after 9/11. I was the only Western journalist there when the US Marines fired indiscriminately into a crowd of demonstrators, leaving many dead and injured and turning the city into the centre of the rebellion in the Sunni Triangle. I was one of two British journalists who made it into Saddam's hiding place when the Dictator was finally caught (and the only one to get into Osama bin Laden's lair in the mountains of Afghanistan, but that's another story).

I've had tea with Tariq Aziz, flown guns to the north of the country with private armies and watched wives and mothers clinging to the skeletons of loved ones pulled from the fetid earth at mass graves.

I've met American and British servicemen and women, spooks, SAS men, private security contractors and mercenaries, and heard their stories.

I've met ordinary Iraqis all over the country, and heard *their* stories.

Some days, I've seen death and horror really close up, and I've come near to being killed myself. I've had some of the funniest and most bizarre moments of my life on the same days.

That's the kind of place Iraq is, and this is that story.

Chris Hughes, *October 2006*

2001
Beginnings

My brother rang just as I pulled my car onto the M4 motorway outside London.

'Hello, mate,' he said, breathlessly. 'I've just got off the phone from our New York office. A plane has just gone into the north tower of the World Trade Center. Do you know anything about it?'

Patrick works as a broker in the City. I listened as he described scenes of chaos in his office: everyone was glued to their mobiles, frantically emailing or scanning the Reuters news feed. Many of them had friends and family working in the States, some of them in the WTC.

'Haven't heard anything,' I said. 'I'll give the news desk a call. If it's anything major I'll let you know.'

I dialled the *Mirror* desk's direct line. It was busy.

Thirty seconds later, my mobile went a second time. It was Patrick again.

'Chris,' he almost shouted. 'Christ, it's massive, mate! Another plane's gone in and hit the other tower... looks like terrorists.'

Click. His phone went dead. Not a lot of time for niceties and pleasantries in the City.

Fiddling with my radio, I called the news desk again. This time I got through to an executive. I could hear pandemonium in the office around him.

'Two planes hit the twin towers,' he yelled. 'Huge terrorist attack. We're watching it on TV now. Come back to the office immediately.'

Click. Not a lot of time for niceties and pleasantries in tabloid journalism, either.

I pulled into some services. I was ten minutes from Heathrow – I'd been heading to Bristol on a nothing job – and there was no way I was turning round and heading back to Canary Wharf. Once they'd got their heads together, they'd start looking for someone to send to New York, and I was surely closest to the airport. This was shaping up to be the biggest story of my career and I didn't want to miss out. Sure enough, my phone went again. It was a typically abrupt call. 'Hughesy? Right, get to Heathrow. We're getting you on a plane to New York as soon as possible.'

It was September 11, 2001. A group of young Muslims had boarded four planes in America and hijacked them. Two of the planes were flown into the twin towers of the World Trade Center in New York, the first ploughing into the north tower at 8.46am and the second smashing into the south tower at 9.02am. A third hit the Pentagon and the fourth crashed somewhere in Pennsylvania: they'd been planning to hit the White House but they ended up destroying a field.

The whole thing happened around lunchtime, our time.

I always carry my passport and a small overnight bag – we live in hope of being sent abroad – so I pulled out of the service station and headed straight for Heathrow, though, by the time I'd got there, George Bush had banned all flights across the Atlantic. The airport was crawling with newspaper hacks, TV crews, radio journalists and photographers. I said my Hellos, tried to find myself a seat and sat down to wait.

And wait.

Three days, two paperbacks and too many fatty, stodgy airport meals later, the ban was finally lifted. The first flight over was to Toronto, a jumbo packed with returning Americans and British journos. It was a moving introduction to what we would find in New York – many of the American passengers had either lost family or friends in the outrage, they were in tears as they boarded and a priest held a mass on board at 30,000ft.

In Toronto, my colleague Rosa Prince and I hired a people carrier and drove down to Buffalo, where we caught a flight to New York with a couple of *Daily Mail* people and two or three others. As our plane arrived over New York, we could still see the smoke from Ground Zero, and fighter jets circling the area like birds of prey. We landed to find a city in shock and mourning, full of grim faces and gritted teeth.

Journalists see some horrible sights and you can become jaded, even cynical, after a while.

The aftermath of 9/11 left no room for that sort of nonsense.

The sight of the smoking remains of the World Trade Center towers at Ground Zero, and the knowledge that thousands of people had died there in the most horrific circumstances, was utterly shocking.

We attended dozens of funerals, packed with weeping people, each one becoming harder to handle than the last. The hardest day, for me, was that of the service for the NY Fire Service Chaplain Mychal Judge. Judge had been killed by falling debris as he knelt to give the last rites to a dying fireman outside the burning towers. His funeral was a staggering event. Three thousand people packed the church and the surrounding streets; inside, the solemn bravery of the men and women of the Fire Department, the dignity of his brown-robed fellow priests and the dusty, grimy faces of those who'd come directly from the site were tremendously affecting. I was outside, filing to a copytaker (reading my story over to a typist back in London), when the coffin arrived with Judge's fire helmet, the word 'Padre' written on it, resting on top. The bagpipes started blasting away just to my left and next to me a fireman, fresh from Ground Zero, his face and uniform filthy, began sobbing openly, tears pouring down and leaving white tracks on his dirty cheeks.

I felt tears stinging my own eyes and I turned away, asking the copytaker to wait as I composed myself. It was a weird feeling: I didn't know Judge and I was there to report on events, not to get emotionally involved. I was oddly embarrassed but, as I welled up, I saw I wasn't alone. Many of the other journalists, British, American and others, were crying. Among them was a photographer from another London tabloid, a good friend who I'd known for years. He caught me looking at him. 'It doesn't get much worse than this, Chris,' he said.

If only he'd been right. It was all going to get a lot worse.

Over the next few days, we went through all the standard newspaper operations. British relatives flying in to New York had to be met at JFK airport by reporters hoping for a few words or a photograph to add to the bottomless well of grief and anger that was filling the papers. Churches, hotels and hospitals were watched around the clock, community leaders, politicians and police were interviewed and re-interviewed and we were sent on wild goose chases all over New York State looking for British angles to the story.

Ground Zero itself was still smouldering and the smell of smoke and burnt human beings crushed into concrete, steel and office furniture hung over the city in clouds. Thousands of visitors filed past the site every day, tucking into bagels and doughnuts while NYPD officers ushered them past as though on crowd control at Disneyland. We watched, voyeurs watching the voyeurs, in case something news-worthy happened.

It was the biggest story any of us had covered. By day, we picked over the bones of the Manhattan end of it until it was a dry husk. By night, we crowded the bars alongside exhausted rescue workers and workaday New Yorkers, theorising and arguing until the every nook and cranny of this cataclysmic event had been exhausted.

The same names came up time and time again: George W Bush and Osama Bin Laden.

The same question was on everyone's lips, too: *What will Bush do next?* Whatever he did, we knew it wasn't going to be half-hearted and that it would focus on the Middle East.

It was some months before his famous 'Axis of Evil' speech would definitively name Iraq as a target, but most people already knew that Saddam Hussein's regime was in Bush's crosshairs. He had got it into his head that the Iraqi President was the evil genius behind a Muslim plot to overthrow the West. This flew in the face of the available evidence; Saddam was undoubtedly evil but, while he had street cunning, he certainly wasn't a genius. And he wasn't exactly a hard-line Muslim, or all that popular with anyone else in the region. The idea that he was cooking up an Islamic Armageddon with Osama bin Laden was laughable.

But the American President wasn't about to let a small thing like the available evidence get in his way. It looked as though 9/11 had given Bush Jr the perfect opportunity to go back to the desert and finish what his dad had started.

On September 20, 2001, I stood with the rest of the world's press outside St Thomas' Church on Fifth Avenue as Tony Blair, former US president Bill Clinton and UN secretary Kofi Annan attended a memorial service inside. Smiling men in black overcoats examined our camera gear and bags as we waited in the cold, wondering what Blair was going to say.

As they came out of the church, Clinton hung back and Annan went for his car. Blair, ever alert to a photo opportunity, switched on an earnest, grave expression and headed for the media. We could see the smoke of the pyre of Ground Zero a few miles away across town as he spoke, with his hands by his sides, in sombre tones. His stuttering speech was clearly designed to sound Churchillian, statesmanlike. Some felt it sounded phoney and trite. Whatever, it was very pointed.

'My father's generation went through the Blitz,' he said. 'There was one country and one people which stood by us at that time. That country was America and those people were the American people. As you stood by us in those days, we stand side by side with you now.'

Well, that didn't leave much room for doubt. Whatever the Yanks did, the British would be doing it with them.

He walked off to his waiting car, leaving behind a flurry of activity, dozens of journalists punching in the numbers of their news desks to file this momentous and slightly presidential speech.

As I waited for the *Mirror* desk to pick up, 3,000 miles away in Canary Wharf, the chatter around me bubbled with the words 'Afghanistan' and 'Iraq'.

I was called back to London that day.

* * * * *

By the time I got back to the office, the *Mirror* already had a four man team on its way to Afghanistan. I'd had my eye on that trip so, feeling slightly cheated, I asked where I was going. Piers Morgan called me to one side. 'Hughesy,' he said. 'Forget Afghanistan. I want you to be the first fucking Western journalist into Baghdad after 9/11. I don't care how you do it. Just get in there.'

That was a tall order; only North Korea and the Moon were tougher to get to. But I started badgering the Iraqi consular office in Queens-gate, London. Every few days I would turn up at the shabby former embassy near Hyde Park, under the baleful eye of several hundred security cameras and, I imagine, the secret service agencies of two dozen nations, and demand to see Saddam's man in London, the elegant, greying Dr Mudhafar Amin. At first, he refused to see me. After a while, I wore him down and he would at least give me a hearing, smiling sweetly while I put my case. Over a dozen times we sat sparring in his office, a sparse, high-ceilinged, echoing room adorned with pictures of Saddam and a 4,000-year-old stone bust of the snake-headed goddess Medusa which sat, staring at me, on a wooden cupboard nearby. He would offer me a coffee and spout Iraqi propaganda with a smooth smile and a knowing look. He would remind me he loved and admired Britain and that he was a reasonable man. Then he would apologise and explain that, for the time being, the visa was being refused at the Baghdad end.

I tried everything – the *Daily Mirror*'s anti-Iraq war stance, the promise that we would investigate the UN sanctions against trading with the country and their effect on the poor children in the south, even common or garden begging. In desperation, I considered offering a bribe. I doubt it would have done any good. Saddam didn't want to give us a visa and that was that. It wasn't as though Amin could really pull any strings or cut any corners. He had a family back home and Iraq's feared Mukhabarat secret police were ready and waiting to exact revenge on the wife, children or parents of anyone who caught their eye.

This wasn't good. Piers was a pretty fair boss but this was his pet project. In tabloid newspapers, you don't tend to fail on too many editors' pet projects. If you do, you start looking for a new job.

Then someone suggested I try George Galloway.

Back then – before the days of *Celebrity Big Brother* and licking milk off Rula Lenska – the perma-tanned Galloway was best known as a bumptious, self-important Labour MP who was the Iraqi regime's best friend in the UK; he was in and out of the country so often that some had nicknamed him the Member for Baghdad Central. Famously, he'd had a skin-crawling, televised meeting with Saddam in which he had told the dictator, as one moustache to another, 'Sir, I salute your courage, your strength, your indefatigability.' This was a phrase which had had half of Britain looking for a sick bag and the other half a dictionary. I wasn't sure what I thought of the balding Scot, but I was a tabloid journalist under pressure. I'd have done a deal with Satan himself if it got a result, so George Galloway presented no serious problem. Not really expecting any success, I lifted the phone and called his office to see if he could help.

His connections in Iraq were obviously somewhat better than those enjoyed by the country's official representative in London. Within the hour, he had called me back saying I could travel to Baghdad with him in two weeks, and that there would be no problem with the visa.

He wanted no guarantees and nothing in return, just my word that I would listen to him talk about the prospect of war and the UN sanctions which were making conditions impossible for many Iraqis. His now-estranged Palestinian wife, Amina Naji Abu Zayyad, had family in Jordan and he would be visiting them before meeting me in Ruwayshid, a Jordanian shanty town close to the Iraqi border.

This was great news.

Naturally, I presented it to Piers as a journalistic triumph all of my own making.

Then I set about booking a flight to Amman in Jordan.

So Many Ways To Die

There are so many different ways to die in Iraq.

Some are exotically brutal, like the televised beheadings, driller-killings and mass stranglings which are now the last word in terrorist chic among the country's insurgents. Others are more mundane – tribal squabbles that end in tears, disease and malnutrition, natural causes.

But even with all that going on, I wouldn't mind betting that one of Iraq's most common causes of death is still road accidents. They're not particularly careful drivers.

We met up with Galloway at Ruwayshid after a two-hour drive from the Jordanian capital: me, a few charity workers, *The Guardian*'s Ewen MacAskill and the DJ and journalist Andy Kershaw, who was putting together a radio programme. Our three-vehicle GMC convoy had pulled into the tiny town and stopped at a drab-looking kebab shack to wait for the MP. Half an hour later he arrived, emerging from a darkened saloon car with his trademark Havana cigar poking out from beneath that bushy moustache and those baggy eyes. He was full of bonhomie, and seemed almost proprietorial about the country we were about to enter.

'Welcome, and greetings brothers!' he said, a broad smile cracking his face. 'Leave your mobile phones here' – he nodded towards the kebab stall. 'You're not allowed a mobile in Iraq.'

Reluctantly, we handed our phones over to the grease-spattered owner. 'Don't worry,' said Galloway. 'They'll be fine with this chap. He takes everyone's phones.'

We got back into the vehicles, and Galloway led our convoy to the Al-Karama border crossing, where we were ordered to a carpeted room while a team of guards turned over our vehicles and bags. I sweated slightly as I watched them: though I'd passed my standard mobile over, I'd retained my satellite phone, stashed in the bottom of my holdall. They cost thousands of pounds, and I didn't fancy explaining to the office that the last time I'd seen it, it had been in the hands of a kebab seller. To my surprise, it wasn't found. What was found was about a hundredweight of condoms, which spilled out of one enormous optimist's suitcase onto the floor. The guards cackled, gleefully, before confiscating the contraband contraceptives.

'You no sex in Baghdad,' said one, wagging his finger at the embarrassed bloke. 'You no sex here.'

After a while, another guard walked over. He pointed at the Westerners among us and – a malicious grin written all over his unshaven face – screamed one word: 'AAAEEEEDS?'

Our Jordanian driver stifled a giggle. He had explained the set-up to us earlier, in his broken English. If we said we had AIDS, we weren't allowed in. If we said we didn't, we would be required to undergo a mandatory blood test with a massive, blunt-ended needle that left your arm black for a fortnight.

The border guard twinkled at us, enjoying our discomfort. 'Test nooooowww!' he bellowed.

'Absolutely no chance,' said someone, and we all shook our heads in agreement. 'No way.'

'OK. Baksheesh of twenty dollar,' he said.

It was the first of many small bribes we'd be asked for: US dollars were the greenback grease of the country's black economy. We handed the cash over and our papers were stamped HIV-negative. Why they'd gone through the elaborate charade, I don't know. I'd have handed over $100 straight away just to get out of there.

Then we were in Iraq. I had achieved Piers' goal of being the first journalist in Iraq, post-9/11.

At least, the first western journalist.

OK, the first Western *newspaper* journalist (I suppose Andy Kershaw's a journalist).

Well, apart from Ewen MacAskill from *The Guardian*, that is.

Then began the nightmare drive through the desert to Baghdad. The possibility of ending up as a smoking corpse in a smashed up car flitted through my mind more than once as our little convoy of 4x4s roared after Galloway's limo.

I had no idea where we were. All I knew was that we were somewhere in Iraq, somewhere dark, barren and terrifying, and partway through an overnight journey of 600 or more kilometres. I was absolutely exhausted but wired to the eyeballs with adrenalin and goggling alternately at the road and our driver, a speed freak with a casual approach to steering and a penchant for leaning out of his window to hurl abuse at other motorists.

At one point, we stopped for *chai*, the ubiquitous Iraqi tea served in small glass tumblers with a mini-mountain of sugar piled up in the bottom. My legs trembling, and not with the cold, I walked away from the car and stared into the empty heart of Iraq's gritty, wind-blasted western desert. There was a strange light a few miles away, out there in the nothingness.

The Jordanian driver noticed me looking.

'Bedouin tribe,' he said, cupping a steaming glass of *chai*. 'They move up and down here. I watch them for many days. One day, here. Next day, 30 kilometres away. Next day, somewhere else.'

'How do they make a living?' I asked.

'They sell many things,' he said. 'Carpets. Lambs. Goats. Live only in desert, just come out to barter, then go back. They have nothing. Very poor.'

I shivered as I watched the firelight, imagining the simple desert folk huddled around those guttering flames.

They must have been able to see the lights of the cars and lorries tanking it along the road and it was an odd, slightly unsettling, clash of cultures. There I was, standing on this 21st century asphalt, with my satellite phone in one pocket and my airline ticket in the other, and a fridge full of poncey Japanese lager back in London, and there they were, stuck out in the middle of their ancestral nowhere, with barely a camel and a finely-woven silk rug between them, living as their people had for centuries.

Unless the Jordanian was bullshitting. Maybe they had Land Rovers and Sky TV? One thing was for sure: if they did, they needed to start watching the news channel. This place was going to be crawling with American armour and grunts from Nebraska and Iowa some day soon and I couldn't see them stopping to go around three nomads and their goat.

Then it was back into the car to resume our nightmare journey. We had dozens of near misses and close shaves until the sun started coming up at around 5am; then what had been merely terrifying in the darkness became petrifying. As the dull light washed across the flat, grey-brown wasteland on either side of the road, I could see the remnants of hundreds of horrific crashes – battered cars and lorries, bits of engine, wheels, roofs, doors and other unrecognisable chunks of blackened metal lay everywhere. As dawn turned into morning, and we came closer to the capital, the road got busier and busier. Eventually, all six lanes were filled with battered old cars, pick-ups full of workers and gleaming SUVs, all weaving in and out of each other at frightening speed, like extras in *Death Race 2000*.

And finally we were in the outskirts of Baghdad, driving through verdant, almost biblical, palm groves and past ramshackle farms that looked as though they'd not changed in hundreds of years. After a few miles, that blended into the suburbs, a concrete confusion of housing estates interspersed with a vast Middle Eastern Spaghetti Junction of urban motorway exits, underpasses and overpasses. Everywhere were giant mosaics of Saddam, or vast, painted murals, or huge statues; in each, he was striking some heroic or thoughtful pose. Clearly, this was no shrinking violet. Soon, we slowed into the interior of old Baghdad. Here, the streets were a chaotic blur, the pavements packed with people selling fruit, vegetables, animals and wares, much of it spilling onto the road. The signature smell of the Middle East – a sweet, humid, fetid scent of rotting produce and the smoke of lazy barbecues – drifted in through the AC vents. Shoe-shines were every hundred yards; these were the lowest of the low in Iraq, where showing another person the soles of your feet is the biggest insult possible, right up there with cursing a man's moustache.

The city was teeming with business, bursting with roadside deals and market-place transactions; for centuries, the people of this region have bartered, traded and made money. Baghdad is sliced in half by the Tigris, and its waters have always brought merchants and their trade up and down to the city, where donkey carts and camel trains would be waiting to continue into Asia and Europe. It was once the trading crossroads for the Middle East and beyond, its crop fields dubbed 'the granary of the world'.

Children ran alongside the car, laughing and waving, and every other patch of rocky waste ground was full of more youngsters playing football.

Our home for the week was to be the Al Mansour hotel, a 'five star family establishment with all the facilities you could wish for'. If you had very, very low expectations, maybe. It was a depressing, shabby, smelly place, with dim lighting, dirty windows and groaning lifts. The sheets on my bed were stained, the room freezing and within hours of arriving I fell ill with a chronic case of the runs.

My room had a smoggy, murky view of one of the main bridges over the Tigris. It was manned at each end by bone-thin men in brown, Republican Guard uniforms who sat inside antiquated anti-aircraft guns pointed optimistically up at the sky. All over Baghdad, similar mounted gun positions were being set up on rooftops, the sweating soldiers serenaded by the wailing of the calling to prayer that wafted over our heads five times each day. I looked at the gun nearest to me, and remembered the news footage of American smart-bomb attacks in the first Gulf War. Maybe Saddam hadn't watched the news? A decade on, facing smarter bombs, stealth technology, more satellites and deadlier warheads, what sort of chance did he think these raggedy-arse conscripts, with their rusty old cannons, were going to have?

We had been assigned a minder and a driver by the Iraqi Information Ministry, a pair of green-suited spies who were our almost-constant companions for the next few days. They were friendly, on the surface, smiling and amenable. But underneath there was a sinister steel about them. We persuaded them to take us to Saddam City, the heaving slum of the Shia underclass, whose young men had been forcibly drafted into the Republican Guard to fight in the war against Iran. In the build up to Gulf War I, the media had sold these guys to us as evil, ten-foot tall über-warriors who would eat US Marines for breakfast and SAS men for tea. As so often seems to happen, it wasn't quite like that: I met only a lot of polite, diffident, skinny and limping men who had been marched at gunpoint to the frontlines of Saddam's stupidest mistakes. Some of them told me they were praying for the Americans to come again, so that they would have the chance to die defending their country; curiously, they always had one eye on our minders as they spoke. *Mirror* photographer Arnold Slater and I shook off the minders one afternoon, diving into a taxi and heading for Baghdad's famous Sadoun Street markets. We spent an hour wandering around the darkened, draped tunnels, drinking *chai* and buying trinkets, before leaving. Outside, the two burly men in the ubiquitous green suits were waiting. They drew alongside, smiling. 'Now we go back to the Al Mansour perhaps, sirs?' said one.

In the evenings, they drove us to restaurants like the Black and White, a favourite haunt of Iraq's privileged and famous and the regular eaterie of the now-departed UN weapons inspectors. Smartly-dressed waiters would bring us lamb kebabs and houmous, amid a hubbub of conversation and laughter which denied the perilous closeness of war. You could bring in crates of Amstel or Heineken, bought for $10 or $12 from the local newsagents, where they were kept cold in a false bottom of the fridge. The waiters would shamelessly demand baksheesh for corkage, and the Iraqi foreign ministry officials accompanying us would smile to themselves at our vulgarity: fine single malt whisky was more their kind of thing. It was surreal, sitting there supping cold beer and tucking into kebabs, and knowing that your table's GPS co-ordinates were probably already programmed into a smart missile somewhere.

The point of the trip, for me, was to get a feel for the country the Coalition was soon to invade, and to produce colour pieces – extended news stories – for the paper.

For Galloway, it was a chance to show a national newspaper the effects of sanctions and to put his case for peace. He'd always been a controversial figure, even before his *Celebrity Big Brother* days, and I could see why. At first glance, it was easy to dislike him: many felt he was just a puffed up, verbose, big-head with a questionable relationship with the Iraqi dictator. As I got to know him, however slightly, I began to feel this was a misplaced view. I think he was genuine in his affection for this odd country and in his desire to see war averted at almost any cost, and a lot of what he said made sense. The problem was that it was him saying it: he had an unstoppable ego and a weakness for over-egging the rhetorical pudding that tended to get in the way of the message.

He had arranged for us to visit a hospital in Basra, to see the combined effects of Allied depleted uranium munitions left over from Gulf War I and the sanctions which restricted medical supplies. We went down there on a No Fly Zone-busting Iraqi Airways' flight with a hundred Iraqis who were visiting family in the south. The plane was a rust bucket with wings – well, the return journey only cost $6 – and I tried not to think of the combination of incompetence, lack of spare parts and American missiles that might come between us and a happy landing at the other end. The Iraqi inability to queue was plain to see as we landed. As soon as the wheels touched the ground, with the plane still bowling down the runway at 160pmh, all of the locals leapt out of their seats and scrummed towards the exit door, pushing and shoving, lashing out and cursing each other. The plane came to a halt, the ground crew rammed a set of steps carelessly against the side of the aircraft and the Iraqis flew down the stairs, some tumbling head over heels onto the concrete runway in their eagerness to get to their relatives.

'*Fuck* me,' said someone. There wasn't much to add to that.

At the bottom of the steps, a forty-strong welcoming committee had lined up, waiting to greet the famous George Galloway and his entourage. Most men in Iraq sport moustaches, and every male official in the line had a particularly enormous, bushy specimen; they got ever more extravagant as you headed along the line. Andy Kershaw was ahead of me as we walked along the line, shaking hands. Like me, Andy had started out with the Arabic hello – 'Salaam aleikum' – but was beginning to revert to English.

'How you doing?' he'd say.

'Hello, nice to meet you.'

Suddenly, he stopped, and stage-whispered over his shoulder, 'Christ, Chris, wait till you see the muzzy on this one!'

I looked past him and saw a man with a draft-excluder on his top lip.

We both stared, and – we'd been out on the razz until the early hours and were hopelessly hungover – started giggling helplessly.

There was a pause, and then lines of teeth appeared from the middle of the hair and a huge smile cracked across the face of the head of the Basra Ba'ath Party. He was proud as punch and happy to acknowledge the shock and awe in which we held his 'tache.

We were whisked off to the hospital, where we were shown film footage of children suffering with serious birth defects. Many scientists believe these are caused by radiation from the depleted uranium-headed tank-buster missiles and shells I mentioned earlier. These super-tough munitions, twice the density of lead, smash through tank armour like a knife through butter, igniting inside at around 6,000°C. Everything inside the tank is vaporised and often sucked out of the other side through the exit hole. The detritus of the kill is said to leave a creeping plague of radiation behind it – some describe it as 'aerosoled cancer'. I'm no specialist in this field (or many others), but there was certainly something unpleasant happening there; each week, babies were being born with an eye missing, with no nose, with exposed stomachs. And none of these children survived long, because UN sanctions against Iraq meant many basic medications were banned.

All of this was explained in a lecture by a female nurse. We sat in silence, until Kershaw suddenly stood up and started speaking. 'I'm sorry,' he said, 'but since no bugger else is going to ask this, I'll do it. How come Saddam can build so many palaces and these kids are suffering like this?'

The nurse stopped in her tracks. She stared at him, horrified. Our Mukhabarat minders shifted in their seats and fidgeted, not knowing what to do.

'Sit down and don't ask questions like that!' shouted Galloway. 'This poor woman could be shot for answering you. You must know that?'

Andy sat down and the incident was brushed under the carpet, but it was a telling illustration of the problem with going to Iraq under Saddam as a journalist. You couldn't ask the questions you needed to. All you really got to see was what Saddam's henchmen wanted you to see. It was better than nothing. But not much.

As we sat at Basra Airport, waiting for the flight back, Galloway gave us an answer, of sorts, to Kershaw's query.

'Yes, he has many palaces,' he said. 'But they were built using local materials, paid for with Iraqi currency and labour. The medicines they need have to be imported, and paid for in dollars. That's what you should be focusing on.'

The New York-based committee dictating UN sanctions policy would not allow these treatments in because they had potential military uses, in that they could be used for treating battlefield casualties. It made some sort of sense, but for me it did little to resolve the essential contradiction of Iraq; the man in charge of this place was speeding from mansion to gilded mansion, while children died in the dirt outside. And I was there as his guest.

After a seemingly interminable wait in this lino and strip light hell, we wrestled with a new bunch of flailing Iraqis to get to our seats and set off back for Baghdad. At one point during the flight, an attendant emerged from the cockpit with a look of vague concern on his face. I checked that the wings were still in place and tried to forget it. But after we had landed, I asked one of Galloway's acolytes what had happened.

'There was a US fighter alongside,' he said. 'He told the pilot he was going to shoot us down if we didn't return to Basra.'

'Bloody hell,' I said. What a story that would have been. 'Galloway and *Mirror* man dead in Iraq crash' – I'd have been absolutely *guaranteed* the front page.

'What did the pilot do?' I asked.

'Apparently he just shrugged and grinned.'

That's Iraq for you: lots of ways to die, and they're not scared of any of them.

2002

I Shall Never Go To London Again

I got back to London feeling reasonably pleased with myself. The *Mirror* had run my stuff as a front page story and a spread inside, describing me, only slightly disingenuously, as 'The first western reporter in Iraq after 9/11'.

Our main picture was of the mosaic in the doorway to the Al Rasheed hotel; the tiles formed the face of George Bush Snr and the legend '*Buch is criminal*' (sic). Iraqis would wipe their feet on it every day as they passed through the door, a calculated insult to the man who'd kicked Saddam out of Kuwait a decade earlier. I tried to convey the underlying tension and the sense among locals that war was inevitable, that the WMD hunt was just a sideshow. 'There will be blood on the streets,' one youth had told me. How right he was.

But every cloud has a silver lining: Piers loved my copy. Tabloid journalism is a strange trade: job security is minimal, results are everything and memories can be short. If you haven't had a good 'hit' in recent weeks, it's very easy to become paranoid.

The repercussions of the World Trade Center attack were still reverberating around the globe. George Bush Jnr was making it plain he thought Iraq was involved somehow and was charging around threatening to invade everywhere. The UN weapons inspectors weren't getting anywhere and, as the weeks dragged by, war became all but inevitable.

With that in mind, Piers decided a second visit to Iraq would be a good idea.

The *Mirror*'s Head of News, Richard Wallace, called me over. His instructions were simple enough. 'Chris,' he said, 'get over there, get a chat with Saddam and ask him if he's got weapons of mass destruction.'

As a tabloid reporter, you get sent on many different kinds of job.

Some are reasonably straightforward: 'Go to this address and interview Mr X.'

Some are trickier, but doable: 'Go to this address and interview Mr X about his affair with Mrs Y.'

Some are absolutely impossible, and 'Go to Iraq and interview Saddam Hussein about his nuclear, chemical and biological arsenal' falls into this last category.

Richard's a bright guy – he would go on to become the paper's editor when Piers Morgan was fired – and a seasoned operator. He knew as well as I did that, barring a miracle, I was not going to get a cosy, *Hello*-style sit-down with the Iraqi president ('A Relaxed And Happy Saddam Welcomes Us Into His Lovely Palace And Shows Off His Extensive Collection Of Nerve Agents'). But the request had been handed down from on high, so we had to give it our best shot.

Galloway again did the honours and, after the same nightmare journey, with another lunatic driver and another skipped AEEEDS test, I was back in Baghdad.

The streets looked the same – a cosmopolitan mix of men in traditional Arab robes, veiled women, kids in jeans and teenage girls in short skirts, even the occasional Iraqi with curly red hair, probably the descendants of ginger Scots who would have served in the British Army there a century and more ago. But I got the sense that people were more nervous, keen to do their business as quickly as they could and get home.

I asked the Iraqi Ministry of Information for an interview with the President – I think I heard them laughing as they put the phone down. Saddam wasn't going to be talking to the *Daily Mirror* today, tomorrow or in the foreseeable future. He had other things on his mind, apparently. But I happened upon the next best thing by chance the day after we arrived. Galloway attended a conference, making one of his typically overblown speeches calling for peace and denouncing Bush and Blair, and Saddam's number two, Tariq Aziz, was in the crowd. If we couldn't get to the president, he would make a great stand-in. Aziz was one of the most intriguing men in the upper circles of power, an avuncular, slightly tubby, white-haired figure with thick specs who was known as 'Mr Magoo' among the foreign press. He had helped form Iraq's Ba'ath Party in the 1950s and had stayed close to Saddam's side ever since; unusually, for a member of the government of a predominantly Muslim country, albeit a secular one, he was a Christian, a Chaldean Eastern Rites Catholic. His real name was Mikhail Yuhanna: he'd adopted 'Tariq Aziz', which means 'Glorious Past', years before to make himself more acceptable to the country's Islamists. In a country where the streets ran red with the blood of those murdered by the ruling regime, it was hard to imagine his hands were entirely clean. But he seemed a very personable and reasonable man; even after the war, when he was in custody, I found ordinary Iraqis willing, albeit grudgingly, to exonerate him from the worst excesses of the regime. I imagine there was little he could have done to reign in his leader, who was tyranny personified. Saddam had killed senior colleagues and even family members before now and it wasn't beyond him to dispose of Aziz – and his wife and children – if the mood took him.

Galloway took to the stage and made a barnstorming speech in front of a thousand delegates from all over the world. To my horror, he then turned to me. 'The London *Daily Mirror* newspaper is here today,' he said, with a flourish, 'and its reporter has promised me personally that he will denounce this evil war on the front page of that newspaper tomorrow!'

I'd said no such thing. Feebly, I opened my mouth to protest but I was drowned out by spontaneous cheering. I seem to remember a lot of African delegates started slapping my back and giving me the thumbs-up. But as I felt the blush receding from my cheeks, I saw that Aziz was leaving, a knot of grim-faced guards around him, and the way out was past us. There were no other journalists around. *Mirror* photographer John Ferguson and I stood up and were immediately wrestled back to our seats by the guards. I could understand why; the leader of the Northern Alliance in Afghanistan had recently been killed by two 'reporters' who had hidden a bomb in a TV camera and blown him up along with themselves. But Aziz noticed the altercation, and approached us.

'You are the journalist from the *Daily Mirror*, are you not?' he said. 'How can I help?'

The minders, grim-faced, slackened their grip and Fergie started banging frames off. The bodyguards edged forward on the balls of their feet but Aziz motioned to them to leave him be.

'Sir, does Iraq have weapons of mass destruction?' I asked.

He smiled again. 'No, we do not.' He launched into a lengthy and, frankly, rather dull explanation of the country's position vis a vis the United Nations and when he stopped to draw breath I butted in again.

'If Iraq is invaded, will Iraq fire missiles at Israel?'

'No,' he said, looking grave now. 'Every drop of blood spilled will be spilled on Iraqi soil.'

We chatted for five more minutes before he politely excused himself and walked off.

I was elated. We had our exclusive interview, with pictures. Our rivals would be steaming and the office would be delighted.

The next day, a general invitation was extended to the Western journalists in Baghdad to attend the concrete Ba'ath party headquarters to interview Aziz properly. We were picked up at our hotel and driven at speed in a convoy through the streets of the city by the Iraqi secret police; I felt guiltily important as I watched people dodging out of our way or averting their eyes in fear but, as we arrived at the HQ, the centre of Saddam's power base, that mild sense of pomposity crystallised and fractured when it dawned on me that being important in Iraq brought its own problems as well as privileges. That feeling, that I might be in the crosshairs of a US missile, came to me again.

We congregated in Aziz's modest office. He looked tired and resigned – he must have known the game was all but up – but he roused himself as the questions started flowing, batting them off with the dexterity of any politician. Most of the questions were about weapons of mass destruction and UN resolutions but we'd had all of that the day before anyway. All I was interested in now was the whereabouts of Saddam, and we wouldn't get anything on that from Aziz. The dictator was constantly on the move, fearing air-strikes and treachery amongst his own men, popping up now and then for a spot of rabble-rousing in some city market place or other.

Someone raised the issue of Tony Blair's 'WMD dossier', which was due to be published shortly. The Prime Minister had boasted that it would contain details of where Saddam was making and storing his chemical and biological arsenal and it was an important plank of Blair's justification for getting involved in a war with Iraq. Aziz denied, all over again, that his country had such weapons, though he did it with the air of a man who knew it would make little difference to his future. Then he made an offer: he undertook to take us all to any three of the locations identified by Blair within hours of the document being published. We seized on his pledge, even if it was actually something of a stunt. The chances of a bunch of Fleet Street reporters being able to uncover proof of anything, one way or the other, were fairly slim. I certainly wasn't going to be able to tell weapons grade uranium from a lump of Battenberg cake but the chance to visit the secret sites would make dynamite copy, nonetheless.

Before we left Aziz, I asked him, 'How often do you speak to the president?'

'As often as needs be,' came the answer.

'And *how* do you speak to him?'

I was hoping for a steer on where they met, but Aziz sidestepped me neatly.

'In Arabic, of course,' he said.

Meeting over, we returned to our hotel and set about filing our story and sending pictures back via our smuggled satellite phones.

With war drawing ever closer, I felt very nervous. If we were caught, we could easily have been accused of spying and that didn't bear thinking about. The best we could hope for was that they'd be confiscated and we'd be chucked out of the country, hopefully without too much of a roughing up. But we had no choice: there was no other way of getting your copy or pictures back to the office (I'm not quite sure how the Iraqi authorities thought we *were* filing our stuff, actually). It wasn't a technical walk in the park either; the thick concrete construction killed our signal, so Fergie had to lean out of the window as far as he could, holding our two dishes while I held onto his legs, the only thing between him and a rapid descent from the 11th floor onto more concrete below. It was early evening, and a deep orange sun was slowly disappearing behind the shabby, off-white buildings around the hotel, but he was very visible; we just had to hope no-one looked up.

As he leaned out, we could see a dozen other journalists halfway out of their own windows doing the same thing. For some reason – perhaps it was the ludicrously amateur nature of our collective attempts at stealth, maybe it was the nervous tension – we both started giggling. Like adolescents. Mid-giggle, John suddenly stopped, and said, 'Bollocks... look down there!'

I craned my neck. Down below, sat around the pool, were a group of burly Serbs partying with a bunch of curvy women in skimpy bikinis. Who they were, and what they were doing there, I never found out – Saddam had a good relationship with Serbia, and its citizens didn't need visas to get into Iraq – but at that moment one of them spotted us and started pointing. My blood ran cold for a second, and then it froze: a cortege of limousines approached the hotel from a lane at the back and drove towards the underground entry tunnel. It was widely rumoured that Saddam visited the hotel and that there was a deep bunker beneath it where he and his regime held secret meetings. For a heart-stopping minute, we watched the line of eight cars drive slowly down beneath the hotel. Now we were *sure* to be discovered. The story and pictures disappeared into the ether, and Fergie scrambled back into the room. Both of us were wide-eyed with the adrenalin and I could feel my heart banging in my chest. We sat in silence, waiting, wondering what to do. But nobody came.

Finally, we relaxed.

After half an hour, I called the news desk and an executive picked up.

'Hi mate,' I said. 'I've just filed 1500 words on Tariq Aziz. He's given us all the usual stuff but there's a great line – he's offered to take us to any of the sites Blair identifies as WMD centres in this dossier next week.'

'Yeah,' he said, sounding slightly distracted and not particularly interested. 'I'll have a read. Call me back in half an hour.'

Exasperated, I said, 'Mate, it's quite hard to phone from here, you know. Could you just...'

'Hughesy, I'll have a read. Call me back. Go and get a beer.'

'Well, it's not that easy to get a beer, either,' I said, but the line had gone dead with a click.

Tabloid newspapers are great at breaking down complex stories and encapsulating them in an easy, digestible form, and I love the immediacy and drama of the newsroom. But the downside of this can be a short attention span and a restless urge to move on, an unwillingness to linger and go into detail. I didn't blame the exec, he'd be juggling 20 or 30 stories, and by the time I got back to him I was sure he'd have seen the potential in this one, stunt or not. But it was frustrating.

Fergie and I had another story in our sights, though.

We'd been asking our 'translators' for permission to visit an ordinary Iraqi home. I wanted to find out what they thought about the prospect of war; I was pretty sure we'd get the party line, about being happy to die for Saddam and all that, but it had to be tried.

Karim, my man from the Ministry, kept blocking the idea. 'Impossible to arrange,' he said. 'How I find suitable family? It will take weeks.'

'Look, Karim,' I said, 'I'll just walk half a mile that way and knock on a door.'

'No, no, Chris,' he replied. 'Is not possible. In England could I do this? The way things are between our countries?' His sceptical face made it clear he thought not.

'Karim,' I said, 'an Iraqi journalist in London could go anywhere he wanted and talk to whoever he wanted, any day, any time. Honestly.'

He smiled indulgently and shook his head. 'No, no, not now. I don't think.'

That night, a big football game between two Baghdad teams was being held in the city. It was a major grudge match, and the last, in all likelihood, before Gulf War II broke out. Maybe we could cover that? Karim agreed so, after sundown, we made our way down to the Al Sh'ab stadium. It was bursting at its concrete seams with screaming men and boys, yelling, chanting, banging drums, setting off flares and jumping up and down. I noticed one youth was wearing an Arsenal shirt… then I saw a Liverpool one, then someone in Manchester United colours, even kids in England shirts, which was strange, given that we were about to go to war with them.

Then the players came streaming out of the tunnel and onto the pitch and one particular part of the stadium went completely wild, grown men screaming like wild things and surging forward in excitement. Even the Special Police Guard, standing every 20 yards and pointing their snub-nosed machine guns at the crowd, were smiling and laughing at them. This was their Kop, where the hardcore Al Zawa fans had gathered.

'Can we get in there?' I shouted to Karim, half hoping he'd say no. I pondered the English equivalent: a load of Iraqi journalists piling into the crowd behind the goal at Millwall, say, as England prepared to be blitzed by a load of bombs from Baghdad. How would that go down?

Karim nodded.

'Er... will we be OK?'

He laughed. 'It will be fine. There are no hooligans like Europe. We do not have that sorts of things here. We like only football.'

So we picked our way down through the crowd as the game started. People were slapping me on the back and, as word spread that we were there, they started cheering us. 'British, British, British', they chanted, and then 'Beckham, Beckham, Beckham.'

It was weird; they must have known that our tanks were massing with the Americans a few hundred miles to the south, ready to roll into their country, and yet they were welcoming us, almost ecstatically. There was no obvious outlet for dissent against Saddam's regime, of course. Perhaps this was their way of expressing their desire to see the tyrant overthrown. Perhaps they actually *wanted* the war?

At the front of the surging crowd, an old man got out of his seat to let me past, with a slight bow and an extravagant and statesman-like flourish of his hand. 'Welcome, sir!' he said. It was so formal and considered that I almost thought he was being sarcastic but I went along with it all the same and shook his hand. He started a kind of jig, jumping up and down and grinning like a nutcase, and this proved a cue for the rest of the nearby fans: soon they were all dancing like that. It was insanity, Iraq as free as it could be, just for a couple of hours, one Friday evening. I started chatting to a man in a dirty grey robe with Saddam's face painted on the front. He was a farmer, he told me, and he had travelled 200 miles up from near Basra to see his team play.

Pointing at his leader's image, he shouted in a guttural voice, 'SO-DOM, SO-DOM... he very good, he very strong.'

He looked at me with an increasingly aggressive expression and an Iraqi police officer appeared at my elbow. 'Sir, everything is OK with you?' he said, giving the farmer a glare. Instantly, his face creased into a grin and he began shouting 'Bora bedan nefdeike ya Saddam!' (*'With our hearts and our blood we would die for you Saddam!'*). The chant soon spread throughout the whole stadium; whatever that strange situation had been, it was diffused.

I joined the cop by the side of the pitch and he started talking to me through the side of his mouth, as if he was being watched.

He said his name was Abdul and added, 'It is dangerous for me to talk to you. I am usually at the Revolutionary Bridge which I guard during the daytime. I have visited London some years ago, and I wanted to try out my English. I speak well, yes?'

Speaking out of the side of my mouth, I said, 'Your English is very good. What do you think about all of this?'

He shrugged. 'I don't like football so this is a little boring for me, to be honest.'

'No, the war?'

He paused for quite a while. Then he smiled thinly. 'I think I shall never go to London again,' he said, and walked off to stare at the crowd again.

Shortly after that, the game was over. Who won, and what the score was, I couldn't say. I followed as both sets of fans wandered outside. They kept their distance from each other, whistling in derision, shouting and waving their head-dresses mockingly at each other. But there was no violence, despite the fact that the large police presence had gone. A young boy ran up to me and handed me a programme of the game, grinning shyly before running back to his father; the man waved, and the pair of them danced away into the night, arm in arm. I wonder where they are now?

Karim and I watched as the crowds drifted away.

'How are they getting home, Karim?' I asked.

'They walk,' he said, looking at me in surprise.

'How far?' I said.

'Maybe 10 miles, maybe 20,' he replied. 'Some have car or motorcycle, of course, but not many.'

I whistled under my breath. It was a little different from watching my local side, Chelsea. Most of them looked like they had absolutely nothing but the clothes they were wearing and the worn-down sandals on their feet. They had no money – their *thaub* robes had no pockets, anyway – but their faces had been full of smiles and laughter. I found it all quite poignant. These Iraqis, sons and fathers, brothers and grandfathers, had just taken part in what was probably the very last truly enjoyable mass occasion Iraq would see for many years.

Karim coughed, and placed his hand on my elbow, nodding his head towards the waiting limousine, and we slowly picked our way through the departing masses, many of them still dancing and waving their head-dresses.

* * * * *

The next day, the news desk told me Blair had unveiled his Weapons of Mass Destruction Dossier in The Commons.

The Iraqi Ministry of Information summoned us all immediately to the office of Mohammed Uday, the man who would help facilitate our visits to the factories or storage areas of our choice. Between us, we identified three sites and put them to Uday, a serious-looking, slightly scary man, who was rarely without a cigarette. He nodded. 'OK,' he said. 'If you have any questions ask them now. There will be no time when we are at the installations.'

A reporter stuck up her hand. 'Will we be able to take soil samples?'

The last British journalist to have concerned himself with Iraq's soil had been the *Observer* reporter Farzad Bazoft. A decade or more earlier, he had wandered into the desert and collected samples from sensitive military sites. I imagine he thought it was a fairly harmless thing to do. Saddam took a different view. Bazoft was caught, arrested, beaten for weeks and then executed as a spy, despite pleas for clemency from around the world.

The room went quiet and all eyes turned to the reporter. On one level, it seemed a fair enough question, the sort of thing you'd put to an MoD spokesman in Whitehall without even thinking about it. If the Iraqis had nothing to hide, why not let us take samples? We could have them analyzed back home and that would give us a better indication of whether or not they were telling the truth.

In pre-war Iraq, though, it was a mad thing to ask. This was an intensely paranoid and frightened place, where fathers informed on sons, secret service men and spies were everywhere and public hangings were commonplace. It was the acme of authoritarianism and no-one – least of all some government functionary – was going to go knocking on any doors asking, actually, do you mind if we give these British reporters a bit more access?

Uday collected his thoughts and then addressed the woman, smiling mirthlessly. 'I think, dear, since we all remember what happened last time, we will not be doing that.'

His refusal was not an indication that they actually had WMD: it was the only answer he could give.

The usual convoy took us out to the three selected establishments, all factories on Blair's target list. We were shown around, and were free to poke our noses into nooks and crannies and ask questions.

One run-down factory legally made dynamite, among other things, which raised a few eyebrows among some of my colleagues.

'Well, we are allowed to produce dynamite and other conventional weapons, you know,' said the manager, defensively.

As we stood in an outbuilding, a reporter asked, 'Do you make phosgene?'

Phosgene, a deadly gas used in World War One, has a number of perfectly legitimate industrial uses but was on the banned list because of its military potential.

The manager, who looked very uncomfortable with our presence, explained that phosgene was indeed a by-product of work at the factory. 'It's part of the process,' he added, 'but we cannot collect it so it's not important.'

'What happens to it, then?' said the reporter, suspiciously.

'It just goes out into the atmosphere, harmlessly,' said the man.

The journalist wasn't happy and made it clear he thought the man was prevaricating.

'Look,' he said. 'I need to nail this – it's very important.'

The manager finally lost his patience. 'Believe me,' he snapped, 'I know it is very important. It is very important to me because when the bombs come from the sky and onto this factory I will be standing right where we are standing now. That is my job. I will be here and all of you will be somewhere else.'

There was an awkward silence while he recovered his composure.

He was clearly under enormous pressure and I found the whole thing faintly embarrassing. British journalists – I include myself in this – can be incredibly insensitive at times. We arrive at places, take pictures and demand to know things, often with a minimum of manners, and then depart. An hour later, we've filed our story and we're in the bar, or moving on to the next town, and it's all forgotten. For us.

I wandered off and had a nose around, trying to engage the other staff in conversation. The place looked fairly industrial, as had the other two, but they could have been manufacturing Pot Noodles for all I knew. Still, it wasn't a total waste of time; I felt there were clues and hints in the nuances of speech, facial expressions and body language of the staff, and I came away feeling as certain as I could that there really were no WMDs at the three sites. What there was, was a lot of very frightened people.

We all dutifully filed stories saying we'd visited the sites and had been told there were no WMDs but, apart from a little colour and bylines saying '*I was there*', we could have sent them from our hotel rooms. The very act of their allowing us to go had been interesting, for such a closed and secretive society, though. It showed that, even at the highest levels, they were genuinely scared. As with the fans at the football game, I tried to imagine the scenario in reverse: Iraqi tanks and planes are parked up on the French coast, waiting to come over, and a bus load of Iraqi journos demand a guided tour of our factories first? Somehow, I couldn't see it.

Our time was almost up, but the regime had laid on a final treat for us: a fashion show, of all the bizarre things you might organise in the weeks before you get invaded. It was being laid on in Babil – more commonly known in the west as Babylon – fifty miles south of Baghdad. We were picked up in the usual limousines with the usual curtains drawn across the rear windows and set off at the usual extremely high speed. Most of Saddam's cabinet were going to be at the show, and it seemed as if the whole of southern Baghdad knew their leader might be on his way past; for a 30-mile stretch along the main highway heading south out of the capital, men lined the streets, not a space between them, armed with AK-47 assault rifles and rocket-propelled grenade launchers. As we passed, each man, some in uniform and some in traditional dress, snapped to attention and saluted our cars. It was an extraordinary sight, a show of strength designed to get a message across to someone, presumably via the medium of us: Iraq was preparing for a bloody battle. Indeed, many of these men – many of them the Sunni Muslim diehards, the Fedayeen – would soon perish in fierce but doomed fighting just south of here.

Soon the urban sprawl of Baghdad petered out and the crowds were replaced by the sight of Saddam's armoured defences. Our cars slowed down as we entered a rougher part of the road, densely palmed on both sides. Suddenly, it cleared completely and we were out in the open: as far as the eye could see was bare scrubland that had recently been cleared, and hundreds, maybe thousands, of Soviet-built T-72 and older T-55 tanks dug in so deep that you could only just make out their turrets. Earth berms had been piled up high in front of each one, and the guns were elevated high as if saluting the Iraqi leadership.

Fergie grabbed his camera but the Mukhabarat driver waved his finger sternly and barked, 'La! La!' ('No! No!')

It was an awesome sight, in one sense, but despite their great numbers, it all looked hopeless. They had no chance. Just over the horizon were billions of dollars-worth of Apache helicopter gunships, tank buster planes, super-accurate artillery and far superior US tanks. Saddam could have had a million T-72s, two million, even; the only difference would have been in how long it took the Yanks to destroy them.

After a mile or so, we passed the last line of tanks and, shortly after that, we hit the outskirts of Babil, where thousands of people were heading for an amphitheatre for the outdoor fashion show. We pulled up outside the arena and were ushered into a waiting room just in time to see the entire Iraqi cabinet, minus Saddam himself, enter the crowd. They strode in and took their seats, a huge scar of green uniforms slashing down the middle of the crowd. Taha Yassin Ramadan, vice president of Iraq and one of Saddam's closest aides, ambled proudly onto the stage, joined by four machine-gun-toting heavies. Huge arc lights came on, the two sides lit up like daylight while the centre, where the Iraqi leadership was sat, was left in the dark so potential assassins could not see them. Ramadan rambled on for about half an hour in Arabic – about what, we never found out, though I imagine it focused mainly on death to America and giving your blood for Saddam, that sort of thing.

Our interest – my interest anyway – perked up once the models appeared, loads of gorgeous women sashaying up and down the catwalk as the crowd cheered.

My mildly lustful reverie was broken when a colleague from another paper leaned over to me. 'Imagine what this looks like from 40,000 feet up, Hughesy,' he said. 'One F18 could take out virtually the entire Iraqi War Cabinet. I don't think they'd care too much about a handful of reporters, do you?'

For the third time, I had a crosshairs moment. I lost all interest in the models and started thinking about my flight home.

2003

Swept Aside

On March 20, 2003, at about 2.30am, Bush and Blair launched their long-awaited war on Iraq.

I'd love to be able to say I was on the front line when the tanks started rolling into Iraq, bravely filing copy like a heroic war correspondent as the shells dropped all around me. Perhaps I'd have picked up a small shrapnel cut on one cheekbone, just a trickle of blood oozing down my dusty features as I stared, like Lawrence of Arabia or that bloke in *Apocalypse Now*, out into the desert.

Unfortunately, it didn't work out like that.

I'd spent the intervening months since my return to London watching the inevitable war draw nearer, despite all the peace marches and the international condemnation. I'd covered the political shenanigans – dramatic statements by Hans Blix, theatrical ultimatums by Bush and Blair – but the real action was three thousand miles away and I wasn't there.

Once it had become plain to everyone except Saddam that it was all about to kick off, the news desk had put together our war team. The plan was simple enough. Tom Newton-Dunn was sent to join the troops, Alexandra Williams flew out to a position just over the Kuwaiti border and our deputy political editor Bob Roberts headed to cover events from CentCom, the US centre of operations in Qatar. Richard Wallace had been promoted to US Editor and had flown to the States to watch events from Washington and New York. And I would be in Baghdad, dodging missiles and bombs and filing amazing, probably award-winning, copy about the battle for the capital and the race to capture Saddam.

But we all know what happens to the best-laid plans. Unfortunately,

I fell victim to the ferocious intra-officer rivalry between the *Mirror*'s news and features desks. Each department wants to be the one to bring in the big stories; it's a creative tension which works in the paper's interests. The Iraqi regime had started making a limited number of visas available and Matt Kelly, the features editor, had arranged for one of his writers, Anton Antonowicz, to go out to Baghdad a month previously. Ostensibly, Anton was there to produce a series of 'colour pieces' – descriptive backgrounders that run to greater length than news stories. The idea was that, as war drew nearer, Matt would pull Anton out and I'd replace him. But it never happened and, with one *Mirror* man in the capital, I couldn't secure an additional visa. I had to watch in frustration as virtually everyone else in London started catching planes to the Middle East.

I finally admitted defeat a day or two before the war began.

'I'm just not going to be able to get a visa,' I told Conor Hanna, the news editor.

He wasn't best pleased.

'Fucking Anton's going to be doing it all,' he said. 'You have to be there.'

But it was impossible.

Anton filed some great stuff, with excellent pictures by Mike Moore, but that didn't help me. When the bombs started falling, I was sat on my backside in the office, twiddling my thumbs. I had been put on the night news desk rota and I spent the first hours of the ground invasion collating all the copy coming in from the Middle East. It was tremendously frustrating: all the bylines, all the twisted glory, all the fun... it was all going to be elsewhere. Professionally, things hadn't been going that brilliantly. My most recent hit had been the earth-shattering news that the film director Michael Winner had been rushed to hospital with a suspected heart attack. Unfortunately, it turned out to be a nose bleed. I mean, obviously, I'm delighted for Michael that he pulled through. I'm sure he's a lovely man, and his films... well, I'm sure he's a lovely man. But it didn't do me a lot of good – the story ended up buried amongst the puzzles and cartoon strips at the back of the paper.

I needed to get out there, somehow.

I kept on trying other avenues and, finally, a few days after the ground war started, the RAF agreed to give me accreditation to join the British end of the operation. I'd be hooked up with a helicopter outfit running missions in the south, they said. This was fantastic news: it wasn't Baghdad, but it was much better than being stuck in Canary Wharf.

First I had to undergo nuclear, biological and chemical warfare training with the army on Salisbury Plain. It was part of the deal if you were travelling with the MoD. This felt mildly hypocritical: the *Mirror* had been very forthright in its view that Saddam didn't actually possess such weapons, so running around in a gimp suit and a gas mask in preparation for facing them was slightly contradictory. But we had no choice and, anyway, I didn't want to stake my life on a few *Mirror* editorials. Donald Rumsfeld had recently said that not only did he *know* there were WMDs in Iraq, he knew *where* they were. Maybe he was right.

The NBC warfare centre was a cluster of anonymous buildings that looked more like school classrooms than the nerve centre of Britain's anti-WMD training. There were a number of other journalists on the course with me, and the usual air of levity pervaded. That was dispelled, slightly, when we were shown pictures of the blistered and burned corpses of gas attack victims. Gruff sergeants threw us into tear gas chambers and fitted us with our own 'Noddy' suits and masks, which looked more like bondage gear than anything else. They lectured us on what to do if someone shouted 'gas, gas, gas', how to drink water through a mask and how to treat the victim of a bio or chemical assault. Most of it went in one ear and out the other, to be honest. All I remember is an expression called 'blot, bang, rub', a chant to remind you how to deal with nerve agents. You 'blot' with paper, I forget what the 'bang' bit means and you 'rub' something into the affected area. The 'something' was given to us in talcum bottles but I have no idea what it was. Despite our less than professional approach, the instructors were very patient with us. A couple of sergeants spent an hour or more trying to fit my gas mask, endlessly poring over computer read-outs and adjusting straps as I sat in an indoor tent breathing through a tube funnelling in air from outside.

'You sure you haven't got a funny-shaped 'ead, sir?' one kept shouting. 'I'm sure you 'ave.'

Finally, I was ready for war, though it was getting a little late for that, if the relentlessly upbeat American reports from Iraq were correct.

A day later, I was on a commercial flight to Kuwait, weighed down with several bags of normal clothes and hand luggage full of the British army's gimp gear, which the on-board stewardesses found highly amusing.

At Kuwait airport I caught a cab to the Sheraton, and soon arrived breathless at the hotel where I met up with fellow *Mirror* reporter Alexandra Williams, a friend of mine who had already distinguished herself in Afghanistan and other Middle Eastern trouble spots like Gaza and the West Bank.

Swigging casually from a bottle of water, she smiled at my agitated state. She'd already been there for three weeks.

'Hughesy,' she said. 'How's things?'

'Not bad,' I said. 'Listen, I can't stop. I'm just going to drop some gear off and meet this RAF bloke who's getting me embedded with some helicopter squadron.'

Alex didn't quite fall on the floor and roll around cackling. She did give me a weary, and slightly indulgent, smile, though.

'I think you've been wound up, mate,' she said.

'Eh?' I replied.

'I think the RAF are winding you up. If you're going out with them I'll be very surprised. They did the same thing to me.'

It seemed as though someone was extracting revenge on us for our newspaper's anti-war stance.

Mirror photographer Chris Grieve walked over. He wanted to know if I'd thought to bring any booze with me.

'No, mate, sorry,' I said. 'I'm supposed to be joining up with some helicopter squadron… they told me booze was banned. But it seems like maybe I'm not, actually.'

Chris, a good friend, howled with laughter. 'Not you as well,' he said. 'Book a room for at least two weeks, because you're not going anywhere.' He walked off, shaking his head.

As Alex and Chris had predicted, I spent the next week and a half just waiting. Every day, I'd meet up with a supercilious RAF officer to put my case for being allowed out on missions into Iraq with them.

He'd listen patiently, a slight smile on his lips, before turning me down with a flourish – 'Awfully sorry, old boy, no can do at the moment!' – and walking off.

By now, the ground war was over. The Americans were in Baghdad, Saddam was on the run and the early scenes of joyful Iraqis celebrating in the streets were being shown around the world. I'd missed all of it. To make matters worse, Anton was coming out of Baghdad and needed relieving. I was only an hour across the border but I was stuck there, and, because the visa issue was out of the way with the US military in control of the borders, the office had organised Gary Jones to replace him, all the way from London. Whilst I silently wished him a safe journey, I wasn't exactly praying he'd get loads in the paper.

I just needed to sort out this idiot from the RAF or find another way up north.

But unfortunately for me, Gary started producing stories from Baghdad and the RAF idiot stayed resolutely idiotic.

After a couple of weeks, the officer sent me to CentCom to replace Bob Roberts. CentCom, the US Central Command base, was at a secret location somewhere inside Qatar. It wasn't exactly a glamorous posting unless you really, really like US Marines, but it was better than Kuwait. I flew south and met up with *Sun* reporter Tom Worden, who was also going to CentCom, and we checked into a hotel in Doha, the capital city.

The next morning, we hired a car and drove out together to the base, a heavily-guarded, 20-square kilometre facility in the grey desert half an hour outside the city. Razor wire fences stretched as far as the eye could see; beyond the fence sat dozens of squat, metal buildings the size of tennis courts.

CentCom wasn't a fun posting. Every day, after queuing for hours in the heat and undergoing a rigorous search, we'd file in to a press conference to hear US Army Brigadier Vince Brooks put America's slant on the war. As far as I could tell, the whole thing was a big PR scam, a sham designed to convince the world that the US military were being open and above board about everything. Vince was fine while he was getting across his message, which was that all was going according to plan. Each day he'd show new footage of various successes and talk in broad terms about the brilliance of the campaign and the American military generally. But if anyone ever asked any difficult questions the shutters came down straight away.

'I can't answer that at this time,' he would intone, gravely. 'That information is classified.'

Not that I asked any difficult questions, you understand. Brooks was terrifyingly articulate and thoroughly on top of his game and at least 50% of the British press people at CentCom (myself very much included) were just hacks desperate to get out of there. None of us wanted to stand up in front of the world's media and stumble through an inane question under Vince's steely gaze.

'Yes, sir!' he'd bark. 'You... over there!'

The poor bloke would stand up, mopping his brow and trying to read the sopping wet, shredded piece of paper in his hand.

'Er...'

'Where you from, please?'

Mumbled response.

'Speak up! Can't hear you!'

A few of the TV heavyweights would swivel to watch, while Vince's eyebrows went ever higher and the sneer on his face set like concrete.

We used to toss coins, hoping to avoid the dubious privilege of being the representative of Her Majesty's Tabloid Press who would table that day's laughable enquiry.

My solitary effort was hideously embarrassing.

'Chris Hughes...er, *Daily Mirror*, er, London. Is it... er... true... er... [nervous cough]... excuse me... that supplies up to US troops heading to... er... or already in Baghdad... er... aren't getting through quickly enough? Could you, er...?'

'No, it is not and no, I could not. Next question? Yes, you madam, over there...'

Most days, the main story seemed to be that the Americans had caught or killed another member of their strange pack of villainous playing cards, featuring leading members of the Iraqi regime. They all seemed to be uncles of Uday and Qusay Hussein, Saddam's psychotic sons.

'Today, this man was captured,' Vince would say, triumphantly, pointing to the knave of hearts on a screen. 'The apprehension of this gentleman is a significant result for the Coalition.'

We'd all dash into our tiny, air-conditioned press room and search the internet to find out what we could about the unlucky prisoner.

'I can't believe it!' someone would shout. 'It's another one of Uday's uncles.'

'Did Uday ever shoot him?' someone else would call out.

'Er… wait a minute… yes! He was shot by Uday at a barbecue in 1989 but recovered and was given a senior post in the Iraqi army when Saddam found out.'

The next day, the four of diamonds would have been killed in a gun battle with US Marines.

Back into the air conditioned room and onto Google.

'Christ! This one was shot by Uday as well. He blew his foot off at a party, it says here.'

'Shouldn't we check it's definitely a new one?' someone would say. 'Surely *all* of his uncles can't have been evil? And surely Uday can't have shot *all* of them?'

But they were, and he had.

I got chatting to a Major one afternoon. We were getting on famously, so I thought I'd dig a bit about CentCom.

'So, what exactly goes on behind the scenes here, Major?' I asked.

'Well, I can't tell you that, sir, that information is classified.'

'OK, I understand. But what do you actually do yourself? What's your job?'

'I can't tell you that, sir, that information is classified.'

'Hmm. What's this place actually called? What was here before CentCom?'

'I'm sorry, sir.'

'I'm not asking for a grid reference or a post code or anything, just the name?'

'What's a post code, sir?'

'It's a collection of numbers the post office uses to identify an address.'

'Oh, you mean, like a zip code?'

'Yes, that sort of thing.'

'I'm sorry, sir, that information is classified.'

'Are we closer than 300 miles from the Iraqi border, or further away than that?'

'Do you have map of the Gulf States sir?'

'Yes, I do, but this place looks like a bunch of sand, from my calculations.'

Enigmatic smile and silence.

'OK. We are actually still in Qatar, though? Can you tell me that?'

'I can't tell you that, sir, that information is classified.'

I gave up, laughing.

Wherever we were, I might as well have been a million miles from where I wanted to be.

On my second Saturday there, Tom Worden and I had filed our stories and made for the beach near the hotel. We'd bribed a waiter to bring us ice buckets full of cold lagers every hour and a half and were getting pleasantly mellow, and unpleasantly burned, when my phone rang.

It was Conor Hanna, the news editor.

'Hughesy... where exactly are you?'

Conor is a very sharp bloke, and a human lie detector. I couldn't bullshit him, but I couldn't say I was getting drunk on the beach, either. News editors don't like that sort of reply.

'Er... I'm near the hotel.'

'*Near* the hotel?'

'Er... yes. Near the hotel.'

'How far from the hotel are you exactly?'

'Er... let's see. Four hundred yards?'

'So you're basically *at* the hotel?'

'Yes.'

Short silence. I knew he was imagining my pasty body lying in the sand next to a bucket of ice-cold Amstels.

'OK, whatever. Listen, we need you to go to Baghdad.'

'Fantastic.'

'Gary Jones has got to come home. His mum's ill. Give him a bell, he's booking you a drive into Iraq from Jordan. Get yourself onto a flight there as soon as poss. Call me when you get there.'

Then the phone went down with a crash.

I set about paying my drinks bill and trying to sober up.

* * * * *

There were few signs of the recent hostilities as we crossed the border and headed along that familiar highway through Iraq's western desert, but from a hundred miles outside Baghdad, it started.

The burned-out and blackened skeletons of Iraqi tanks and armoured personnel carriers absolutely littered the desert. The bristling, macho show of strength organised by Saddam, which I'd seen just a few months earlier on the way to that weird fashion show on the outskirts of Babil, had been brutally brushed aside in a matter of hours by George Bush's hi-tech army.

They hadn't just cleaned up Saddam's military forces, either. Civilian buses, lorries and cars were everywhere, too: buried in the central reservation, skewed across the highway at crazy angles, or overturned and smashed up in the desert. They were absolutely riddled with bullets, windscreens smashed, bonnets up, the occasional blackened corpse still inside.

I'd never seen anything like it before; it was fascinating, and sickening at the same time. I tried to put myself in the place of the American soldiers and airmen who had led the charge for Baghdad. I could understand they wouldn't have wanted to take any chances and they must have been worried about suicide car bomb attacks. But, still: at least *some* of these people must have been ordinary Iraqis trying to get home before it all started. It was a hell of a way to win hearts and minds.

Looters had obviously come scavenging through in the wake of the Americans. Every car that hadn't burned had been stripped of its engine, every boot lid was up, every door open, any valuable contents spirited away. That just served to remind me what a risky journey this was. The area ought to have been sterile and safe after the US Army had pushed through – it looked like they'd killed pretty much everyone in their way, after all. In fact, it was anything but. The Yanks had advanced so far, so quick, that their rear echelons had been left miles behind. Back where we'd come from was one lot of soldiers, and two or three hours in front was another. In between there was just me, my Jordanian driver, Mohammed, and bands of marauding bandits. These outlaw gangs had followed in the US slipstream, hiding out in the desert and swooping down in 4x4s to rob and murder. The hotel bars in Kuwait, Jordan and Doha were full of tales of people stripped, shot and left to die by the side of the highway. Defenceless, unarmed people, like me.

I looked out of the window as we sped past more burning tanks and cars and thought back to the fear I'd felt on my first two trips here, dicing with death at 100mph along this very road. I felt 10 times more frightened now. I'd had a conversation with a Special Forces soldier the night before. He had looked askance at me when I'd told him I was planning to try to head for Baghdad.

'You are *absolutely* sure about that, are you?' he'd said. 'You know the situation out there in the desert?'

Sitting in an air-conditioned Amman hotel bar, a cold beer in my hand and Fleetwood Mac being piped overhead, the likelihood of being robbed and murdered had seemed so remote. I'd said I thought we'd be OK.

'My advice is, wait for a convoy and join up with them,' he'd said, before walking off, muttering and shaking his head.

Why hadn't I waited for a convoy? It was literally anarchy out here. I scanned the horizon, looking for dust plumes or other unwelcome signs of life.

Occasionally, Blackhawk and Apache helicopters screamed over our heads. I didn't know whether to laugh or cry: as long as one of them was in the area we were probably safe from the bandits but, on the other hand, every ten yards was a car just like ours with about 1,000 rounds in it.

Hours passed and I actually started to get bored. Surprisingly, there are only so many times you can see the remains of a fried-up T72 and its cremated crew before ennui sets in. With nothing but the roar of our tyres on the asphalt and the occasional word from Mohammed to keep me going, I almost forgot about the robbers. Then Mohammed braked suddenly, peering into the distance. I followed his gaze; my heart jumped, my stomach fell and my head went all sort of wobbly. Ahead of us, maybe half a mile away, I could see human figures spilling across the road, arms waving. I felt a horrible chill run through me and my mouth went dry. As we drew closer, I could see they held assault rifles and pistols.

'Don't stop!' I shouted. 'Turn back! Drive round them!'

Mohammed ignored these contradictory suggestions and continued to slow. The men, seven or eight of them, were wearing green parkas and hoods or balaclavas hid their faces. I screamed at Mohammed: 'Do not fucking stop!'

We were just outside the town of Ramadi; this was one of the early trouble hotspots, an extremely dangerous place in which to find yourself.

Unbelievably, he started laughing at me.

'OK,' he said. 'Is OK. This are friends.'

'Friends?' I said.

'Yes, this are men from police,' he said. 'They are army men.'

There was no way he could have known this as far as I could see, but it was too late. We were nearly upon them and, as the car slowed almost to a halt, I considered jumping out and legging it. There were pros and cons to this: I *do* go to the gym now and then but, on the other hand, I smoke. They'd catch me within about a minute and a half. I slumped lower in my seat.

Mohammed wound down his window and one of these blokes leaned in, grinning at me and looking at my bags on the back seat. I'd spent two hours buying loads of provisions in a superstore in Amman the night before – tins of beans, tuna, spaghetti, bottles of water, loads of chocolate, processed cheese in tubes – and he was eyeing them with interest.

My mind raced back to the stories of roadside death I'd heard. At that point I'd have taken a quick bullet to the head reasonably happily; the possible alternatives didn't bear thinking about. But he then looked away and took the papers Mohammed was proffering. He did seem to be reading them, too, which, presumably, bandits wouldn't bother doing. My spirits rose a little.

Amazingly, the papers were handed back and the guy waved us on our way. He even saluted us.

I was literally shaking with adrenalin and fear, and it took me an hour or more to calm down; by then, we were pulling into the outskirts of Baghdad.

It was so much quieter now than I'd seen it before. The street sellers had crept back to work but they were fewer and further between and nowhere near as busy. People hurried by on the streets, keeping their heads down; there was little sign of the gossiping knots of men you always saw, sitting in doorways, chatting and laughing over their hookah pipes and cups of sweet *chai*. Mohammed had to slow to a crawl to weave around piles of rubble, cars turned inside out by missile hits and craters in the road. Collapsed buildings lay sprawled across the pavements, nothing but the bricks and breeze blocks left, everything of any value looted. Loud bangs were going off, both nearby – I ducked instinctively many times – and in distant parts of the city, and sporadic small and heavy arms fire could be heard everywhere. American armoured vehicles patrolled the streets, soldiers sweeping the people with their machine guns, eyes hidden behind mirror shades.

I'd missed something pretty big, that was for sure.

We were heading for the Palestine Hotel, but the journey took us an hour more than it should have; bridges were smashed to pieces, roads were blocked and moving quickly was impossible. Eventually, we drew up to the hotel, weaving through a huge demonstration, hundreds of Iraqis screaming up at American tank commanders hunkered down in their turrets. On the ground, infantrymen, hands on their guns, eyed the skyline nervously, looking for snipers. The Palestine, a pinky-orange high-rise close to the centre of the city, overlooked the spot where the enormous statue of Saddam had stood before it was ripped down by US Marines as they stormed into Baghdad. With the Sheraton opposite, it was the main base for the hundreds of media teams in town, though I'd never stayed there before.

Stepping out of the car, I met an old friend, the *Sunday Mirror* photographer Phil Coburn.

He wore his habitual world-weary look, a look I had first seen whilst chasing a minor celebrity in Las Vegas many years before.

'Hello, mate,' he said. 'Heard you were on your way.'

'On my way?' I said. 'I nearly got skinned and buggered to death out there.'

He seemed to find that highly amusing.

'Have you seen Julian?' I asked. This was Julian Andrews, the *Daily Mirror*'s photographer in Iraq, and the man with whom I'd be teaming up over the coming weeks and months.

'Yes, he's over there somewhere, covering this thing,' said Phil, nodding at the seething, bubbling demonstration, and wrinkling his nose. 'Hasn't got a cat in hell's chance of getting it in the paper. I'm staying over the road in the Sheraton. See you later.' And off he went.

The entire area around the Palestine was protected by a ring of razor wire, tanks and American servicemen. Much as I was no fan of the US military, I am a massive hypocrite and I found their presence very comforting. Someone loosed off a machine gun a hundred yards away and I ducked. It's important to get used to it quickly, and to stop flinching over every whizz and bang, if for no other reason than to avoid being patronised by the nearest moron. An American civvie was standing just to my left and he patted me on the shoulder, grinning. 'Hey, buddy,' he said. 'You get used to it, man, you get used to it.' He looked into the distance and I studied him for a moment. He was about 19, with the full 'Nam thing going on: cap sleeve T-shirt, webbing, pouched trousers and desert boots. I wondered how long he'd spent in front of the mirror, working on just the right level of dishevelment, perfecting that thousand yard stare.

He looked back at me, the grin returning as he took in my spotless flak jacket and clean, pressed linens. 'So you just got here, right? I can tell, man. Everything's cool. Stick around, I'll show you the ropes.'

'Right,' I said, and wandered into the hotel lobby to find some locals to help me with my bags and boxes.

As we struggled to the lift, Julian caught up with me.

'Alright mate?' he said. 'Journey OK?'

We got into the tired-looking lift and set off for the 16th floor, the cables and motor groaning and clanking all the way.

The *Mirror* had taken a suite at the Palestine, which sounds very grand. It wasn't. Julian pushed open the door to 1635. We had interconnecting rooms. Some time in the 1950s they had probably been the height of Baghdad fashion. Now, they were filthy, dusty, off-white shells. Apart from a sofa and a couple of small tables, the furniture had been removed and the windows had also been crudely taped up; the idea was to prevent anyone inside from being ripped to pieces by flying shards of wood or glass in the event of a missile strike. That might sound slightly paranoid, but an American tank had fired a shell into the hotel a couple of weeks before, hitting a room a few floors below ours which was being used by Reuters. A Ukrainian cameraman was killed almost outright and a Spanish journalist in the room above died half an hour later, bleeding to death despite emergency surgery.

We had mattresses on the floor and everything else – clothes, food, water, equipment – was stacked in the corners.

Julian must have seen the sceptical look on my face. 'It's better than most, mate,' he said.

I dumped my stuff with Julian's, splitting it between the two rooms – the logic being that if one room was done over we might have the rest to fall back on – and walked out onto the rickety balcony. Below me, in the glow of a gathering twilight, lay the Tigris, which wends its way from eastern Turkey down through Iraq to Shatt al Arab and the Persian Gulf. Across the river lay the main American camp, sprawling across what had once been Saddam's favourite Baghdad palace. In the distance, plumes of smoke rose into the sky, feeding the hazy fug enveloping the whole country. The streets were full of colour and life: chanting Iraqis, American armour and troops, the revving engines of cars and motorbikes. The 'pop-pop-pop' of automatic gunfire sounded repeatedly, sometimes nearby, sometimes way across the city, punctuated by the percussive bang and flash of explosions, or the whizz of flares shooting high into the gloaming. Dogs howled and rooted through the rubbish which was piled up everywhere: this was a pungent early sign that the Coalition had made a serious error in failing to prepare for governing the country after the fighting was over. Another sign – our generator, powering our laptops, recharging batteries and giving us light during the frequent power cuts – sat alongside me on the balcony, chugging away like a trials bike and belching petrol fumes out into the air. As well as refuse collection, the Americans had failed to restore reliable electricity and water.

I breathed in deeply, and immediately retched. Whatever wasn't just left to rot by the side of the road was being burned in old oil drums or pits, and a choking smog of dust, diesel and petrol fumes and burning excrement and rubbish had followed us all the way up to the 16th floor. It was everywhere; I soon found out it gave everyone 'Baghdad flu', a euphemism for a kind of fever you got from breathing in an aerosoled mix of charred faeces, animal corpses, rubber and plastic. You couldn't wash it off; it burned your throat and you wore it like a coat.

The twilight lasts for fleeting moments in the Middle East, and night fell quickly. Phil came knocking on the door, armed with several cans of lager, a Mars bar and Steve Boggan, then a senior feature writer on London's *Evening Standard*. We shook hands and then the other three descended on my boxes of provisions like famished wolverines. Once you're taken out of your normal environment, of London pubs and restaurants, daily papers and TV, it's amazing just how interesting a box of pretty ordinary food can be. This lot had been here for a few weeks and I watched them assessing each purchase like restaurant critics, shaking their heads at this, nodding knowingly at that. The chocolate got big nods, as did the beans, but the spaghetti was put to one side. (Too messy, apparently.) Phil and Steve were unhappy with my choice of spirits – Jack Daniels – and wanted to know why I'd not bought 'proper whisky'. The lack of vodka didn't go down at all well.

Julian selected some tins of tuna and beans, and a pot of chilli sauce, and set about making our evening meal on a paraffin stove wedged between two sandbags on the veranda.

I took the opportunity to phone the office back in London. They'd be keen to know that I'd arrived safe and well.

Conor Hanna picked up.

'Hi, it's Chris…'

'Chris who?'

'Er, Chris Hughes.'

'Ha, ha, Hughesy, got you. So have you found Saddam yet?'

'I've only just got here, like, literally, an hour ago. The desert's crawling with bandits and we were nearly…'

'Yeah, yeah, yeah, whatever. Give us a call when you get Saddam.'

Click. The phone went dead. The concern for my welfare was heart-warming.

Julian had finished warming up the food so I joined the others, and we sat round on old crates or the floor, chatting and getting slowly drunk.

Phil had some interesting tales to tell. He had arrived a couple of weeks earlier, joining a convoy. Not far from where Mohammed and I had been stopped earlier that day, outside Ramadi, Phil's convoy had been sprayed with automatic fire.

'The bastards hit a few cars but nobody was hurt,' he said. 'It's a really bad area, that. The Yanks just aren't patrolling the road at all and they could do it easily with helicopters. It's become the dodgiest part of that journey.'

I told them about my own experience; sharp intakes or breath all round, with a few raised eyebrows. I suddenly realised how lucky I'd been. If those seven or eight men had been the wrong seven or eight men, I would have been dead by now. It put me off my dinner, slightly.

I walked back out onto my balcony. Groups of helicopters, Blackhawks and Chinooks, thud-thud-thudded across the face of the harvest moon. Chinooks, the huge, two-rotor lifting workhorses, rarely came out in daylight, because their size and their cumbersome, lumbering nature made them targets for everything from opportunistic small arms fire to missile attack. I watched a trio of Blackhawks, better armoured and much more manoeuvrable, heading for an area that was sending up a column of black smoke, blotting out the stars in the dark blue night sky. Down below, one of the huge M1 Abrams tanks dotted around our compound groaned to life and set off, trundling down the road in the same direction. It was at once comforting and frightening.

Julian must have guessed what I was thinking. 'It's not completely safe here,' he said, as I walked back in. 'But we can move around fine as long as we're sensible. Best of all, the desks are pretty much leaving us alone to get on with it.' He got up and carried our dishes to his bath tub to wash them.

I was knackered and ready for bed, but sleep was hard to come by. We left the windows open, because the air-conditioning was louder than the generator and gave off worse fumes; the incessant, Bonfire Night flash-bang of the skirmishing outside kept me awake for hours before, eventually, I drifted off.

Lunatics, Horses and
Very Bad Men

I woke not long after dawn, feeling horribly groggy and wondering where I was. I'd only had a few beers the night before but I felt like I had the worst hangover of my life. The combination of broken, fitful sleep, the muggy heat, that godawful stench coming up from the streets below and the tension and fear of the previous day had given me a really good kicking.

I got up and staggered around in my boxer shorts, trying to find my way to the loo. I had a quick shave; one thing I didn't want was a 'war beard'. Some guys like to let a bit of stubble develop as a sort of shorthand witness to the difficult and dangerous conditions they're working under. It makes me wince, and is perhaps the ultimate crime for a British tabloid journalist. One or two of my colleagues had filed stuff from Afghanistan, with picture by-lines of themselves sporting a few days' growth. They'd been torn to pieces in the office when they'd got home.

Brushing my teeth and peeling my eyelids apart, I made my way out onto the balcony. It was around 6.30am but the sun was already up and the temperature was rising. It wouldn't stop until it reached 120 degrees or more: a sapping, irritating heat that was tough enough for us but much worse, surely, for the American squaddies in their tanks.

Shielding my eyes against the brightness, I could see the city below coming to life. Donkey carts and cars were nudging their way past the hotel, soldiers watching them carefully, and muezzins were calling the faithful to prayer in the distance. There were flies everywhere and that

47

stink, worse outside than in, was rising with the smoke of a hundred little fires burning in every direction.

We had satellite dishes set up on the balcony, tied to sandbags, so we had excellent internet and email access. I sent off a couple of emails while listening to the BBC World Service on our short-wave radio to make sure I was abreast of the wider situation and hadn't missed anything important overnight. There wasn't much chance of that. The only story in town, as far as the *Mirror* was concerned, was Saddam being caught, and I couldn't imagine the US military keeping that one quiet. As soon as it happened, they'd be driving around outside with loudhailers, cracking open bottles of champagne and high-fiving everyone in sight.

I glugged down a half litre bottle of water and watched weary-looking engineers from the world's TV networks set up their equipment on the sun-scorched lawns of the Palestine for the day's work. Nearby, in the shade of straggly palm trees, their reporters were already polishing their copy, reports on the gun battles and skirmishes from the previous night. I could see tents in the grounds where other news teams were living under the protection of the American security cordon around the hotel. There were several thousand newspaper, TV, radio and security workers packed into an area the size of a football pitch. I hadn't felt particularly lucky when I walked in here last night, but Julian was right: it was luxury compared to a tent.

Ex-Special Forces men, earning a fortune providing security to the TV crews, stood around in little groups. They were trying hard to blend in but you can spot these men a mile off, mainly from their unofficial 'uniform': chinos, training shoes, mirror shades and binoculars, and fishing waistcoats with pockets stuffed with maps and equipment.

Julian had been out for 15 minutes. He came back in.

'What's the plan then, mate?' I said. 'Where's Saddam?'

He grinned at me. 'Yeah, right,' he said. 'Let's get going. I'll introduce you to our driver and the translator.'

I went to my pile of clothes and picked up a pair of trousers and a short-sleeved shirt. There's an unspoken dress code amongst journalists, from the tabloids, anyway, a kind of war-reporting chic: scruffy, casual and hard-wearing was the order of the day but any kind of military gear was definitely out. Combat trousers were generally a no-no, for much the same reasons as war beards. I ignored the gas mask and blue plastic NBC warfare suits; the suits, particularly, looked ridiculous (the ex-SAS men who guarded the TV crews seemed to find them particularly amusing) and I wouldn't have been seen dead in one, if you'll pardon the pun. I did pick up my Kevlar helmet and blue body armour, though. These presented you with a difficult balance. On the one hand, you didn't want to look macho or terrified, and both were possible, depending on whether you strutted or scuttled. But on the other hand you didn't want to look dead, either, and this was also possible if you didn't have the kit with you at all. I opted for the usual British approach: helmet hung from my belt, jacket slung over my shoulder. (As the situation deteriorated, I became less fashion conscious, or more cowardly, and wore it openly and often, as on the front cover of this book).

Down in the lobby, two men stood waiting for us, smoking red Marlboros.

Julian made the introductions.

Nibras, our driver, was a Sunni Muslim who came from an engineering family and lived in Mansour, Baghdad's Kensington. A small, stocky man, he looked totally unArabic, more Greek or Turkish, with his pale skin and light brown hair.

Adil, the translator, was a total contrast, a rake-thin, dark-skinned man with thick, black hair. He was a Shia from the slums of Al Sadr (the Saddam City I'd visited pre-war, hastily renamed in honour of the murdered Shia Cleric Mohammed Al Sadr).

Pre-war, their paths would hardly have crossed; there was no love lost between the majority (85%) Sunni Muslims and their Shia brethren, in Iraq or, indeed, throughout Islam. The division between the two sects – a religious argument relating to the succession of leadership following Mohammed's death – has developed over centuries, hardening into a feud which, occasionally, spills out into violence. In Iraq, there were potent political and social factors which aggravated this already explosive situation. The Sunnis, though actually the minority in the country, were the ruling class. They had prospered under Saddam, getting the best jobs, education and housing. The majority Shia, on the other hand, had been downtrodden and oppressed under the dictator. (Later, relations between the Shia and

Sunni groups in Iraq would descend into virtual civil war, but Adil and Nibras, both intelligent and personable, showed no hint of this tension.)

Like most Iraqi men, they gossiped constantly, and this – with their quick wits and Adil's good English – made them excellent assistants. The gossip network in Baghdad had become extremely sophisticated under Saddam. It hadn't been safe to talk on telephones – most homes didn't even have one – because the Mukhabarat were constantly monitoring lines, and the answer was to pass whispered stories and rumours around tea shops and markets. News travelled incredibly fast: you could tell a man something in the south of the country and within days, sometimes hours, it would have spread like wildfire across the whole of Iraq, though you needed to filter out the Chinese whispers, exaggeration and lies to get anything like the truth.

'Adil,' I said, after we'd all shaken hands and swapped names. 'I think Julian has told you the main reason for us being here is for when they arrest Saddam.'

'This will be a very happy day for me, Mr Chris,' replied Adil.

'Me too,' I said. 'But in the meantime, we're on the look out for stories for the paper.'

Adil had been working with Julian for a while; he knew the sort of thing we wanted. He conferred quickly with Nibras and the pair of them slipped out of the hotel and into the crowds outside.

Julian grinned. 'They'll be back in a sec,' he said.

In a different life, these guys would have been excellent tabloid reporters; unearthing titbits of news was something they were born to do, and they loved it. Within minutes they had returned, beaming.

'There are 900 psychopaths which has escaped from Baghdad hospital and they are killing people all over the city,' Adil told us, proudly.

'Yes, many mad peoples,' said Nibras, nodding enthusiastically.

That sounded promising.

Adil's eyes suddenly widened. 'Oh!' he said. 'And also Uday Hussein's horses have been found close to my house.'

Both tip-offs were worth following up, and both were near to Al Sadr, the run-down city of a million people where Adil had spent his entire 41 years.

'OK, sounds good,' said Julian. 'Let's go.'

We clambered into Nibras's BMW, his pride and joy. It was fairly new – he'd bought it in Syria a few months before – and it had a mobile phone in the front. It didn't work, but Nibras liked the look of it.

'It is safe where we're going, I take it?' I said.

'Totally safe. As long as you with me,' said Adil.

Nibras winked at us and pulled out a black 9mm pistol he had stashed under his dashboard.

'Very safe with me also,' he said.

'Bloody hell, Nibras,' I said. 'Where did you get that?'

'From home, of course,' he replied.

'Could you put it away, please?' I said. 'You're making me a bit nervous.'

Grinning broadly, he replaced the pistol. From then on, he would pull it out and wave it around from time to time; I never knew whether he had the faintest idea how to use the thing.

We decided to follow up the tip about Uday's horses first, since it would probably appeal more to the office. Uday was a cartoon thug who made excellent copy: he was just like his dad, only without the modesty, self-restraint and kindness, and his stable had been home to some of the finest Arab stallions in the region. Before it had all gone horribly wrong for the Hussein family, he'd loved nothing more than to ponce about on his ponies pretending to be a cowboy. Finding them would make a cracking story.

As we got to the outskirts, Nibras slowed down and Adil leaned out of the window, chatting to locals who were ambling along carrying water and other provisions on their shoulders.

'It's down here,' he announced, telling Nibras to take a left turn into a muddy track which led onto a patch of waste ground. We came to a halt and a group of rather fat men walked towards us.

Adil leaned out of the window to ask them if they knew where Uday's horses were.

The men looked at each other, giggling conspiratorially.

'Nam, nam,' said one. *Yes, yes*. Then he patted his belly and said something in Arabic back at Adil. Adil looked at Nibras and all of them burst out laughing. The laughter continued for several minutes, until

51

Nibras and Adil were holding each other for support and looking like they needed oxygen.

Julian and I sat in the back, patiently, and the fat men slowly stopped laughing. One of them leaned inside the car and pointed at us, saying something to Adil. He shook his head, tutted, and wound the window up, almost pushing the Iraqi out. Nibras did a hurried, jolting u-turn on the wasteland and away we drove.

Adil turned in his set. 'There are no horses left, I am afraid, sirs,' he said.

'Why's that, Adil?' I asked. I can be quite slow sometimes.

'Those men ate them,' he replied. 'Them and their friends have many... how do you say? Many curries.'

It was time for me and Julian to start sniggering, which set Adil and Nibras off again.

When we'd all calmed down, I said, 'What else was he on about?'

His face became grave. 'Oh, they were bad men, Mr Chris,' he said. 'Very bad men. They were asking who you are and whether you have things to steal. They want to rob you and kill you,' he said.

I sat back in the seat, feeling mildly sick. I looked out of the window at the bustling streets of Al Sadr. It dawned on me that we'd come out this morning with hardly a care in the world and driven into this place with two men we hardly knew. The people looking into the car right now, just a thin-skinned door and a sheet of glass away, were dirt poor, resentful and armed to the teeth. Life was cheap here, and the life of a Westerner was cheaper still. I sank a bit lower in my seat and resolved to be a little more careful in future.

As we set off on the trail of the missing 'psychopaths', I toyed with the idea of filing the story about Uday's gee-gees being scoffed. On balance, I decided against it; I was sure it was true but sod's law said agency pictures of them alive and well and munching hay in a stable in Tikrit would appear the next day. There's always a fine line between what a journalist 'knows' and what he or she can prove, and editors, who are notoriously allergic to being embarrassed, tend not to be too sympathetic if you go with your instincts instead of cold, hard facts.

The asylum – I'm sure there's a politically correct word for it, but this was what it was known as locally – wasn't far. Within 20 minutes, we'd pulled up outside; it was a collection of around a dozen, single storey, greyish, concrete buildings in an enclosure about half a mile square. There was a general air of dilapidation – paint peeled off the window frames and doors hung open, their hinges loosened. Weeds grew from the bases of the walls and on the roofs. The compound itself was a palm-groved area which had once been surrounded by 10 foot high gates and wire fencing. Someone had battered down the gates and they were lying crushed into the lane leading to the hospital's main entrance. The wire fencing had been largely trampled into the ground, too, and an abandoned wooden watch tower, some 30ft high, overlooked the scene.

Inside we could see people running around, others chasing them; from their clothes, it was clear nurses were trying to catch patients.

Tentatively, Nibras nosed the car over the flattened gates and drove along the road. We rounded a corner, not knowing what to expect, and came across an extraordinary sight. Standing in our way was what looked like a filthy dirty, raggedy-clothed scarecrow holding an M16 assault rifle and wearing a US army helmet. The spindly, gawky figure had dark green teeth and, as we approached, it flashed them at us in a broad smile.

'Cooeeey! How ya doin' today?' it shouted.

We stopped, all of us staring at this weird apparition.

'I said, Howdy, guys! How ya doin'?' it repeated.

I looked around. There was no sign of any other US military personnel in the area. In fact, we'd not seen any for miles. Could this *really* be an American soldier? He walked up to the car and leaned in. Nibras recoiled at the smell: the guy obviously hadn't washed for days. I stepped out of the car. The soldier proffered a filthy hand. I offered mine and he grabbed it and held on, shaking it madly, staring at me with bug eyes and a manic grin. He looked about 19.

'What are you doing here, mate?' I said.

'Well, sir, I'm kind of guarding the place,' he replied. 'My unit left me here a couple of days ago. They're coming back for me real soon.' He sounded hopeful, but not certain. 'Least, I think they are.'

'You're here on your *own*?' I said. The real insurgency wouldn't start for months but this guy was absolutely not safe here alone, on the edge of Al Sadr. His army had recently killed thousands of Iraqis and invaded their country, and just down the road were a million people, at least half of whom regarded America as the Great Satan whether or not they'd just kicked Saddam out. 'Is that wise?'

The grin dropped from his face for a moment and was replaced by a look of frightened doubt. 'Well, everybody's being real friendly to me,' he said. He looked around, scanning the horizon. 'I hope my buddies are coming back for me soon.' He paused. 'I'm from Wisconsin,' he said. 'Do you know it?'

I said I didn't. He was the saddest-looking soldier I have ever seen, caked in filth, obviously hungry. I had no food but I gave him some water.

He told us he had been part of the advance party into Baghdad a few weeks ago and was now part of a security detachment tasked with guarding various installations all over the city. But there was nothing worth guarding here. We watched as he chatted to a few Iraqis who had gathered nearby, curious at our presence. He was very polite and courteous to them but it wasn't long before he gravitated back to us.

'Hey,' he said, grinning that green grin again. 'You guys're taking pictures of me, hell, I wanna take one of you!' He pulled out a battered disposable camera and snapped us. 'I love this country,' he said, stowing the camera back in a grubby pocket. 'These people are so friendly.'

I asked him where everyone was and he pointed to a building nearby. 'Most everybody is gone now,' he said. 'They escaped. But there's some folks in there. One of them's a reporter, I believe.'

We walked round the building; an attractive blonde woman in her 30s stood in the shade of the concrete wall, interviewing an older woman who appeared to be a nurse. I listened in; from her accent she sounded French. I looked at my watch. We had plenty of time, so I stood back, waiting patiently for my chance to interview the nurse.

Suddenly, there was a scream from within the building, and one of the inmates came running out, giggling madly and clutching his clothes, chased by two orderlies in white uniforms. They caught him and persuaded him to go back into the building, smiling at us apologetically as they did so.

Then Julian nudged me. 'Oh, Christ, Chris… have a look at this!'

Behind and to our left, a huge Iraqi man in a dirty blue robe was emerging from the undergrowth. He was staring intently at the French woman, a look of demented concentration on his face. He was stooping as he walked slowly nearer to her until, about 15ft from us, he stopped. He lifted his robe, his face breaking into a huge grin, and started masturbating furiously in front of us. His eyes were still fixed on the French girl, his tongue hanging out like a cartoon wolf. She was oblivious. What could we do? We held our faces in our hands as we tried not to laugh – for some reason, international social protocol had to be observed, as if all the social norms weren't being shattered anyway.

An orderly ran out of one of the buildings, shouting and swearing in Iraqi, and shooing the panting, gurning man into the palm trees, where he finished matters off and collapsed to the ground with a groan.

At that moment, the French woman turned round. She really was gorgeous. 'Sorry for taking so long with my interview,' she said, smiling. And off she walked, unaware of the bizarre little scene which had played out behind her.

The nurse she'd been talking to had seen the whole thing; she looked at me, raised her eyebrows and shook her head in a melancholic way.

'Some of the lunatics are still here, then?' I said.

'This is one of the unexpected problems of the war,' she said, in excellent English. 'The Americans came through here and destroyed the army and the police. All of our security guards fled, also. But of course the Americans left and carried on to Baghdad centre. So all the criminals in this area waited until they had gone, and we had no-one protecting us. Then they smashed down the gates and came into the buildings.'

'What were they looking for?' I asked.

'Drugs, equipment… anything of value,' she said. 'Curtains. Chairs. Everything they could carry.' She paused. 'Also our girls, the nurses,' she said. 'Many women have been raped by these criminals since the war came. There is no law now, so they break into buildings and rape and steal.'

'And the patients have escaped, too?'

'Exactly,' she nodded. 'It's not a problem if they come back for their medication. But many don't come back and, anyway, many drugs were stolen and we are running out of them now.'

'What about the nurses?' I asked.

'When the bad men were outside I gathered all of the remaining nurses together,' she said. 'I said to them, "All of you who are virgins and not yet married can go home tonight. Those of us who aren't will remain because our patients need us." Those young girls need to remain intact for their future husbands. But someone had to stay.'

Her voice cracked and she looked at the ground. I suddenly felt terribly intrusive. She must have had tremendous strength and courage, and devotion to her patients, to remain here. The manager of the hospital had walked out and was standing next to us, listening; he interrupted the interview and spoke to the nurse. She hurried off into a nearby building without looking at us, her head down.

'I would prefer it if you left her alone now,' he said. 'She is very upset with what happened, as we all are.'

'How about the patients?' I said. 'We were told that they have been killing people?'

'Many of them are very dangerous,' he replied. 'I cannot say what they have done. I only know that if they are here and they are medicated, they are controllable. Many of them come back every day for food and treatment but the numbers are falling and our drugs are running out. Without medication... well, you saw the behaviour of the gentleman a few moments ago.' He shrugged his shoulders.

Julian had been walking around the building, taking photographs, and he returned. 'I'm finished if you are, Chris,' he said.

I was. Something horribly unearthly had happened at this tragic place, a place trying and failing to maintain a veneer of normality, and it was giving me the creeps.

I thanked the man and walked back to the car, where Adil and Nibras were leaning on the bonnet, smoking and chatting.

As we drove away, I wondered, uneasily, whether the generals and politicians who had devised and fought so stunning a military campaign had given any real thought to what would follow? I couldn't see how the Americans, who couldn't even get the water and electricity back on properly, were going to resupply this place. And what about the other asylums dotted around the country? Or the maternity wards? Or the casualty departments? I'd been dubious about the war before; now my doubts were deepening.

On the way back to our hotel, we called at one of the city's many gun markets. These were impromptu little affairs; a group of men would set up among fruit sellers' stalls, or simply plot up on a patch of ground and open the boots of three or four vehicles. You could buy almost anything you needed; AK47s and automatic pistols were anywhere from $30 to $50 a piece, rocket propelled grenade launchers and heavy machine guns, or trendier machine pistols like Uzis, a little more. Ammunition was thrown in and prospective purchasers would test the equipment by loosing off a full magazine into the air or at a wall. The Americans were keen to stop this trade and it was always amusing to see the traders react when a patrol approached. A small boy would sound the alarm and guns would be chucked into boots, or covered with blankets; within 10 seconds, everyone would be strolling round whistling, or kicking pebbles and tin cans, looking far too nonchalant.

I watched them haggle and barter for a while as Julian took some photographs. Sure enough, a US patrol did come into view and all was hastily cleared away. But I reckoned we'd seen 40 guns bought and sold in a quarter of an hour. Everyone was arming themselves, and some of these people weren't particularly pleasant. Then I suddenly thought about the lone GI back at the mental institution. The last thing I'd seen as we drove over the flattened gates was him, on his own, standing chatting with locals. What the hell was going to happen to him? Surely, the Americans *must* have been heading back to pick him up? If so, they'd better be quick about it. I wondered how long it was before some very bad people heard that there was a US soldier alone inside this compound. I wondered if he'd ever see Wisconsin again.

* * * * *

Over the next few days, the hotel filled up and up until it was bursting at the seams. Mostly, the new arrivals were TV and newspaper journalists or technicians, and their security minders. But there were a fair number of weird wannabees, too. All men, and nearly all American, they would introduce themselves as 'war correspondents'. Some were easy to spot, shameless scroungers, braggarts and war vultures who were always asking to 'borrow a few bucks' or sleep on your floor. We were quick to get rid of them. 'Oi, mate,' Julian would say, to some idiot spouting on about '*Aye-Rak*'. 'Fuck off.' He's a hard-looking bloke, Julian, and they usually got the message.

But others were clever; they wore the right clothes, knew the international lingo of the newsman and had good cover stories. They could sucker you into believing they were for real. One such moron was a fat, big-haired Septic Tank called Josh.

We had fallen into the habit of taking the lift down to the sixth floor to join the ITN boys for a few drinks in the evenings. We would bring our own beers, stow them in their fridge and sit around swapping gossip and passing on tips. Josh began to show up, sitting down with us and talking loudly about the last major story he'd covered in some far-flung troublespot, while helping himself to our lager. He was an irritating big-head, but I assumed he was some big-shot from CNN or NBC and tried to ignore him.

One night, standing on the ITN balcony, I got chatting to their security guy, an ex-SAS Scouser, B (I'm withholding his name at his request).

'Do you know who this Josh bloke is?' I said, nodding my head in his direction.

'No idea, mate,' said B, in surprise. 'We thought he was with you.'

Phil, our friend from the *Sunday Mirror*, went quiet.

Later it emerged that Josh had been staying in Phil's room, borrowing money off him and poncing food; Phil had assumed he was part of the ITN team in some way. It turned out he didn't work for anyone; he was just another sick war tourist. He'd had his last drink with us, but he'd had a good couple of weeks at it.

One evening another Yank approached me in the street. He was holding a camera and he stopped me from passing by standing in my way.

'What do you want?' I said.

'Are you from the British press?' he asked.

I said I was, and he pulled out a little pocket digital camera.

'I got some great shots here,' he said. 'How much?'

I had a look. They were rubbish.

'Not for me, thanks, mate,' I said. Then an amusing thought occurred to me. 'Mind you, you ought to show them to Julian Andrews.

He's the London *Daily Mirror*'s photographer. I reckon he'd pay you around ten grand for that lot.'

His eyes lit up and off he trotted to our room, where I knew Julian was still packing up his cameras.

Half an hour later, Julian joined me in the street, grinning. 'You tosser,' he shouted 'You sent that fucking American twat to see me. Ten thousand pounds he wanted. What a muppet.'

There were dozens of these nutcases in the hotel, all getting off just on being there. It wasn't hard for Julian to get his own back on me.

A day or so later, a skinny little Canadian in his late twenties offered his services to me while I was paying our weekly bill at reception.

'I understand you're looking for a proper writer to work with you, to help you along with your words,' he said. 'I think I'm your man. I am good with English and I am a journalist.'

I could see Julian laughing in the background.

'I think someone's pulling your plonker, mate,' I said.

'Pulling my what?' he said.

'Someone's having a laugh at your expense,' I said. 'Him, over there.'

He turned to look at Julian.

'But he said you were a struggling journalist who couldn't write properly,' he said, mystified.

'How would he know?' I said. 'He can't read.'

The Canadian drifted away, reluctantly; for weeks afterwards, I'd catch him looking at me with an expression of disdain on his face, like I was the one pretending to be a reporter and not him.

The mickey-taking was fairly relentless. I'd not long split up with my girlfriend and, while Iraq wasn't the best place to find yourself a new one, there were a few attractive sorts – blonde French journalists and the like – hanging around the hotel. One girl had caught my eye: she was absolutely stunning, slim but very curvy with beautiful eyes. She was always well-dressed and perfectly made-up and she seemed to be part of one of the foreign TV crews. I happened to mention to Julian that I liked the look of her. Perhaps the first rule of journalism – ahead of 'always carry a pen' – is, Never, *ever*, mention that you fancy someone. Once something like that gets out, it's a nightmare in media circles, which resemble a sort of club for 13 year olds. Julian was straight over to the ITN security guy, B, and his ex-SAS mate Bob (I'm withholding his surname at his request), who was looking after Channel 4, and they all started giggling at me.

Just then, she stalked past in her high heels, nose in the air, looking utterly unapproachable. Mine weren't the only eyes that followed her, I can assure you.

For days, Bob, B and Julian wound me up mercilessly.

'She's some Italian TV bird called Sophia something,' B would say. 'She's really up for it, mate. You can tell by the way she looks at you.'

'I think you're in there, Chris,' Bob would agree. 'I'd have a crack at her if I was you.'

'Nah,' Julian would say. 'He hasn't got the bottle.'

Eventually, more to shut them up than out of any hope of success, I wandered over to her. She was standing outside the hotel, looking amazing in sunglasses and a tight skirt. The three of them were hiding behind a palm tree, cackling like naughty schoolboys.

'Hi,' I said. 'Sophia, right? How's things? I'm Chris, by the way.'

She looked me up and down with a terrific sneer; I'm an optimist by nature, but I began to feel quite pessimistic about my chances.

Eventually, she spoke.

'You know Warren T. Busheimer (or something)?' she asked, in an accent I couldn't quite place.

'Er... no,' I said. 'Who's that?'

'He TV producer,' she said. 'American.' With that, she walked off, muttering something to herself.

I turned round to find three grown men rolling around in the scrubby grass in front of the hotel.

That evening we were standing on our balcony having a drink, when B grabbed my arm. 'Here, Chris,' he said. 'Come here and see this – your bird's down there.'

I looked down and saw 'Sophia' disappearing down the road with two American squaddies before going into a bombed-out building with them.

There was cackling all round and it quickly developed into hopeless guffawing when they saw my face.

Bob was the first to recover. 'She's a prossie mate – we've been watching her for weeks. She does about two every hour.' He glugged at his lager. 'If I was their sergeant major I'd be demanding to know if they've caught anything off her yet.'

'Her name's Fatima,' said B. 'She used to sort out the regime, Uday and all that lot.'

Julian just chuckled into his beer.

I'd been had, though not by Fatima.

She was just one of the many working girls plying their trade in Baghdad's hotels and in the secret brothels in the back streets; with thousands of US soldiers and private security men around, most of whom hadn't seen a woman in months, there was a strong demand for their services and they did a roaring trade. This dropped off significantly after a US Special Forces man found out the hard way that the girl he'd been seeing wasn't quite as friendly as he'd thought. They found him one day, chopped into about a dozen pieces and left in a couple of black bin liners by the side of the road.

Not long after, Fatima disappeared. A car pulled up outside the Palestine and three Iraqi men jumped out and grabbed her by the hair, dragging her towards the vehicle. I didn't see it happen; those who did say she fought like mad. But they bundled her inside, screaming, and drove her away. Her body was never found.

* * * * *

Phil Coburn, our *Sunday Mirror* colleague, had been disappearing every day for a couple of weeks. He kept telling me it was nothing special but it was obvious he was working on what is known in Fleet Street parlance as a 'secret squirrel': an exclusive story.

It turned out he had been venturing into the South Baghdad badlands looking for an Iraqi family that had been badly shot up in a fire fight between US Marines and Iraqi troops at the beginning of the war.

It had been a terrible incident. The father, Haytham Rahi, was shot in the leg, his wife was killed and their four-year-old daughter, Tghreed, had lost an eye. It had created one of the war's iconic pictures: that of the father, covered in blood and cradling his wounded daughter.

The image had struck a chord with Coburn's editor Tina Weaver and he had been told to track down the family.

It's worth stopping to think about that for a moment. Imagine the danger he was putting himself through; unarmed, unescorted, he was travelling through some of the world's most dangerous towns and villages, knocking on doors, asking questions. There must have been at least a 50% chance of him being kidnapped and killed.

Anyway, eventually, he'd found the Haytham Rahi and he had agreed to pose for photographs with his daughter and to be interviewed.

Phil's problem was, he had no reporter to handle the words.

He approached me one morning. 'Look, Chris,' he said. 'Any chance you can come with me and do this interview? My office are happy if yours are.'

Back home in England, the *Sunday Mirror* would never allow a *Daily Mirror* reporter anywhere near one of its stories. We are owned by the same company, and will share a pint and a laugh with each other in the evenings. But working hours are a different matter; the rivalry between newspapers is tremendously fierce and cuts across all links and ties. (Rivalry is immense even *inside* the office. A friend who works on the *News of the World* tells the tale of how a team from the NoW news desk arrived at an address to find staff from the same paper's features operation already there; they were working on the same story and didn't realise it. A fight ensued.) But this wasn't back home in England. Out in Iraq there was a sense of shared hardship and danger, and favours were commonplace.

'Of course, mate, no problem,' I said.

He came closer, looking conspiratorial. 'There's one other thing,' he whispered. 'Can I borrow your translator Adil as well? It's just that mine's a knob. Every time I take him anywhere he annoys everyone. He's more likely to get me killed than anything.'

His man was slightly out of earshot and out of sight, just standing in the corridor.

'What's wrong with him?' I asked.

Phil shouted for his guy to come into the room. I did a double take. The idea is for your translator to blend in. This bloke looked more like an extra from *Miami Vice* than an Iraqi. He wore bright blue plastic sandals with white socks, tight, stone-washed blue jeans and a lurid orange T-shirt with the words *EAT ME* emblazoned across his rather chubby frame. His ridiculously frizzy hair was topped with a baseball cap bearing the legend *BUGLE BOY*.

Phil said, 'Introduce yourself to him, mate.'

I shook the guy's hand, putting my right palm across my heart in the typical Iraqi greeting. 'Hi,' I said. 'I'm Chris.'

'Hello, my friend!' he beamed. 'I am Coco!'

I turned to Phil. He looked really fed up. 'See what I mean?' he said.

Coco really was a clown. He spent the next five minutes bragging to me. 'I am ex-military,' he said. 'I very tough. I not afraid to die – I take Mr Phil everywhere.'

Phil shooed him out and then told me that every time they knocked on a door the ludicrous Coco would say, 'Leave this to me,' before barging into the home. He'd be booted straight back out and Phil would spend the next 10 minutes apologising for his translator to family elders.

I couldn't really say no to his request to borrow Adil.

That day, we drove to the house where Haytham and his children – Tghreed, and his baby son, Hussein – were staying with relatives, a three-bedroomed villa in a desperately poor suburb of Baghdad, with raw sewage running through the streets outside. Twenty of Haytham's male relatives, who had travelled 200 miles from the south to oversee our interview, crowded into the living area. Tghreed, a pretty little girl despite her lost right eye, giggled and smiled at the camera, snuggling up to her father. Haytham – dressed in a traditional Arab robe and barefooted – ordered a boy to serve us *chai*. On the walls were two faded pictures; one was of the Shia idol Imam Ali, cousin of the prophet Mohammed, the second a dusty photograph of the Ayatollah Mohammed Al Sadr, the Shi-ite Muslim leader murdered by Saddam's thugs and after whom Al Sadr was named. A well-beaten, threadbare Arab carpet covered the earthen floor. There was no furniture. We left our shoes outside and sat cross-legged, hiding the soles of our feet and drinking the warm, sweet tea the boy had brought in tiny glasses.

Women's voices could be heard through a drab curtain separating us from the rest of the home; we would not be allowed to meet them.

A tribal leader, dressed in a white robe and traditional head-dress, hushed the room and beckoned Haytham, a 34-year-old civil servant, to begin his story.

Speaking through Adil, he explained how, on Day Two of the ground war, he and his wife Rbab, 27, had loaded the family into their battered, coffee-coloured Volkswagen saloon and set out for Basra. They'd hoped they would be safer down south. After 200 miles, close to a village called al-Fajer, they saw military positions ahead.

Cradling his daughter and playing with his worry-beads, Haytham said: 'I saw the troops and thought they might be Iraqis. Then I realised that they must be American and I felt safe because I never believed that they would harm civilians. I slowed down and stopped. We started to get out of the car because I wanted the soldiers to see our baby and daughter, so that they would know we were a family. As I got out, the shooting started and I was hit about five times. I could see the bullets hit my wife: her blood was all over her. I screamed at them to stop. My daughter was crying about her eye – which I later realised had been hit – so I grabbed her.

'I crawled into a ditch, crying out to my wife but she didn't reply. I knew she was dead. Her blood was pouring downwards mixing with the blood of my daughter and myself. You cannot imagine what it was like.'

He paused, wiping his eyes and gathering himself. 'After some time, a tank came bearing down on us and my daughter was screaming that it would crush us. They even lowered the big gun to point straight at me. I got up and they stopped two metres from where I was standing. It was then that I collapsed.'

The American troops had handcuffed him and shoved him roughly to the ground, but once they realised he was unarmed they had medevac-d the family to Kuwait, where Haytham and Tghreed were operated on and cared for over the next three weeks. The little girl's right eye was lost but she and her father had otherwise made a full recovery. Baby Hussein had been uninjured.

Haytham spoke quietly, with tremendous dignity, and it was impossible not to be moved by his story.

He said: 'I have no hatred inside me, not even anger towards those people who shot at us. I forgive them totally. We have suffered a great deal but now I want to rebuild my life. The sadness I feel is something for the past. I believe in Allah and I also believe what happened was his will. It is part of the Iraqi way to move on and deal with these things. It makes us strong and gradually I feel I will be happy again. I have two beautiful children and even though my daughter was wounded in the eye, she is still very special. She has suffered and lost a great deal but her spirit has kept us all going. Her strength and love of life is unbelievable. When I see her smile I want to weep with joy that she survived. I just want her to be happy and look just like her friends. Maybe one day she will have an operation to make her wounded eye look better.'

I asked how he was coping with the loss of his wife.

'Losing my wife made me very sad,' he said. 'Can you imagine what it is like? But I have to be strong for our children. In my head, I have dealt with the loss of Rbab. She was the best wife and mother a family could have had, and of course I love her and miss her. But now Tghreed and Hussein are my future. They are everything to me. Things have changed a great deal but now my job is to take care of my beautiful children. That's what my wife would expect of me and that is my duty.'

We sat in silence for a few moments and then I thanked him for his time before we left and started back to the Palestine.

I was troubled. I'd seen the wrecked civilian cars on the western desert highway, and now I'd heard a first-hand account of one of those incidents. Assuming Haytham was telling the truth – and why would he lie? He was asking for nothing – I simply couldn't understand how well-trained troops could have opened fire on a family in a car in daylight. He'd been getting out of the vehicle, for goodness' sake, and they'd been in a tank. It all felt badly, badly wrong.

His courage and honesty had been breathtaking, and soon the world would know his story.

And Phil and I had had a good result too. Phil's hard work had paid off, and we'd get a double-page spread in the *Sunday Mirror* with this story; that was what it was all about, wasn't it? The geopolitical ramifications of the war, the minutiae of 'events on the ground', even the slaughter of civilians… these were matters for others to consider and deal with. All I had to do was report the news I came across.

An hour later, back at the hotel, all thoughts of my spread vanished.

'Bad news about your Jordanian driver, mate,' said one of the security guys as we knocked back some cold beers on the balcony that night.

'What… Mohammed?' I said.

'The guy who brought you in,' he said.

'Yes, that's Mohammed,' I said. 'What about him?'

'Haven't you heard?' he said. 'They found him this morning. Shot dead on the road outside Ramadi. Apparently, they'd stripped him naked and stolen everything, even his clothes.'

I turned away, shaken. It wasn't as though Mohammed and I had been friends. But he was a good guy, a family man with kids, just trying to earn a living. I thought back to that day when we'd been flagged down by that group of armed men. He'd seemed very relaxed then, complacent even.

I'd raised it with him as we got nearer to Baghdad.

'You need to be really careful out here, Mohammed,' I had said. 'I know you're making a good wage out of ferrying people in and out of here but it's not worth dying for.'

'No, Mr Chris,' he'd replied. 'Is fine. I am friend to the Iraqi people.'

In my experience, the Iraqis hated the Jordanians. 'Are you sure?' I'd asked, dubiously.

'Yeeees,' he'd said, grinning.

We'd both got really lucky the day he'd driven me in.

Now his luck had run out.

To Be A Pilgrim

The satellite phone started bleeping as I lay on my mattress.

I was shattered; we'd been out all day, working on various promising leads and watching them all turn to dust and trickle away. Someone had promised to show us a cache of weapons abandoned in a truck by some insurgents but when we got there the lorry was empty. Then we'd moved on to a house where stolen works of art were said to have been left by looters who'd later been killed. Again, we drew a blank. The day had progressed in that general vein until we'd called it a day in the late afternoon. The heat was oppressive, the flies were everywhere and I smelt of burnt excrement. To be honest, if you'd offered me a flight out of there at that moment I'd have snatched your hand off. I'd been in Baghdad two weeks now, but it felt like two years.

I looked at the phone and then my watch; it was 7.30pm local time, so 4.30pm back in the office. Couldn't it wait till tomorrow? But the phone carried on chirping at me. Ah, well. We were supposed to be heading down to the ITN room for a balcony barbecue at eight-ish, so I'd got to get up anyway.

I rolled onto the floor and crawled to the phone.

'Hello?'

'Hughesy?' It was someone on the news desk.

'Yes.'

'Have you found Saddam yet? Piers keeps asking.'

The tone was half joking, but I wasn't in the mood. I wanted to say: *I'm sure Piers is keen on me finding him. Every editor in the world is keen on finding him. I'm keen on it. Around five thousand journalists in Iraq, the entire US Army, the whole of the Iraqi population, Tony Blair, George Bush and Ant and bloody Dec are keen on it. In fact, the only person on the planet who isn't keen on Saddam Hussein being found is Saddam Sodding Hussein.*

I didn't, though. What I actually said was: 'It's not that easy.'

'I know, mate,' said the disembodied voice. 'Just asking.'

The lucky bastard would be clocking off in a couple of hours, probably going out for a few pints, maybe a curry and then home to clean sheets and a comfortable bed.

'Listen, we need you to go to Karbala.'

'Where the hell's Karbala?'

'It's in Iraq, mate.'

'Well, ye-es,' I said.

'Look,' said the voice, bouncing down from space. 'I've sent you a wire story on the email. Have a read and crack on.'

The phone went dead.

I turned on the laptop and waited for the email to come through, listening to the gunfire and general craziness going on outside. The rebels had stepped up their activities in the last few days, killing several US soldiers and kidnapping and murdering Iraqi policemen. Car bombs had become a regular occurrence. *I'm a 40-year-old bloke from the Wirral*, I thought to myself. *What the hell am I doing here?*

The news agency piece arrived on my screen.

It was short.

Millions of pilgrims were expected to descend on Karbala, one of Shia Islam's most famous and holy cities, for a festival of… blah blah… denied under Saddam… blah blah… religious fervour… helicopter gunships.

I rubbed my eyes. Actually, this was quite interesting. I read it again.

For hundreds of years, Shia pilgrims had made an annual journey to Karbala to commemorate the anniversary of the death in battle of Abi Abdillah al-Husain, a grandson of the Prophet Mohammed, in 680 AD (or 61 AH, as the Muslim calendar has it). The festival of Ashura, which traditionally culminated with a mass gathering at Husain's grave, was of enormous significance and many worshippers would whip and beat themselves in a frenzy of religious ecstasy. For almost three decades, Saddam's regime had denied them the right to carry out the pilgrimage. Whenever they tried, the dictator's assault helicopters would swoop in on them and cut them dead in the street. In their dozens and more. With Saddam gone, hundreds of thousands would be flocking to Karbala the next day.

I closed the story. Could religious faith really drive people to mass in the streets even as those deadly choppers swarmed above?

A note attached by the news desk just said, 'Go and have a look'.

I Googled Karbala. It was around 70 miles south of Baghdad, and looked a beautiful place: golden-domed minarets, exotic-looking mosques and, as the focal point, the spectacular tomb of al-Husain.

It would make a change from the filth of Baghdad.

* * * * *

We left early the next morning, taking the almost impassable country route south from the capital to try to avoid as much of the traffic as possible. Even then, the roads were noticeably busier than normal; eight or ten people squeezed into cars, pick-up trucks and lorries with the backs full of pilgrims, others on donkeys, pushbikes or just walking.

I'd made some notes and read them as Nibras drove. Karbala was, effectively, Iraq's Mecca and Medina. Most of the country's Shia icons were buried in tombs within the town and it had become known as the City of Sacrifice and Martyrdom.

Adil, a Shia himself, sat in the front passenger seat, beaming from ear-to-ear with excitement.

'It's the first time in 25 years,' he said. 'Nobody from my family has ever been to the festival of Karbala. This is a great opportunity for me to see it.'

As we neared the city, the roads were choked with people, women dressed entirely in black and trotting along carrying days' worth of provisions on their heads or shoulders, the men smartly-dressed, looking serious, and marching along, their heads nodding like those of chickens to the rhythm of their prayers.

Adil turned to me. 'Many of these people have come from hundreds of miles to be here,' he said. 'They come from Pakistan, Afghanistan, Saudi Arabia. Many Iranians, too. Even some from England.'

Nibras pointed to a group of young men who were dancing along the street in a kind of synchronised hop and a skip motion which seemed to be punctuated with a bigger jump after every three skips. With this jump, the men would cross their hearts and then slap their heads three times. They looked like a group of Morris Dancers Tangoing themselves. My eye caught Julian's. Like me, he was fighting a smile at this strange sight. But something about the pageantry and seriousness of it all stopped us both.

'What are they doing that for?' I asked Adil, nodding at the head-slappers.

'They are punishing themselves for not rescuing Abi Abdillah al-Husain, peace be upon him.'

'What happened to him?' I asked.

'He was slaughtered by his enemy,' he replied. 'But he died with a sword in one hand and the Koran in the other.'

'Nasty,' I said.

'Yes,' said Adil. 'The evil Caliph chopped off his head, his arms and his legs.'

'It's a bit late for a rescue then, isn't it?' I said.

Adil shot me a reproachful look. I hadn't meant any offence: it was the sort of sarcastic, off-the-cuff remark I'd make a hundred times in the office. Adil's look was a reminder that I wasn't in the office.

As the men trotted along, I heard their chant over the sound of the engine: 'Bora bedan nefdeike ya Husain.'

With our heart and our blood we will die for you Husain – the chant I'd heard many times in Iraq, though before always sung in praise of Saddam.

The outskirts of Karbala were lush and green, the sides of the roads densely-palmed and the open fields bursting with leafy alfalfa. It was busier still, here, and we slowed to walking pace: everywhere there were broad smiles, laughter and chatter, along with the dancing and head-slapping. People were starting to notice us – our white faces stood out in the back of the car – and occasionally they would bang on the windows. Adil would wind the window down and talk briefly to them and they'd go away happy.

'What did you say to him?' I asked, after one such incident.

'Chris, he want to know who you and Julian are,' he replied. 'I say you are journalists from England who have come to see Ashura.'

'Don't they mind the fact that we're not Muslim?' I said.

'Not at all,' said Adil. 'They are happy for you to be here. It is not important if you are not believers. In fact, I tell them you are Christians. They are happy, it doesn't matter.'

So much gets said and written about Islamic fundamentalism, and most of it is negative and brutal. But Islamic fundamentalism doesn't get much more hard-core than this was and these people – whose country had just been invaded by Westerners – were accepting us happily. Kids ran along the side of our car, offering us bottles of squash, which we waved away, apologetically. Our stomachs weren't used to the kind of bugs that live in the Iraqi water and we'd been warned to avoid local food and drinks. But Adil smiled and accepted the gifts for himself and Nibras.

We had to stop at one point, where the road narrowed. Two little girls smiled shyly at us and then ran into a house, shouting to their father that foreigners were arriving in a big car. The man ran out and burst into tears, screaming in Arabic and throwing himself on the car as though he was hugging it.

I recoiled slightly. 'What's he saying, Adil?' I said.

'He is thanking you for coming to Karbala,' said Adil.

I smiled nervously at the man. The side window nearest to Julian was dripping in his spittle as he shouted Islamic verse, alternating with 'Shukran, shukran' (thank you, thank you). Adil was glaring at us both, as if daring us to mock the guy. He needn't have worried; it was a humbling, affecting performance.

As we drew into the centre of Karbala, we realised there were more than just hundreds of thousands of pilgrims here – there were millions, in a city smaller than Chester. (Final estimates on day one were seven million).

Around 11am, Nibras dropped us off and we arranged a rendezvous point if anyone got lost.

We looked around. Everywhere in the main square there were men – no women – dancing and slapping their heads. Near to the tomb, now, some were using chains and knotted ropes on themselves – occasionally, we'd see someone with blood pouring down his face. The strange incongruity of this struck me: 60 or 70 miles north, Westerners were now being targeted by death squads, soldiers and policemen were dying almost daily and the streets were becoming increasingly unsafe. Iraq, generally, was sliding towards a state of anarchy and was, in parts, perhaps the most dangerous place on earth. And here I was, in the middle of a Shia hotbed, with a frenzied crowd all around me, watching this unfold like some sort of tourist. I looked at Julian. He seemed to be thinking the same thing. We were utterly at the mercy of the crowd – there was no ex-SAS back-up, no 999, no British Army Warrior to quell the trouble if they turned on us. The only security I'd seen was provided by a few unarmed Iraqi police officers and a few men in robes dotted about the rooftops with AK47s. And yet I felt under no threat from anyone.

Suddenly, there was a shout behind us. A man in robes came trotting down the street motioning for everyone to get out of the way. Twenty yards behind came a baying mob of about 100 men waving bloodied scimitars. It was a frightening sight: the screaming swordsmen were heading straight for us, their faces contorted with fury. Julian and I darted into an alleyway, looking desperately for a door. There was none. I turned round: Adil was stood by the side of the road grinning and clapping at the men as they stormed past, on their way. He caught sight of me, cowering against the wall, and shouted over. 'It's OK, Chris! It's OK, Julian! They do not want to hurt you! They are just practising for when they have to rescue Husain in the big battle!'

The relief was enormous: my legs were wobbling and my heart beating like mad. We rejoined Adil and carried on, part of the surging crowd pressing ever closer to the tomb. The nearer we got to the shrine, the worse the self-harm became. Here, everyone seemed to have a chain in his hand and some men were whipping themselves with swords.

I've covered many demonstrations and riots as a reporter, in London and around the world, even as far away as Kathmandu. I know that head and face injuries often look far worse than they really are – blood streaming down a face often comes from a tiny cut on the scalp. But some of these people were literally gushing the stuff; the ground was slippery with the gore of pilgrims wherever you stood. It was beginning to look like an abattoir or some sort of medieval battleground. Many of the worshippers had clearly been taped up before returning to the fray; their bandages were stained red and dripping.

We passed a group of about 30 men in their 20s, who stood in an extended circle, whipping their heads with chains; they looked trance-like as the blood flew, splattering everywhere, sometimes onto the ecstatic faces of the onlookers. We kept our distance; there wasn't much AIDS in Iraq, given the closed nature of the country, the strong sense of sexual morality and that horrible AEEEDS test at the borders. But there were an awful lot of other blood-borne diseases around that a Western constitution might not be able to take.

We approached the main mosque and joined a queue which rapidly developed a life of its own, an impossible crush that almost carried us off our feet. It was like being sucked into the narrow part of a white-water river: I tried to get out, news stories from the past of hundreds dying in crushes just like this filling my head, but there was no way of breaking free. It was horribly stifling, a steaming, sweating, baying mass, and there were people fainting in front and to the sides. Some, the lucky ones, were hauled upwards and passed over heads to safety. Others were trampled underfoot and left behind.

For several minutes, we had the life squeezed out of us as we headed for the tiny gates of the mosque, where a terrific logjam was building up, before we were spat out on the other side into the main square. Panting, I got away from the melee, Julian following. Backing against a wall, I looked around: there were at least a thousand men kneeling in the main square, praying, and others were joining them all the time. It was an amazing spectacle and the hairs on the back of my neck rose up.

We had been told there were first aid rooms, so we followed a trail of blood. It didn't take long to find them. Built into the side of the crumbling mosque walls were open rooms where the poor had been housed; now, these were filled with wounded men being stitched up and bandaged. We stood in the entrance to one of them, people squeezing past us, grinning in sheepish acknowledgement that they may have been a little over-zealous, before skipping back into the crowd and starting to hit themselves again.

Inside, one of the doctors – speaking perfect English – told us he had treated more than a hundred people that morning and that he was now beginning to bandage up some who were returning for a second time. It was only midday.

Julian nudged me and pointed at the floor. A man lay at my feet, sopping-wet bandages around his forehead and streaks of dried blood all over his face. He was grinning up at me, raising his eyebrows as if to say, 'Hi.' In the gloom – none of these rooms had proper lighting – I saw that he was actually hog-tied: his hands were roped behind his back and then lashed to his feet, which were also strapped together.

Horrified, I looked up at the doctor.

'We had to do this,' the medic said, stitching up a wound in another man's scalp. 'I know it looks bad. But if we didn't tie some of these people they would knock themselves unconscious and literally bleed to death. Some of them are hitting themselves so hard they could damage their brains with the repetitive impact on their skulls. We are very worried about them, actually. We don't want anybody to die through celebrating, do we?'

'Is it OK if I talk to him?' I asked.

'Of course,' said the doctor, with a shrug. 'If he wants to talk to you it's fine.'

Through Adil, I started questioning the man at my feet.

'Is this true, what the doctor says, that you are tied up for your own safety?' I asked.

'Oh yes,' said the man, proudly. 'If I was not tied up I might really hurt myself.'

He looked like he'd fallen through a set of patio doors.

'You already have hurt yourself, haven't you?' I said. 'Would you whip yourself more? Until you bled to death?'

'Yes,' he replied. 'Of course. But I am happy.'

'Can't you just be happy without whipping yourself? Doesn't it hurt?'

'You ask about hurt?' His eyes burned. 'You would not understand.'

'When is it safe to untie you?'

'I asked the doctor, when he tied me up, to untie me when I fall asleep.'

'You actually *asked* the doctor to tie you up?'

'Yes, of course – otherwise I would harm myself.'

All the time, the man was grinning despite the discomfort he was obviously in. If I'd been talking to a drunk in London, I'd have struggled to keep a straight face. But, weird as this was, it was, somehow, not funny. We thanked them and left the doctor and his weary helpers to carry on patching up the never-ending stream of bleeding pilgrims. We headed for the main exit out of the courtyard that held the kneeling worshippers. After once more suffering the horrible crush to leave, we made for our car and, as we walked, I noticed Adil's hands and arms twitching with the beat of a nearby march that was led by a drummer. He clearly wanted to join in. He caught me looking at him and stopped.

'Why do they do it, Adil?' I asked.

'They are remembering the death of Husain,' he said. 'As he suffered, so they suffer.'

We found Nibras waiting with the car at the rendezvous point and we were soon on our way out of the city. As we reached the outskirts, people were running out of their homes, desperately waving us into their driveways.

Adil and Nibras politely declined, but Adil explained what was happening. 'These people have heard you are from Britain,' he said. 'Now that you are returning from Karbala they know that you are true pilgrims who have visited the place of the shrine of Husain. They would like you to stay in their home and offer you refreshments while they clean all of your clothes for you.'

'Why?' I asked.

Adil shrugged. 'So they can take the dirty water from your clothes and pour it onto their crops in the fields,' he said. 'Offering the water of pilgrims to the fields will mean that their crops will grow better than ever this year. The fact that you and Julian have come from so far away gives your water extra value as you are true pilgrims.'

'But we're not Muslims,' I repeated.

'That doesn't matter,' he replied. 'You are pilgrims now.'

As we started on the road back to Baghdad, I realised we had just witnessed an explosion of freedom among the Shia people. For them, this was a very special time in Iraq's history. For the first time since I'd seen those iconic TV pictures of Saddam's statue coming down, I wondered whether the anti-war movement had been wrong.

As we got back to the capital, though, my feelings hardened again.

Here, there was no infrastructure, no law and order, and the malaise that had settled over the country was gradually turning to anarchy.

Insurgents were already stirring up the ancient hatreds between the Shia and the Sunni, between the different tribes, and between all Iraqis and the coalition invaders. The jungle drums were beating across Iraq, the rumour machine working flat out. People were talking, angrily, and the demonstrations across the country were getting bigger and louder and more frequent.

Not long after, the very young men we had seen guarding the rooftops of Karbala with their AKs and narrowed eyes had joined the Shia rebel groups and were following firebrand Shia clerics like Moqtada Al Sadr, son of the murdered Mohammed Al Sadr. In Central Iraq, in places like Fallujah and Ramadi, west of Baghdad, the Sunni groups were already rousing themselves.

Much of this anger was starting to be directed against American soldiers. The Americans had a brilliant war-fighting army, the best the world has ever seen, but they had been utterly unprepared for the post-war situation and that was becoming clearer by the day. Occasionally, they got it right. They had kept their distance from the Shia for the whole week-long celebration at Karbala, for instance, and I hadn't seen any violence. But outside that period, I saw them making huge mistakes, every day, in their behaviour towards Iraqis. A large number of civilian deaths had occurred during the invasion, with some estimates suggesting they had run into many thousands. I think the more pragmatic Iraqis would have accepted at least *some* civilian deaths were inevitable in this, as in any, war (though, obviously, arguments about the legitimacy of the war and the lengths to which the troops had gone to establish the identity of the targets they were hitting would rage on). But what was arousing the anger, even that of the moderates, and quickly turning them against the Western troops, was – as much as anything – the casual, low-level disrespect those troops showed these proud Iraqis. Whenever we drove through Baghdad, we were forever having to brake sharply, or pull to the side of the road, to allow some American convoy of Humvees or other personnel carriers to pass. The lead vehicle in the US convoy would stop at a junction and the gunner on 'top cover' would swivel round, pointing his .50 calibre machine gun right at your windscreen, waving furiously at you to move further away from their vehicle. Often these gunners would be wearing scarves around their faces, and goggles to protect their eyes against the wind and blowing sand; I understood this, but it had the effect of dehumanising these men, so that you felt very threatened by them. Many times, I sat in traffic jams, looking at the faces of the subjugated Iraqis in their cars or standing on the streets, watching the convoys roaring past. The armoured vehicles would disappear on their way, leaving clouds of dust and diesel fumes in their wake, and a lot of angry, impotent people. It irritated us; it must have infuriated the Iraqis.

It wasn't hard to imagine these people going home in the evenings and swapping tales of disrespect and contempt. It was creating a fertile bed for the insurgency to grow.

Bodies In A Car

I awoke with a start; it was about 5.30am, and someone was banging on our doors, shouting. I could hear frantic footsteps pelting up and down the corridor outside.

It was as though 50,000 volts had just shot through my body: I went from asleep to wide-awake and trembling with adrenalin in about a second and a half. I jumped up – I'd taken to sleeping fully-clothed, with my boots lying next to the bed so that I could slip into them easily if we thought we were about to be robbed. I'm not sure what difference I thought footwear would make in that eventuality; it was just one of those mildly irrational, almost superstitious, things you did in Iraq.

I ran to put my ear to the door, listening.

I could just about make out the sounds of terrified people dashing about over the noise of my own blood pumping in my ears. My heartbeat was around the 200bpm level: if you wanted to devise the perfect conditions for bringing on a coronary, you wouldn't have to look much further than putting a slightly unfit, hungover, 40-year-old smoker in a hotel he thinks has just been overrun by Iraqi insurgents.

Slowly, I tried to calm myself down. No-one had burst in with an AK yet and the banging seemed to have receded; it was further down the corridor now, though it still sounded urgent, as if someone was trying to wake all the guests.

I opened my door and saw tired-looking heads popping out of other rooms all along the corridor. The man in the room next to us was from a Japanese television network.

'I think we're being overrun, Chris,' he said.

A hotel porter sprinted round the corner.

'The Americans have gone!' he was shouting. 'The Americans have gone! Everyone is running into the hotel! There is much danger now! Much danger!'

Bloody hell! We *were* being overrun!

I ran to the window just as Julian emerged from the adjoining room. 'What's going on?' he asked.

'Not sure,' I said, looking down below. 'They're saying the Yanks have buggered off.'

It was true. The American tanks had disappeared during the night, and the crowds that usually thronged the razor wire defences around The Palestine were pouring through the gaps and towards our hotel reception.

'Fuck!' said Julian. He ran for our pile of belongings.

We'd planned for this many times, though I don't think we'd ever actually thought it would happen. 'If we do get attacked,' Julian had said, 'we leave everything except the absolute essentials.'

The essentials were as much food and water as we could carry, our passports, money – we had thousands of dollars with us, for paying Adil and Nibras, buying supplies and bribing locals – Julian's camera and our Thuraya satellite phones. These were amazing things, rented by the *Mirror* from a company in London. You could use them anywhere in the world, and they also provided details of your exact position via the GPS network. I was particularly attached to mine and never let it out of my sight. Julian, who was more relaxed than me, thought I was paranoid but my view was, if it all really did hit the fan and I ended up having to do a runner somewhere out in the badlands, at least I could phone someone – the British Army, the US Marines, a mate in London, whoever... just to let them know where I was. That, I felt, would give me a fighting chance.

Hurriedly, we filled a couple of rucksacks and left the room. We weren't quite sure where to go, but we knew we couldn't stay put. The former SAS guys looking after the British TV companies had chosen the sixth floor to stay on because, they said, any looters would start on the top floor and work their way down. They might have been winding us up – they knew we were only five floors from the top, after all – but we didn't want to find out the hard way that they weren't.

'We need to get to wherever the Americans are,' said Julian.

'OK,' I said. Where was that, though? They seemed to have

abandoned the hotel completely. Had they all been slaughtered by some sort of rampaging mob? Had there been a massive uprising? My mind was racing as we ran down the stairs. I remember thinking that we could maybe try and make it to the riverside just behind the hotel and try to swim the Tigris to the US bade on the other side. It was a ludicrous thought; the river was wide and the current was strong and we'd never have made it across. But you think ludicrous things when you believe you're in mortal danger.

As we got to a couple of floors above reception, we could hear a full-scale riot going on – people were screaming and shouting and roaring, and there was the sound of smashing glass.

Several American reporters passed us, running the other way.

'Get upstairs!' shouted one. 'Get away! It's going crazy down there… they're going to kill everyone!'

Julian and I stopped and looked at each other.

Despite this warning, neither of us fancied going back up. Who knew who was up there? And what if they set the hotel on fire, or went up floor by floor, systematically executing people? We felt our best hope was to try to get outside.

'Fuck it,' said Julian. 'Come on.'

We hurried down the final flight of stairs, rounded the corner and saw the hotel lobby area was crammed full of Iraqis; some of them we recognised as people who were normally held back behind the wire by the American soldiers. But I couldn't see any weapons, apart from those being held by the scared-looking hotel guards, who looked ready to down tools and run away. The crowd didn't look focused; they seemed more to be chanting and shouting aimlessly and weren't paying too much attention to us.

The only way out was through the mob, so we entered the fray and started pushing our way through, trying to appear calm and confident. It took a long time, probably several minutes, with a lot of jostling and angry shouts in Arabic, before we made it to the front door. As we did so, we saw a few American soldiers had arrived back at the hotel and were busy trying to regain control of the situation.

A senior American officer drove up in a Humvee, just as Adil and Nibras rounded the corner, with worried looks on their faces that changed to relief once they saw us.

'Bloody hell, Adil,' I saw. 'It's good to see you this morning. What the hell is all this about?'

'I think is just a demonstration, Chris,' he said, 'maybe not too serious. But you can never tell. They saying they want jobs, and water, and electricity, and they angry that the situation isn't getting any better. They all saying different things.'

I looked at the disjointed, disparate groups of men still thronging the lobby and the outside of the hotel. There was a lost air about them and it suddenly hit me; they didn't actually know how to demonstrate properly. Years of Saddam's crushing authoritarianism had left them unable to cope with the freedom to vent their feelings in an ordered, united way. They had been institutionalised.

Bob arrived back at the hotel in Channel 4's armoured Land Rover, having been out and about on some early morning recce. In his light-coloured slacks and immaculately styled hair, he looked more like a business executive than an ex-Para who had spent years fighting in Northern Ireland, The Balkans and God knows where else. He was known for taking a very calm view of the anarchic world around us and I watched him taking in the scene as he stepped from the Land Rover. He didn't look very concerned. He smiled and nodded at us. 'Good morning, chaps,' he said. 'And how are we today?'

'A bit on edge, mate,' I replied.

'Oh, I don't think there's much to worry about,' he said. 'The tanks have gone but I think they're coming back. Anything happens, stick with us, we'll get you out of it if it all goes off. OK?'

That was reassuring, but we were still nervous. Ultimately, Bob's loyalty would be to the Channel 4 team who were paying him. If it all went pear-shaped, he'd do his best but we'd be an afterthought.

Eventually the melee inside the hotel died down and order was restored, the crowd dispersing back to the wire after briefly chanting about how great Iraq was. It had all ended with a whimper, not a bang, but as a gauge of how local people were reacting to the general post-war break-down of society and the destruction of the country's infrastructure it was a telling signpost on a worrying-looking road. It felt, to us all, as though it was just a matter of time before there was a serious rebellion of some sort. The day before, we'd heard that armed gangs had been carrying out daylight public executions of former Ba'ath party members and sympathisers in the streets; there were no police keeping order and a warrior nation that had its emotions suppressed for more than 25 years was bursting at the seams.

With the tanks trundling back – we never found out where they'd gone, or why – and more troops on the scene, the perimeter was re-established, though people continued milling and chanting angrily on the other side of the wire. It felt amazingly good to find yourself back in an oasis of safety in all the madness that was taking place in Baghdad and, again, I felt slightly hypocritical that American guns were protecting me. Not so hypocritical, though, that I decided to take my chances outside.

One man beyond the fence was being particularly vocal about something.

'I wonder what he's banging on about?' I said, to no-one in particular.

'Here's a revolutionary idea for a journalist,' said Bob, his voice dripping with sarcasm. 'Why don't you go and ask him?'

As usual, he had a point.

Julian and I approached the man, Adil alongside.

As we got nearer, he started waving, indicating that he wanted us to follow him to see something down an alleyway just on the other side of the street. Adil looked immediately wary, and grabbed our arms.

'I am not sure this is a good thing,' he said. 'I don't know what is down there.'

We passed some US troops guarding the entrance. The man was only yards away; he was pointing towards a car. I looked back. There were soldiers and tanks everywhere. Surely we were safe?

'We'll be OK, Adil,' I said.

We approached the car and the smell hit us from 10 yards away. It was already a hot day and the back of his car was piled high with shattered, burned corpses, just baking in the sun.

It made me gag.

The man was now crying and pointing to the horrendous jumble of flesh and bone in his car, shouting something in Arabic.

All I could think was: *You actually loaded them in there and drove up here with them in the back. My God.*

But Adil was listening, gravely, and he turned to us. 'These people were killed in a housing area about 20 miles south of Baghdad,' he said. 'This man says an arms dump, full of rockets and explosives collected by the Americans, exploded this morning. It bombarded many houses with missiles and blew up some of the buildings, killing many people. These are some of the people.'

I looked at the man, still sobbing and shouting at us.

From his facial expressions and his tone, he seemed to be alternating between blaming us and asking for our help.

'What does he want from us?' I asked, backing away from the car and trying to ignore the smell.

'He says he wants justice.'

I sighed. He wasn't going to get that from us. I found this kind of thing terribly frustrating, even – if I'm honest – irritating. Every time we left our hotel we would be grabbed by locals, yelling at us about some new atrocity or the fact they had no water or jobs. We would explain that we were journalists and could not help and their anger would deepen and they'd scream at us that we *must* help them. The truth, of course, is that there really was nothing we could do. Even getting emotionally or practically involved was wrong: you would just become part of the problem, raising false hopes and – frankly, I know it sounds callous – wasting your own time too. Simply, we couldn't get involved in anything except by filing stories and photographs. At least from that point of view this had legs.

'Tell him we can't help him there,' I said. 'But we'll report it for our newspaper in England.'

It was a Saturday. This had the potential to be a very interesting tale but it wouldn't wait for the *Daily Mirror* on Monday. Rather than let a potential exclusive go to waste, I called the news desk of the *Sunday Mirror*, which obviously had an edition the next day.

I outlined the story.

'Brilliant, mate… can you file it now?'

Why do they always want it *now*?

'No. I haven't even seen the place yet,' I replied. 'So far it's just a few bodies rotting in a car. It might be nothing. Just asking if you're interested in principle?'

'Yes.'

Phone down, into Nibras's car and away we went.

'I hope he buries them soon,' I said to Julian. 'Surely he's not going to drive around Baghdad showing them off to all and sundry?'

Julian laughed. 'Yeah,' he said. 'It's not as if he'll need a hand digging the graves... there's three or four hands lying on the front seat.'

And we carried on in that vein. There's that lazy, shorthand theory, that joking about this sort of thing is the best way to deal with the horror. Maybe that's what we were doing. Or maybe we were just being heartless and juvenile. Whatever, we did it for the next 20 miles. Looking back, I cringe with embarrassment and guilt but it wasn't till we were almost there that I noticed Adil's face. Sat in the front of the car, he was quietly seething about our cruel banter.

We travelled towards a huge column of thick black smoke in the near distance and as we drew near we could hear the crackling of RPG rounds and small arms ammunition overheating and firing into the sky. We pulled up on the side of a freeway overlooking an area of wasteland half a mile across. A fire was raging in the centre of what looked like a blackened scrap heap of molten metal and jagged shapes. This was the ammo dump. On the far side, we could see wrecked houses where – as the man had said – missiles had struck after the heat had set them off. An ITN camera team pulled up alongside us in an armoured Land Rover as a huge boom sounded from the dump. It was a huge, startling sound that made my insides vibrate, and we all dived behind the Land Rover. A large rocket had shot around 30 feet into the air before plummeting to the ground and exploding. Bits of smoking debris flew over our heads and into a nearby field.

An armoured convoy of US troops arrived, scratched their heads for five minutes and then drove off. There wasn't much they could do about it and they probably wanted to avoid a confrontation with the locals who had started turning up and were looking angrily towards them.

Nibras drove his car further up the road to a safer spot while we watched the inferno rage on. But there was nothing much to see apart from a blazing fire and loads of really dangerous things going off every five minutes, so we headed for the houses. We walked in a long arc around the fire and, after fifteen minutes, we got to the housing which

George Galloway, speaking here to Tariq Aziz in Iraq before the war, helped us get into the country.
Picture: John Ferguson / Daily Mirror

Despite their poverty, and the cruelty of the regime, happy, laughing children were everywhere.
Pictures: John Ferguson / Daily Mirror

At a football match just before the war. Many of the Iraqis wore English soccer shirts...

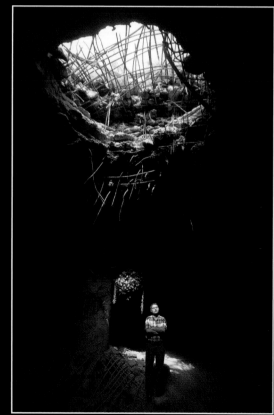

... even as Allied 'smart bombs' targeted their leaders.

Pictures: John Ferguson / Daily Mirror

The mood quickly changed after Saddam was deposed. Demonstrations outside our hotel grew in frequency and fervour: here, a US soldier keeps a look-out for snipers as another protest begins.
Picture: Julian Andrews

Julian Andrews cooks by candle-   head-torch – during a power cut at the Palestine Hotel.

Millions flock to Karbala for the Shia festival of Ashura. We saw no violence and felt no threat, despite the mayhem that was developing nearby.
Picture: Julian Andrews

Houses were wrecked and dozens killed and injured when an ammo dump blew up. Within months of the end of the war, death and destruction, whether accidental or deliberate, was relatively commonplace.
Picture: Julian Andrews

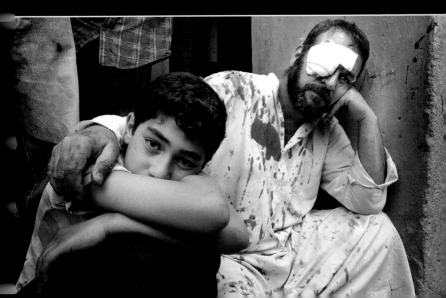

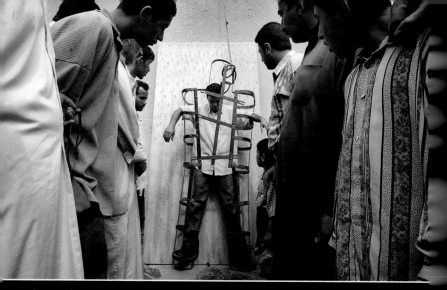

A youth poses for our camera inside a metal torture suit created on Uday Hussein's orders.
People were placed inside it and lowered into a swimming pool where electric shocks were
administered to them.
Picture: Julian Andrews

Two families uncover the remains of their loved ones, murdered by Saddam and buried in the cemetery outside Abu Ghraib.

Pictures: Julian Andrews

had been hit. Close up, it was a frightening sight: whole roofs had been ripped off, sides of homes caved in. Three houses had been completely demolished by a couple of missiles that had self-ignited, flown half a mile and smashed down into them; all that was left were craters filled with water and piles of twisted metal and rubble. A bloodstained man, his eye covered by a hastily-made patch, sat with his arm around his young son. The expression on his face was a strange mixture of fury and resignation: it might take a while, he seemed to be thinking, but we'll get even. He looked chilling.

Adil was very quiet.

Suddenly, a man broke from the watching crowd that was gathered nearby. He hugged Adil and whispered in his ear and each held his hands up to the heavens.

Adil turned to me. 'This is Shakir,' he said. 'He is my older brother. We have many relatives living here but, thanks be to Allah, they are all safe and well.'

I have rarely felt so awful. I thought back to the sick jokes Julian and I had been making on the way down here about that screaming maniac touring the city with his car full of unrecognisable corpses. A dozen people had died here, and at that point Adil hadn't known whether his relatives were among them. He hadn't said a word but had kept quiet and dignified.

'Adil, I'm sorry,' I said.

He smiled, and shook his head, indicating we were forgiven. He was getting used to our strange English ways and we were, slowly, becoming friends.

A group of wounded people, wrapped in makeshift bandages, stood or lay nearby. They were the walking wounded, with bloodied heads and torso injuries that had been hastily treated by local doctors, and who had discharged themselves already from the local hospital. The hospital, I knew, was our next port of call. It's an awful rule of tabloid journalism: you follow the bodies. None of us wanted to go there, but it had to be done. The doctors needed to be interviewed, any loose ends tied up.

The clinic – and it was little more than that – was brimming with people who had sustained various injuries and who were moaning in pain for lack of morphine. Dignified and grave, the doctors showed us from room to room, from patient to patient, never asking their permission, as though accepting that we had some sort of right to enter this very private place. Gradually, we realised we didn't. We were intruding, somehow abusing our positions – big, strong Westerners in a cowed, defeated country. We wouldn't be allowed to do this in England, so why should we here? None of it added to the story and we took no pictures and interviewed no patients; we walked out of the place, the bad taste of voyeurism in our mouths.

I don't believe anyone ever found out the truth about why this stuff went off, killing and horribly maiming so many people. There were two theories – either the Americans had been negligent and allowed a fire to start and ignite the pile of arms, or a local had set off the rockets deliberately to create trouble for the Americans. In a few days, this dreadful story had spread all over Iraq and it certainly did the invading troops no favours. One thing I was sure about: it was a ridiculous, even bizarre, place to leave a huge, unguarded weapons dump.

Back at the hotel, Phil and Steve joined us and we started drinking the rotten Amstel lagers that we had left. Adil and Nibras were tucking into some food from our cupboard, and I joined them.

I still felt some tension from the earlier incident with the man and the dead bodies and wanted to make sure we weren't compounding the offence by getting the beers out.

'Does it offend you if we drink alcohol, Adil?' I asked.

He straightened up and motioned for Julian and me to follow him on to the balcony. He pointed to a small café by the side of the river. A group of Iraqi men were drinking glasses of lager, laughing and joking.

'I used to be one of them for a long time,' he said. 'I would often be drunk and when I went home my father said nothing. Now he is proud I am working for a living, and so am I. No. It does not offend me to see people drinking. I stopped because I wanted to.'

He smiled, and walked back into the room.

Later, after he and Nibras had gone home, I sat on the balcony as dusk fell, drinking a warm beer with a few other media people, and thought about the man who had brought the bodies to us. Earlier on, I'd convinced myself he was just another idiot. Why not just come and tell us about the disaster and then leave? There's an insidious self-importance that affects some journalists in places like Iraq. With your satellite phones, and your pockets full of dollars, and your terribly sophisticated Western sensibilities, you can end up, unconsciously perhaps, looking down on the raggedy-clothed people in whose country you are living. The more I thought about it, the more I realised I had fallen victim to this self-importance. Somehow, I'd thought *I* was at the centre of all this, when I was just an instrument by which these horrors could reach a slightly wider audience. This was just a desperate man, with no idea what to do, a man just looking for an answer to why these people had all just died. For all I knew, those could have been the bodies of his family. Maybe he'd assumed he'd get some kind of action, that we had the power to do something about what had happened, that the sight of the bloating corpses would shock us so much we'd somehow make things better. After all, newspapers use shocking images and words to make their points. Our view – that since we hadn't killed anyone, we were not responsible – didn't translate. We were British, part of the 'Coalition'. Our Prime Minister had egged George Bush on to start this bloody war. Our troops had killed Iraqis who, a few months before, had posed absolutely no threat to them or anyone else. American troops had killed *thousands* of Iraqis, for goodness' sake, some of them civilians. It was British-style democracy that we were trying to export to their torn-up country, the same democracy that had allowed Tony Blair to make the decisions he had made. I hadn't wanted to listen to what the guy was saying, or look at the inside of his car. Once I'd known the basics of the story, I'd shut him out of my mind. I could claim that I was serving the greater good; I'd got another double page spread in the *Sunday Mirror*, after all, and the world (or part of it) knew what had happened. But the truth was that all I had been interested in was a great story.

That's how we see things – as 'great stories'.

The greater good is a by-product of what we do. It's not why we do it.

Bob, the former SAS man looking after Channel 4, wandered over. 'Alright, Chris?' he said.

'Not bad, Bob, thanks,' I replied. 'Funny old day, what with one thing and another.'

'Tell me about it,' said Bob. 'Look at Steve.'

I turned to look and saw one of his colleagues. He looked pale and ill, and was holding a blood-stained bandage to his arm, though he showed no signs of any pain. He was chatting to another security man and, as I watched, he said his goodbyes and left.

'Off to have that looked at by the Doc,' said Bob.

'What happened?' I said.

'Rebels hit them,' he said. 'Three of them jumped in his TV crew's van with AKs. He was unarmed at the time but he disarmed them. Got shot himself for his troubles.'

'Bloody hell,' I said.

'It's just part of the job,' said Bob. 'When three guys jump in your car with guns you have a quick decision to make. Some people get it wrong, back off, do nothing. You need the bottle and the brains to be aggressive and have a go at them and take them by surprise. Do what they're not expecting. Steve had a go and he's lived to tell the tale.'

Instruments Of Torture

As close as we got to Adil and Nibras, we knew we'd never meet their wives. Both Shi'ite and Sunni Muslim cultures are extremely male-dominated, with women subjugated by Western standards; while the men live lives of relative freedom, within strict religious boundaries, the women are given away in arranged marriage to strangers, forced to wear the veil and hidden away at home. In many Islamic countries, they're not allowed to drive, to work or take part in the political process. In Saddam's secular Iraq, this had been less pronounced, and certainly not officially enforced, but it was still the reality for many Iraqi women.

(For some, it went much further than that. After the war was over, with electricity in critically short supply, the Brits in Basra hit on the idea of producing a public information ad to run on TV encouraging people to conserve power. They hired Iraq's leading actor and actress to appear in it and drew up a basic script which called for the 'husband' to come home from work and find the 'wife' busy in the kitchen while the kids were watching TV. Every light and electrical gadget in the house would be on and the husband would take his wife on one side and patiently explain to her that it was important to turn inessential equipment off to save electricity. 'Just act as you would normally,' the Brits told them.

Away they went to make the short film.

A day or two later, they came back, and proudly unveiled the fruits of their labour.

Lights. Camera. Action.

In comes the husband. He takes one look at the blazing lights, strides over to his wife and punches her in the face. She falls

89

theatrically to the floor and he grabs her and drags her into the living room, where he explains about the power situation.

'Er, yes,' said the British officer who'd commissioned the ad. 'Can we make it just a teeny bit less violent?'

The actor – and the actress – looked at him as though he was mad. Like, *I thought you said just act normally?*)

Here is not the place to discuss the subjugation of women in Middle Eastern society but it was something we talked about from time to time with Adil and, as his English improved, Nibras too.

One lunchtime, after a morning spent following up rumours about Saddam's whereabouts – he was supposed to be driving around Baghdad in a taxi – we got talking.

'How come I can never meet your wife, Adil?' I said. 'If I was married and you came to England, it would be no problem – you'd come round to my flat and she'd be there.'

He shifted in his seat, looking embarrassed. 'We don't allow other men to meet our wives because we know what you would be thinking, because you are a man. And that is not right.' There was a long silence, and then we all laughed in recognition of the truth. 'I understand it is different in England, but this is our way.'

'So if you met my wife or girlfriend in London, would you be looking at her in the same way?' I asked.

He giggled nervously. 'It depends if she is nice or not.'

Julian and I laughed. We were about to ask the obvious question – was his wife attractive? – when we caught Nibras's eye. He was wincing and shaking his head, a clear message in his expression: *'You wouldn't ask a Glaswegian from the Gorbals if his wife was fit... don't ask a Shi'ite Iraqi from Al Sadr.'*

So we didn't.

Adil had married late for a Shia – he had been well into his mid-30s – and he talked with great passion about meeting the woman of his dreams, a Kurdish girl from a middle-class family whose father had made it clear he strongly disapproved of their union. Nevertheless, she became his wife and moved into the family home in one of the worst slums of Baghdad, living with the other 22 members of Adil's family. I say 'worst slums', but I don't believe Adil would have lived anywhere else in the world. When he walked through the streets of Al Sadr, he didn't see what we saw – the ankle-high rivers of human sewage running down the middle of the streets, the dead dogs, or the central reservation made of slowly smouldering junk that acted as the local rubbish dump. Nor did he see the masked men standing on the roofs of houses giving us dead-eyed stares and slowly following our progress with the tips of their AK47s. As Adil walked through the filth-ridden, stinking streets, he saw his kingdom: you'd have thought he was just popping into the area to visit his loyal subjects. He grinned at local boys and men, shaking their hands and kissing them on both cheeks as he walked with a loose gait that obviously gave him authority but made him appear like an Iraqi Huggy Bear to me.

We were enormously privileged in being able to visit this place with absolute impunity: American troops would only enter in an armoured convoy, with air cover, if at all. It was possible because Adil's father, despite his poverty, enjoyed an exalted position, like that of a sheikh, in the area.

Once, not long after we started working together, Adil took me to Al Sadr, stood in the middle of a pot-holed street strewn with faeces and garbage and raised his hands to the sky. 'Look at this beautiful city,' he shouted. 'This is my city, my beautiful city.'

I would be lying if I claimed it gave me the same spiritual experience. But I did see people who were the living proof that there can be dignity in poverty, riches in the most surprising places.

One day, Adil and his brother Shakir invited us to lunch at his house.

'Do not eat in the morning, Chris,' said Shakir. 'I want you to be starving when you get here. We are going to make a biryani for you.'

This is Iraq's national dish. Don't try to tell an Iraqi it's an Indian meal: they will get very upset about it.

It was raining, unusually, and Nibras parked his car at the end of a sodden alleyway, telling us that the first gate on the left was the one which led to Adil's home. Around 20 locals were standing in the alleyway to catch sight of the Englishmen Adil had been working for, the British journalists who he had proudly announced would be coming to visit.

We got out, slightly nervously. Imagine the titles sequence for *Coronation Street*, where the camera pans into the back alley behind some working class estate in Manchester. Then turn up the brightness a few notches, remove all the tarmac and add flat roofs: that was where we were standing.

We'd been told we would be fine, that nobody would dare try anything, like a spot of kidnapping, because of the family's respected position locally. Still, I was certainly keen to get to the gate.

Adil met us and ushered us silently into a courtyard, where a carpet had been hung from a washing line to hide the kitchen in which the women were preparing our food.

We took off our boots, great big things that made the sandal-shod kids playing in the courtyard laugh out loud, pointing and running off to tell everyone about the huge shoes these strange white guys wore. A little girl, about three years old and wearing some kind of pyjama suit, shyly pushed her way through the carpet and shouted to Adil. 'Baba, baba.' ('Daddy, daddy.') He picked her up gently and proudly showed her to us before patting her on the head and asking her to tell mum to hurry up with the lunch. His love for the little girl shone from him.

We were ushered into a plain, brick-walled room that had been white-washed many years ago and had no furniture. The floor was of flattened and brushed dirt and an old, recently-beaten carpet was spread out in front of us. The head of the house – 'The Boss', as Adil called his father – was already waiting for us in a darkened corner, wearing a brilliantly white robe and head scarf. A tall, thin man with a greying beard, he nodded at us and greeted us in the traditional way: 'Salaam aleikum.' ('Peace be upon you.')

'Aleikum salaam,' we replied ('Upon you be peace.')

He looked away and didn't say another word to us all afternoon.

We had been warned that there would be no chairs and that we would sit on the floor, so we sat, awkwardly, trying to cross our legs and keep the soles of our feet firmly on the ground and out of sight. Three fading photographs were on the walls; the main one was of the Iranian revolutionary leader Ayatollah Khomeini, the others of two other Shi'ite icons who I didn't recognise. Other male relatives filed in, greeting us and joking among themselves. It was a happy scene and the atmosphere was congenial. Adil's nephew, Ali, walked in, carrying a silver tankard. He filled it with mineral water from a bottle and passed it to me. I took a sip and thanked him.

'Not at all,' he replied.

It was perhaps the politest and most clearly-delivered *Not at all* I've ever heard, and it came from a 16-year-old boy brought up in the heart of the toughest part of the most dangerous city in the most volatile country in the world, after my country had just invaded his. And we think *we're* the superior civilisation.

The biryani arrived, a huge, metal dish full of steaming rice, sultanas, chicken and spices, and Adil's older brother Shakir was at once in his element. He was his father's deputy in the tribal hierarchy and, despite the fact that Adil earned the household money, he called the shots where the sons were concerned. He began ordering his little brother about, telling him to pile our plates high with food and bread, until both of us had to grab his arms and plead with him not to give us any more. Adil handed over cutlery and more bottled water, neither of which the family had use for and which showed how mindful he was of our comfort. Then he pointed to his father, and I rattled off a speech of thanks to the old man for allowing Adil to help us in our work.

He remained impassive. We began to eat – just Julian and I, with the family watching keenly. It was clear that they would wait until we had finished eating, and had left, before they began. I'd eaten breakfast that morning, and began to wish I'd followed Shakir's advice. There was so much of this food and I hated to give offence by leaving any of it on my plate. Not that it was all that hard: I'd been living off tins and packets of rubbish for weeks, and this was delicious.

Halfway through, another older man arrived.

As he walked in, he said his *Salaam aleikums*, and we uttered our responses while trying not to spit sultanas everywhere. He sat down opposite Adil's father and began chatting away to him loudly, apparently about some local matter of import.

Adil leaned over and whispered, 'It's another one of the bosses.'

It's interesting, even amusing, watching older Iraqi men in conversation; they're loud, they speak over each other and everyone else and accompany everything with frantic gesticulations. The two bosses looked as though they were discussing very important matters – perhaps proposals to end a tribal dispute, or plans to make peace with the Sunnis.

'What are they talking about?' I whispered to Adil.

He laughed. 'Just a bit of gossip, as you call it.'

It turned out it was about a neighbour's son, who'd had to be beaten because he had stolen some bread. Later, it had emerged that the poor lad had believed it was his bread – so technically he wasn't an ali baba (thief) after all, and it had all panned out fine in the end. I loved this about Iraq: petty theft was one of the most serious social crimes one could commit. In a poor country, where food and material possessions were scarce and hard-won, this convention was part of the glue that bound them together.

It was an amusing couple of hours.

At one point, Shakir nudged me and began to tell the story of how, one night, a few days after Baghdad had fallen, the family had heard the terrifying pro-Saddam chant '*Bora bedan nefdeike ya Saddam*' from a baying mob outside their home.

For Adil and his family, it had been a truly chilling sound, particularly chanted close by at night and by a crowd of men. At this point, many Iraqis, particularly those who had suffered most under him, could not accept that Saddam was gone. They expected him and his thugs to return to power and to exact a terrible revenge on those who might have supported the invading forces; if this happened, no-one doubted that those in the anti-Saddam redoubt of Al Sadr would be among the first in the firing line.

Ignoring their father's pleas to keep away, Shakir and Adil had peered through their glassless window into the street outside.

Astonished, they burst out laughing and ushered the entire family outside to see what they had seen.

In the muddy street outside they saw a donkey, dressed in a ludicrous imitation of one of Saddam's uniforms and somehow fitted with a huge comedy moustache, being led past by a delighted crowd of Shia teenagers, cheered on by elders and tribesmen.

Saddam City was laughing at the man who had given the place his name, and killed so many of its people.

Adil's relatives were very keen on football, and could barely hide their disgust at my lack of knowledge of the sport. Julian managed to pull us through with his forensic memory of matches going back 20 years, which was more than matched by Adil's own knowledge of the British game. Sitting on this earthen floor, hearing names like Kenny

Dalglish and David Beckham bandied about, and arguments over who had won the 1994 FA Cup Final, I felt a strong sense of disconnection: close your eyes, and it was as though the war hadn't happened, and we were on a slightly adventurous back-packing holiday.

Eventually, we got up to leave, Adil's brother looking hungrily at the food. We shook the hand of each man there, including Adil's father; he never once smiled, but looked proudly up into the air and nodded sagely as Adil translated our rambling thanks and one of his little nephews shuffled up to me on skinny little matchstick legs disappearing into the tops of my boots. And then we were back out into the heat of the day. The sun was bright on the white walls and the morning's rain had all but dried up, leaving the track rutted and baked hard. A crowd of fifty or so neighbours had gather to watch us leave; they pointed at us, laughing and making amusing comments to each other.

Adil's little daughter ran out, shouting 'Baba, baba' and jumping into his arms. He placed her gently down and she climbed into Nibras's car with us. We waved to the crowd and slowly drove away. Twenty yards down the track, Nibras stopped and Adil passed his daughter to a woman who was walking back, saying something to her. She smiled, and nodded and walked away with the girl.

Nearby was a mosque where Adil prayed. The Imam, a fat and jolly-looking man, with a huge white beard and grey robes, wanted to meet us and tell us of some important news. He took both Julian and me by the hand and led us round the back of the tiny, one-roomed building. There, hanging from a wall, was a bizarre object. It was a metal frame, like a sarcophagus, about seven feet tall and shaped like a man, with the limbs, torso and head fashioned out of strips of crudely-beaten iron.

'What on earth is that?' I asked.

Adil spoke to the Imam and then relayed his responses to me.

'It was taken from one of Uday Hussein's offices,' he said. 'It was one of his favourite torture implements.'

It's a hallmark of all of the world's ludicrous dictators that they love to shower titles, positions and the baubles of power on their favourites. Saddam was no different, and he had placed his psychotic son in charge of Iraq's Olympic Committee. Uday doesn't seem to have been much of a man manager, or a sports psychologist, and he wouldn't have bothered with fancy rubbish like nutrition, training and recovery time. No, he'd had an altogether simpler, more old-fashioned way of spurring his athletes on to ever greater heights, and I was looking at it.

'He would put them into this,' said Adil, 'and a crane would lift them up and dip them in a swimming pool. The pool had live electric wires running into it and he would have them switched on.'

'My God,' I said, staring at the contraption. 'What happened to them?'

Adil shrugged. 'Some were electrocuted. Some drowned. Some survived and probably ran quicker next time.'

Once again, a group had gathered around us, men of all ages standing in the courtyard and wincing as the Imam talked.

Julian wanted photographs of the device and we asked if anyone was prepared to 'pose up' inside it to give the images some perspective. A young man of 18 was elected and dutifully allowed himself to be strapped up in the iron suit. Julian began taking pictures, but it soon became clear that the teenager was getting very uncomfortable. He started sweating, and then moaning, and he was quickly unstrapped. His friends, who had been mocking him mercilessly as Julian took pictures of him, now ushered him away, looking embarrassed and vaguely unhappy with us.

'What's it doing here?' I said, when the crowd had gone.

'It was brought to the Mosque because the man who took it thought that was the best place for it to go,' said Adil. 'We had no police to give it to. Where else would you take it?'

The Imam said something else, speaking rapidly and firmly, and Adil listened. Then he said: 'The Imam is furious that it was looted in the first place. Looting is a crime under Islam and he is not happy to have it here. He says he would like you to take it away with you if you want it.'

'To be honest, Adil, we don't really,' I said, looking at Julian. 'It's a horrible thing. What would *we* do with it?'

He shrugged. 'We could pay a contribution to the mosque,' I said. 'To thank you all for co-operating. Maybe that would pay for someone to take it elsewhere and dump it?'

We quickly agreed a fee to go to the welfare fund; the Imam looked delighted.

Looting is taken very seriously by Muslims, even though the ali babas had run riot once the regime was removed. After the war was over, Adil told us, the Imams of Al Sadr had stood in front of their mosques and told the crowds waiting to pray that before they came in they must promise they had not benefited from any of the thieving that had taken place throughout the country. This was an impossible request; people had been buying things at markets with no real idea where they had come from. Certainly, they knew a lot of it must have been looted. Almost as one, Adil said, the crowd outside his mosque had turned tail and walked home, heads hung low because they felt they could not guarantee to the Imam that they had not bought looted produce.

Eventually, word went out that the Imam would forgive the entire congregation, and that they could return to pray – even the ali babas.

Later, Adil pointed out local market stalls which had two kinds of produce; one lot of stuff was labelled 'probably looted' and the other 'unlooted'. The looted gear was cheaper, with unlooted items commanding much higher prices. People who bought looted stuff would shuffle home looking glum, the weight of a huge moral dilemma on their shoulders. Unlooted items, of course, could be carried home with pride. Throughout this period in Iraq, we found that the more poverty-stricken the people we met were – usually the Shia from the poorer parts of Baghdad – the more trustworthy they were.

Adil and his friends were particularly disgusted by the actions of a lot of the troops and reporters we came across, who would openly brag about taking souvenirs and keepsakes from Saddam's palaces, like items of his clothing or personal effects. I though it best not to mention the pair of brass light-fittings I had liberated from the charred remains of one of his bedrooms, which had been hit by incendiaries and high explosive bombs dropped by US planes early on in the war. They'd looked down on the dictator, lounging on his bed, and I imagine he'd fondly appreciated their elegant design a few times. I've never quite managed to get round to hanging them in my flat in London, for some reason – they possess a sort of residual evil, somehow. Not everyone is quite as squeamish as me; an English reporter of my acquaintance walked off with the most hideous pair of trousers possible, a pair of purple-striped baggy pantaloons that had once belonged to Uday Hussein. He loves nothing better than to strut around in these revolting garments at parties, entertaining guests with his witty *bon mots*.

After our visit to the mosque in Al Sadr, we learned that the news and picture desks back in London had quite an appetite for Saddam's torture equipment. Our piece had been given a good show in the paper, so we set about looking for more evidence of exotic, Hussein-related unpleasantness.

Later that week, Adil approached us outside The Palestine, looking slightly apologetic.

'Look,' he said. 'I have this neighbour. He is not a friend. He is not even a very good man. But I think I should tell you that he said to me that he knows a place where Uday minced people up and poured their remains into the river. It's just south of Baghdad.'

'Sounds interesting,' said Julian. 'What does he want?'

'He wants some dollars,' said Adil. A hundred of them, to be specific.

It was certainly worth a look, so the following day we picked the man up from his home in Al Sadr. Adil and he hardly spoke, and I gathered there was little love lost between their families. He was in his 40s, with a lank, dirty-looking beard and straggly hair. He was tubby, too: his backside spilled over the side of the front passenger seat. In a world of skinny people, which Baghdad was, you came to be suspicious of fat men. How did they get the money for all that food? And who was going short to feed their healthy appetites? He sat in the front passenger seat and chatted away amiably in Arabic to no-one in particular, all the way to the location 20 miles south of the capital. I noticed that Adil and Nibras were looking out of the side windows as often as possible and I gradually realised that the man had a breath issue. At that moment, he turned around and grinned at Julian and me, sending a malodorous cloud our way. It almost made me sick; if someone had said he'd spent the morning eating road kill and dog mess, I would have believed it.

'Bloody hell,' said Julian. 'Call the desk... we've found one of Saddam's weapons of mass destruction.'

I laughed, and cracked a few lame gags of my own.

After a minute or two, Adil leaned across us. 'I hear you and I understand what you are saying,' he said. 'Maybe other people do, too.'

We shut up, quickly. It was another little warning that we weren't in London, and that our sense of humour might not be appreciated locally. Julian, slightly red-faced, offered the man a stick of chewing gum; he turned his nose up, snottily, before turning to Adil and raising his eyebrows. Maybe he didn't realise he had a problem.

Eventually, we came to a large field full of knocked-out Iraqi tanks. Leaving Nibras to guard the car, we started hiking towards a copse of trees next to the river, following the fat man. We were, all three of us, excited at the prospect of finding Uday's awful machine, though I was dreading the idea of finding body parts or any other evidence of the horrors it had inflicted.

As we walked, we came across an old man, a 'hadji' Adil called him. He and Adil started chatting, the old man waving his arms first north and then south, making gun firing gestures and 'boom' noises. Adil suddenly burst into laughter. 'Our friend lives very near here. He was actually here in this field when the Americans came over that hill in their tanks. Over there was the Iraqi army. So he had our troops on one side and the Coalition on the other and he was stuck in the middle. He thought *'Who do I surrender to?'* Then he remembered: the Americans won last time. So he thought, *'Forget the Iraqis'*, and ran towards the Americans with his hands up.'

We all laughed and nodded at the old man in appreciation of his story. Adil asked him if there was a mincing machine nearby and he looked puzzled, before pointing to an area behind a copse of trees. Our fat guide set off in that direction, heaving his portly frame through the tall grasses, until we came closer to the copse; then he started getting carried away, running on ahead, panting loudly, cackling with triumph.

And then we saw the terrible mincer, in all its monstrous splendour.

Lying on its side, like a great, slumbering metal giant, blood-red in colour and 10ft high was... a huge red combine harvester.

Julian looked at me and turned to the sweating Iraqi, who was stood in front of this thing with the look of a man with a Pulitzer Prize-winning tale in his back pocket, or a magician who had just pulled off the trick of a lifetime.

'You're having a laugh, mate,' he said and walked down to look at the river.

The man's face fell and he started jabbering to Adil, clearly wondering what was going on. I looked at the harvester. Was it just possible… maybe Uday had used those threshers to slice up the bodies? Perhaps that ramp had fed the offal into the machine before it was spewed carelessly into the water? Could he have baled his victims up? He was just sick enough. Was it – *just* – possible? Julian wandered back over, his cameras swinging idle from his shoulder. He stopped, looking at my face, reading my mind.

'No, Hughesy,' he said. 'No, no, no. Don't even think about it – we're out of here.'

He was right. It wasn't possible. This greedy, cheeky, little toe rag had brought us all the way here, thinking we were stupid, thinking we'd just goggle at this thing and hand over the $100. You could even see dried bales of hay, scorched and bleached by the sun, in the field all around us.

'Sorry, Adil,' I said. 'This guy's trying to take us for a ride here.'

'I know, Chris,' said Adil. He looked downcast, as though he held himself responsible.

'Hey, don't worry, mate,' I said. 'You weren't to know and if we'd not bothered checking it out it would have turned out to be true.'

Julian agreed. 'One of those things, Adil,' he said. 'Happens all the time in our job. No problem.'

We did have a problem with Smelly, though. We paid him a few dollars, refused his indignant demands for the full hundred, and drove back to Baghdad. He was a good deal less chatty on the way, but at least that meant he kept his breath to himself. He and Adil had a huge bust-up in the middle of the street outside the hotel. As we watched, Nibras said: 'Adil very embarrassed.'

The truth was, it had made me and Julian laugh. We gave up on the day, retiring into the shabbiness of the Palestine for a barbecue on the balcony and a few warm Amstels, celebrating another complete waste of time. That night the story of the combine harvester did the rounds in the hotel amongst the journalist community. It was worth being laughed at, though: it earned us a few fresh lagers off the TV crews, who found it all highly amusing.

But the atmosphere in the city was definitely changing now, very much for the worse.

Adil and Nibras had insisted on going home early to beat the darkness that brought new horrors. Gunfire was more frequent now and kidnappings were commonplace, marauding gangs out to make a fast buck with a quick ransom. In the posh district of Mansour where Nibras lived, wholesale looting of family houses had begun. Suicide bombings were becoming regular occurrences – many streets had the charred, twisted remains of a car sitting in them, and the asphalt bore gruesome testimony to these horrific acts: small gobbets of charred flesh were spray-stuck to the road, like chewing gum on a London pavement, until the rats and dogs cleared them away or the sun dried them into dust. Faced with all of this, some of the European TV companies were pulling out, and many of the security men were now walking around openly displaying the guns that had previously being secreted under their fishing jackets. Killings were increasing on the road back to Amman, too. US helicopters, called upon to combat insurgents and protect troops, were making even fewer general patrols along the highway and every day seemed to bring fresh tales of drivers being robbed and killed on their way home. That made us both really nervous: it was our way out of here, after all.

The hotel – that one mad morning apart – still felt relatively safe. The tanks were still there, all around the building, but whenever we asked the Yanks how long they would be staying, they'd shrug.

My thoughts were turning to London.

Mass Grave

Despite the growing risks, Baghdad had been a journalist's dream. You only had to step out of the Palestine and stories would be thrown at you from all directions by the punters who were hanging out on the other side of the razor wire.

Someone would claim he knew that Saddam had been arrested and was being interrogated nearby, or that he could take you to some underground torture chamber that had been newly uncovered, where atrocities had been committed by the Mukhabarat. There would be rumours that US troops had finally found WMDs, or that political prisoners had been discovered, starving to death in previously unknown prisons. People would tell you where the rebels would strike next, or offer to take you to meet a father whose children had been killed by soldiers.

Every day, we would chase new leads and file copy and pictures but, as the weeks dragged on, there was a new tone to the way the news desk were answering my calls.

I would ring the desk at about 9.30am UK time, when they would be drawing up the 'schedule' – the list of that day's possible stories – to take into morning conference. Conference is always taken by the editor; he (or she) sits there and listens while the news editor puts up the stories he's proposing for the next day's paper. The picture editor discusses potential photographs and the features and sports editors lay out their plans for the following day's paper, too. The editor fires out a few tricky questions, dismisses some of the ideas and agrees to others, and makes the final decision – subject to developments during the day – on the content of the next day's edition. Several things are common to every editor I've ever worked for. One of them is a propensity for boredom: if you keep coming up with the same kind of stories every day, they eventually get fed up and they are brutal in letting you know.

In post-war Baghdad, inevitably, a lot of the stories tended to be variations on a theme. While you're out there, surrounded by all this death and suffering, every day bringing something as shocking and awful as the last, it is possible to lose perspective, to get too close to the story. I'd call with what I thought was a good tale. The response would be muted, at best. 'Yeah,' the voice would say, the grimace almost audible. 'Thanks, Chris. I suppose we *could* put that up to him. Look, file it when you get a spare moment.'

Loosely translated, that meant: 'Are you stupid, Hughes? Do you think I *like* getting humiliated by Piers in conference? Please… no more crap about forgotten prisoners. Call us back when you've got something we can impress him with.'

Julian was under the same pressure. Different, more shocking pictures were needed, too.

We spent days chasing shadows.

One Thursday, we took a trawl round the city and came across what looked like a serious incident outside the former Ministry of Information. A group of angry-looking US soldiers were manhandling some Iraqi men to the ground. As we slowed down, we saw an officer take out his pistol and hold it to the head of one of the Iraqis.

'Whooah, stop,' shouted Julian, to Nibras.

He pulled over and we got out, hurrying over.

The officer, red-faced and spitting with rage, was bawling at the plasti-cuffed locals, who looked terrified and were all now kneeling or lying face-down on the ground.

'I ought to shoot you right here, right now, you motherfucker,' he was yelling. 'You sons of bitches, I ought to shoot all of you right now.'

I held up my hands. 'Hold on a minute, chief,' I said. 'What's going on? You can't shoot people in the street.'

He turned to me. 'What the fuck is it to you?' he shouted. 'These are looters.'

The men with him – all of them looking equally furious – pointed their rifles at the four of us.

'Look, can you put those guns down, please?' I said. They looked very close to the edge, pumped up to the eyeballs and ready to blow someone away.

As I started trying to talk to the officer, Adil sidled off to speak to one or two of the Iraqis, who were now weeping in fear. He straightened up. 'Chris,' he said. 'These men say they have not been looting. Why, this man here is even a policeman.' He pointed to one of them, who was face down in the road, hands behind his back. 'He is frightened and angry because the Americans took away his pistol. He has a right to the pistol and he would like to have it back.'

The man was in a police uniform, albeit a raggedy old one. I spoke to the American officer again. 'Look, my translator says they're not looters and this guy here is a cop. You've taken his gun and he needs it back.'

The soldiers looked more hesitant, now, and reluctantly, the officer leaned down and slit the plasti-cuffs. Most of their prisoners got up and sprinted away, but the policeman stayed. 'Give him his gun back,' I said.

'No way am I giving that bastard his gun back,' said the officer, and with a whirl of his hand he indicated to his men that they should get back into their Humvee. Then they were gone, off back to their main base in the old palace.

'Right,' I said. 'We're going after them.' I was full of righteous indignation on behalf of this poor policeman.

We zipped across town to the US HQ and demanded to see the officer. After much to-ing and fro-ing, he appeared. He didn't look pleased to see us.

'Look,' I said. 'This guy is a policeman. You have disarmed him for no reason. You said he was a looter when he wasn't, and he needs his gun back. It's a disgrace. Either you sort this out or we tell the world about what we've just seen.'

The captain glowered at me. Then he shrugged his shoulders and walked over to a Humvee. He came back with the pistol. 'Here,' he said, handing over the automatic. 'Just get him out of here.'

The Iraqi cop grinned from ear to ear and shook our hands before disappearing into the crowds with the .45. As we made our way back to the car, I saw Adil chuckling to himself. 'What's so funny?' I asked.

'Oh, Chris,' said Adil, his shoulders shaking now. 'I know this man, he is from my town. He is a policeman but he is also an ali baba... I think actually he was looting the Ministry, with his friends.'

'You mean we've just re-armed a criminal?' I said.

Adil nodded, tears of laughter running down his face.

I felt pretty foolish. 'What about all that stuff about Islam being against looting?' I said.

'Well, they were just taking furniture and garbage from the old Ministry,' said Adil. 'Is not the same as looting a shop or stealing from a person. And when I see how the Americans are treating them, that I cannot accept.'

Nibras and Julian were grinning. After a while, I began to see the humour in it. We'd made fools of ourselves, certainly: giving pistols to thieves wasn't exactly part of our remit. But the city was crawling with guns and he could have got himself another weapon inside half an hour anyway. Adil and the cop had just been having fun at the expense of the Americans.

That evening, after another largely fruitless day, we were stopped at a checkpoint near our hotel by four US soldiers, scouts who had been at the spearhead of the invasion all the way into Baghdad. They seemed to be decent guys, intelligent and friendly, and reasonably respectful of the Iraqis.

'Man, I'd be pretty pissed if they came into my country,' said one. 'I can understand why some of them are angry with us. We got rid of Saddam but they're still not free because we're here.'

We got chatting. Their biggest issue was dirt: they hadn't had a decent wash in months and all they wanted was a shower. We had running water, and it seemed churlish not to offer it to them. Obviously, there was always the chance that they'd let slip something really interesting.

'You can come and use ours if you want,' said Julian.

They jumped at the chance and arranged to find their way to us that evening.

They turned up at 7pm, bristling with M16 assault rifles, grenades, knives and a bottle of Black Bush Whisky. Nibras had helped us secure a couple more boxes of the nasty, out-of-date Amstels that had been looted from one of Saddam's palaces, so we were all set for a party.

We told them to dump all the hardware in the bath and – while they took it in turns to wash – we all started boozing, like eight lads who had met on holiday in Tenerife or somewhere.

'I can't believe you're not armed,' said one.

'Yeah, we assumed all you guys were carrying weapons,' said another.

'It's not really what we do,' I said. 'I don't know how to use a gun, anyway.'

'So what kind of places do you go to?' asked the first one.

'Pretty much anywhere,' said Julian. 'Anywhere within 100 miles of the city, really.'

'Shit, really?' said the soldier.

'Yes,' said Julian. 'We've never had any problems, to be honest. We went to Karbala last week. We had lunch with some friends in Al Sadr last week, too.'

'Al Sadr?' said another one of the Americans. 'Shit, that's pretty amazing. You know, I haven't really spoken to an Iraqi person, except at a VCP (vehicle checkpoint), since I got here. And we can't go to places like Al Sadr except in tanks and Bradleys.'

'Well, we're not shooting anyone,' said Julian. They all laughed.

The conversation turned to the numerous incidents in which US troops had killed civilians.

'You know,' said one, 'when we were actually pushing up towards Baghdad I even felt sorry for the Iraqi army in their tanks and other vehicles. With the amount of technology we have on our side now they had no chance. We could see them up to 14 kilometres ahead of us, even in the dark. They were being killed before they even saw us. I was hoping they would all get out of their tanks and run away because nobody wants to just kill defenceless guys like that.'

We all had a contemplative gargle of the Black Bush.

Then one of the men said: 'I hear you when you say civilian deaths are a bad thing, they are. Trouble is, how do you tell if a car has a family in it, or a suicide bomber? One night, a message came over our radio when we were just south of Baghdad. *"There's a blue Peugeot hauling ass towards our lines."* The message kept coming over for like five minutes, until there was an explosion somewhere in the distance and the message changed.' He changed his voice to sound like a radio: '*"There's no longer a blue Peugeot hauling ass towards our lines."*'

It was a story we were supposed to laugh at, but we didn't. I understood the point about the possibility of suicide bombers, but what if it had been a frightened family? I thought back to my meeting with Haytham and Tghreed. What if it had been them? The atmosphere changed slightly after that, and the Americans left. At the door, one of them said: 'Thanks for the shower, guys.'

Then they were gone.

* * * * *

Sadly, the Yanks hadn't given us any great news stories and I had a slightly uncomfortable conversation with the news desk next morning. Piers was really only interested in finding Saddam Hussein or finding WMDs, and both were well beyond the scope of myself and Julian. If anything else was going to interest him, it had better be really new and very good.

Just as I put the phone down, Adil arrived for the day.

'Chris,' he said, 'I think I have a story for you.'

There were rumours, he said, that a stash of the regime's files, some of them relating to missing people, had been found in the west of the city. These files were being pored over by Iraqis anxious to find their relatives. Many of Saddam's mass graves were known about but without paperwork no-one had ever been able to match a name with its remains.

Julian and I looked at each other, thinking the same thing: Farzad Bazoft.

Bazoft was the British *Observer* journalist executed as a spy a decade earlier. His body had never been found; if we could discover it – and piece together his final days, how he had died and what evidence the regime had had for the alleged spying – that would be a cracking piece, not to mention some welcome news for his family.

We sent Adil and Nibras off to do some more digging and they returned a couple of hours later. Sure enough, a Ba'ath Party document archive had been found and opened up in a house that had belonged to an army general. It contained a million files or more, and a group of unpaid volunteers calling themselves The Committee for Free Prisoners had set up an office to read through these files and help relatives trace the remains of their loved ones.

We went straight to Nibras's car and drove to the house. When we got there we found scenes of absolute chaos. There were at least a thousand men and women of all ages pushing and shoving outside the building in which the files were being held, with a line of armed men carrying AK47s desperately trying to hold them back. Behind them, a man from The Committee was standing on a table, shouting out names from the files. Some of these people were wailing and beating their breasts; others were just sobbing, quietly. Most touching were those who stood there impassively, blinking in the heat as they listened to the names being read out. The dignity on their faces was heart-rending; occasionally, one of them would meet your gaze. Invariably, they would nod and look down at the ground.

They just wanted, even needed, to know what had happened to their sons, brothers, husbands. I wondered: in Iraq, the truth was very often much worse than what you imagined had happened to people.

In the heat of the afternoon, drinks sellers had descended upon the crowds waving bottles of ice-cold Coca Cola and water at them, even though many of these poor people had no money. Every 20 minutes or so, a woman would scream in recognition at a name, and the file would be passed through the throng to her and her little group. Then they would walk away, three or four people holding each other for comfort and support, to find a shallow grave dug carelessly in some unknown field.

I watched the man from The Committee poring over the paperwork, struck by the strange compulsion that had driven Saddam to keep such meticulous records of his crimes. Each file had a name, a number and a place where the body in question was buried. It described the alleged crime the victim had committed and how they had died. If they had been executed, the method by which they had died – usually shooting or hanging – was stipulated. In some cases, they had been imprisoned for some years before finally being killed; I shuddered to think of the horrors they had endured.

The man was reading out these files one-by-one, and each one was taking him around a minute. I did a quick bit of mental arithmetic. At this rate, with a million files, say twelve hours a day, it was going to around four years to get through them all. We didn't even have four *hours*, so, as gently as we could, we pushed our way through the crowds towards the front. It's the only way to get anywhere in Iraq; they utterly refuse to queue. Elbowing his way ahead, our press cards in his hands, Adil got to one of the leather jackets guarding the front. A moment or two of negotiation followed, a few dollars were passed into various pockets, and we were squeezed through the barrier and into the Committee's offices, room after room filled with thick, green, record books. The organisation's leader, a man called Ibrahim Idrisi, had himself spent six years in prison for joining a Muslim political party, and we sat down and waited for him, listening to the chaos outside.

Almost everything you do in Iraq is accompanied by elaborate, almost ritualistic, ceremony, and this was no different. After a long wait for Idrisi to arrive, we had to stand up when he walked in. We had to wait until he had sat down behind his desk before we sat back down and then I had to make a long and frankly embarrassing speech about how much I respected him, and his family, and how grateful I was for his time.

Finally, I got to the point.

'And so, sir, I humbly ask if it is possible for you to search for the file on the British journalist Farzad Bazoft, who was murdered by Saddam Hussein many years ago?'

Idrisi thanked me for my kind words.

'You know,' he said, waving his hand at the piles of documents stacked against the walls. 'These are only a few of the files they had. They spent weeks shredding and burning before the Americans invaded. It shows how much they had to hide, yes? Imagine the money Saddam spent on all the torture and the prisons and the killings. If he had spent it on his people instead they would have loved him forever.'

Then he stood, we stood and we all walked toward the door, which he opened wide. 'I'm sorry,' he said, with a regretful smile, 'but we cannot search for the file of just one man. But please come back. If we happen across it, I will be glad to let you see it.'

Slightly crestfallen, I shook his hand and we made to leave. As we did so, a worker walked by and collared Idrisi. While he was distracted, we slipped into an ante-room. 'Find the right person and offer them money,' I said to Adil. 'If he won't help us, someone else will.'

Outside, Adil came up to me, smiling. He'd found the right person, a man who worked in the building and came from the same area as he did. He'd struck a bargain: a dollar a day as a retainer and a further $100 for the file on Bazoft. Underhand, yes, sleazy, maybe, but it was the only way to get what we needed. (We kept that system going for about a month, with Adil dutifully returning every day to this grief-filled place to pay the man his dollar and check whether he had found the file. Sadly, he never did and, before long, the offices became a focal point for the early, pro-Saddam rebellion, with ex-Ba'athist thugs shooting at the crowds every day in drive-by attacks. Eventually the building was closed down and the files spirited elsewhere.)

With the hunt for the journalist's remains underway, we could concentrate on the bigger picture. Adil had learned from a member of The Committee that the files showed that two or three thousand bodies had been buried in a graveyard west of Baghdad and close to the infamous Abu Ghraib prison. OK, it wasn't Saddam or WMD, but surely this was a tale that would interest Piers?

We looked at a map and quickly located the site, on the edge of a small town called Al Kirk, some 20 miles west of Baghdad. We made our way through the crowd to Nibras's car and set off, nosing through the wrecked streets to the industrial zone in the north-western outskirts of the capital and then on out into the lush, sparsely-populated farmland beyond. For once, we drove in silence; there was no *craic* being had. I think we were all dreading what we were about to see. A mile or two from our destination, we came across a group of boys having fun, jumping in and out of a deep water irrigation channel. Julian asked Nibras to pull over and we all got out and watched these kids for a while: they looked unusually carefree for Iraqi youngsters, full of peals of laughter and squeals of delight, ducking and splashing each other in the sun. You didn't see children playing here, much. Julian took his kit from the car and started taking photographs of them – they made a nice contrast to all his other pictures from the country, I guess. He must have taken 20 or 30 shots, with the children running up to examine the images of themselves in the digital screen on the camera and then running off back to their mates, giggling all the way.

We didn't need those photos, though; I think we were all delaying the moment when we'd have to see these graves.

When it was time to press on, Adil beckoned the oldest lad over, a boy of about 15, and asked him if he knew where the burial site was. He nodded his head, no longer smiling, and agreed to drive with us as far as the entrance to the place. It was set behind a tree-lined avenue on the side of the motorway; we stopped at the gateway and the boy jumped out, taking ten dollars off us for his trouble and setting off back to the water channel at a run.

'He doesn't want to be seen helping you,' said Adil. 'He is worried it might cause problems for his parents.'

Fear of reprisals was growing everywhere and it was safer for people not to be seen helping Westerners, including journalists. Some translators and drivers had started wearing scarves around their faces to avoid being recognised and identified as collaborators.

We turned into the avenue and two unarmed guards, sitting in chairs, waved us on.

There was a wooded area to our right that went on for about a mile, and beyond that we saw the graveyard. It was an area of bare earth, a couple of hundred yards across, surrounded by a breezeblock wall about five or six feet high, bleached white by the baking sun and topped with grass and weeds. Beyond the far wall was a normal cemetery and, in the distance, Abu Ghraib jail itself.

As we pulled up, there were just two battered old cars parked outside. We were among the first to arrive, which was something of a relief.

Journalists have to do some horrible things: ask people how they feel when their two-year-old has died in a car crash, or doorstep people about a marriage break-up, or cover huge disasters in which many have been killed and injured. When you're young, it doesn't bother you too much (and it never bothers some). But the older you get, the more perspective you develop, and the less you relish those sorts of jobs. Standing outside that horrible, evil graveyard, I didn't relish going inside at all. It felt intrusive and wrong. I was struck again by the contrast between these poor people and myself and Julian, who were (relatively) sophisticated, worldly-wise Westerners, with pockets full of money and expensive gadgetry and, some day soon, plane tickets home. I could hear the faint sound of sobbing from inside the gate; we were going in there to record their grief and, by nightfall, we'd be back on our balcony, drinking warm Amstel and, probably, joking about it all. Where would they be?

But thinking about it wasn't going to do any good. In we went.

A group of men, who were squatting around a shallow ditch, turned towards us. Adil, a grave expression on his face, approached them and talked to them for a while, frequently pointing to us and obviously seeking their permission for us to be there.

Finally, one of the men gesticulated for us to come closer and we walked towards them nervously, fearing what we would see.

At the edge of the shallow grave, the men had placed a white sheet on the dirt; on it, they were carefully, tenderly, arranging the bones of a skeleton to make the shape of a man.

Those bones were all that was left of Hamid Omran. The men were his brother and cousins.

I spoke to them, through Adil. They were astonishingly dignified and polite, shading their eyes from the sun as they looked up at me and answering my questions calmly and politely.

The brother, Abdul, told me that Hamid had been arrested at their home in 1994 by Saddam's secret police, and taken away for 'questioning' on some spurious grounds.

'He didn't like Saddam but he had done nothing wrong,' he said. 'The papers show that they killed him after a year. He was 31 when he disappeared and we have seen no sign of him from that day until this.'

He looked around. 'They massacred people for the whole of the 25 years of that regime,' he said. 'Now we have found my brother, at least we can be at peace. We still have the agony. But now Saddam and his friends will face agonies of their own.'

Carefully, he lifted his brother's skull, and turned it to the side, pointing to a deep depression.

'They hit him here with an axe or something and it broke his skull,' he said. 'But he didn't die from that. They hanged him later.'

Tears formed in his eyes and he looked away in embarrassment, blinking and wiping his face with the back of his hand and placing the skull back into its position by the side of Plot Number 444.

'Shukran,' I said, straightening up and looking away, both to cover his embarrassment and because I was feeling emotional myself.

A man was lingering nearby. He told us his name was Mohammed Mohammed, and that he had begun digging graves here when he was 14, as part of his military service.

'Every Wednesday morning, they had hangings at the prison at dawn and the bodies would come a few hours later,' he said. 'Usually eight or nine, sometimes more, sometimes many more. The oldest graves in the cemetery are from 1983 and the newest are six months old.'

Just before the war started, Saddam had declared an amnesty for prisoners at Abu Ghraib, releasing them.

'There could be three thousand bodies here in total, I think.'

I looked around. The whole field was full of graves, little mounds of earth six feet long by three feet wide, each marked with an Arabic number on a metal plate atop a foot-high spike pushed into the soft earth.

Other cars were pulling up, now, and as we talked to the men, other groups of relatives were silently picking their way through the graves, searching for their lost ones. Every now and then there would be an unearthly howl, or a scream, as a woman found the grave of her husband or son, or a man came across his brother's plot. I watched one of these groups: two or three of them immediately dropped to their knees and started scrabbling with their hands, frantically trying to get to their relatives. Then others, who had brought shovels and picks, began pulling them, forcefully, even aggressively, out of the way, so that they could start chopping and digging at the mounds of earth themselves.

'Please, just scrape it, don't dig,' shouted one man. 'I'm worried he's just below here, I don't want to damage him.'

People were screaming at each other as the atmosphere oscillated between grief and anger.

'Saddam is to blame, only Saddam... the evil, evil son of bitch!' shrieked a man in his 30s, sitting on the ground, running his hands through the dirt on the grave of his only brother. Another man called out: 'You lost one person? We are looking for eight.'

The graveyard was filling up, several TV crews arriving and standing over these tragic little scenes, just another five minutes of videotape of the latest weird happening in this mad country. As far as I could tell, they didn't worry about seeking the permission of the relatives; it's rare for tabloid journalists to feel they occupy the moral high ground, but I was struck by the lack of discretion or empathy these crews showed.

As more bodies were pulled from their graves, it was becoming clear that some of them had not long been there. There was that sweet, putrid smell of decomposing flesh filling the air, and soon everyone within those rough-built walls was beginning to gag, pushing their faces into their shirts to try and mask the smell.

There was a scream from a family huddled 30 yards away. A woman flung herself down, beating the earth and shouting her dead husband's name. A man with her looked over at us and shouted, 'See what Saddam did to us? Why do you come now to write about this now, and not before?'

To our left, another man, stooped and reading the numbers on the rusting markers, a piece of paper held in his fist, fell to the ground with a heart-breaking cry. He crawled over the earth and then on to the adjoining plot, and the one after that, tears spilling onto the ground. Adil spoke to a friend who was trying to comfort him and then returned. 'He says those are the graves of three of his relatives, and that he has ten family members missing in total,' he said.

Men and women from all over Iraq were coming past, some carrying wooden coffins, some praying, others running through the site, searching.

Suddenly, a woman near us howled, a low, piercing gurgle that cut through the background noise of the moaning and crying.

She was middle-aged, and dressed in black, and I watched as she looked up at the sky and shouted something in Arabic before throwing herself, face first, into the rotting remains of what had been her husband or son. She pulled back, rubbing the detritus into her face, wailing uncontrollably. A man kneeling next to her immediately threw up on the ground; another man who was also with the woman pulled her back as she went to throw herself into the grave again, and slapped her hard, full-handed, across the face. Presumably, he intended to bring her out of her trance. It certainly worked. She collapsed to the ground, sobbing quietly, all the energy drained from her. The man who had slapped her stood, picked up a shovel and started walking towards us, waving it in the air, a look of fury on his face.

'We must go now,' said Nibras, grabbing Julian and me by our shirt sleeves and pulling us away. We backed off, beyond the walls, and to the car, leaving behind us a dreadful place where bodies were now being pulled out of the ground like a scene from some low-budget horror movie.

There had been nothing, absolutely nothing, consoling or spiritual about this evil little place, where the living and the dead were being brought together.

As we got to the car, I heard a sobbing behind me. It was Adil.

'These are my people,' he kept saying. 'All Shia, all my people. These are my people.'

A huge weight of guilt fell on us as we realised what we had put him through that morning. He was utterly distraught; we had to help him into the car. Nibras did a quick u-turn and got us out of there quickly, putting his foot down hard and speeding us back along the rough dirt track.

As we left, I dialled the news desk on my satellite phone.

One of the news desk personnel picked up. They must have had a good conference that morning; he was full of banter and cheeriness.

'Hughesy... is that you? What have you got for us then? Found Saddam yet?'

'I've just had a dreadful morning, actually,' I said. 'We've been to this new mass grave north of Baghdad and...'

'Sounds good, mate,' he said. 'Bit different. Piers will like that. Can you file 750 words?'

'Yes, it was absolutely horrific,' I said. 'I'll...'

'Chris, Chris,' he interrupted. 'Hang on a minute, I can't hear a word you're saying. Can you tell that cunt next to you to stop that fucking crying?'

'Er...' I began. I didn't know what to say. I wasn't a million miles away from tears myself. 'Look,' I said, 'that's Adil, our interpreter. We've just... he's just... look, I'll call you later.'

I put the phone down. Now wasn't the time or the place.

So very often in Iraq, terrible sights would be sprung upon you every day, often when you least expected them, and the Iraqis were hard people to shock: there wasn't much they hadn't already seen, and Adil was as hardened as any of them. I looked at him, his face buried in his hands, his shoulders heaving, and felt awful.

All the way back to Baghdad, the main road was dotted with battered little cars and trucks heading the other way, most of them carrying cheap wooden coffins towards the burial site.

I can only imagine how terrible that place would have been a few hours on.

(Later, Julian and I talked with Adil and Nibras about the place. Adil had spoken to many families who had recovered lost loved ones from those little pits. He said many of the corpses being dug up could not have been older than a few months, and it confirmed the widespread suspicions of the Shia people that the Mukhabarat had been settling old scores in the countdown to the Coalition invasion. Most of the bodies had been taken to the holy Shia burial sites in Najaf, south of Baghdad.)

I never heard him speak of the incident again.

Back at the hotel, Julian and I were sitting quietly on the balcony watching the TV crews filing their pieces on the grass below, when there was a knock at the door.

It was one of the American soldiers from the night before. One of them had left behind a magazine full of bullets.

'I need to take those back,' he said. 'I'll be in real trouble if my officer finds out they're missing. We already got grounded because we got back drunk. They're kinda clamping down on that sort of thing right now. We got a sergeant who is being court-martialled because he attended a TV company party in The Sheraton a day or two ago and got wasted.'

We'd heard about this, and that was only half the story. The sergeant had got into a drunken fist-fight with a cameraman, had been ejected from the party and was last seen staggering around the complex, barely able to walk, his M16 over his shoulder, screaming abuse at all and sundry. The Military Police had disarmed him and he was being sent home in disgrace.

'So where you been today?' he asked, genially.

'We went to a mass grave site up near the Abu Ghraib prison,' said Julian. 'They just uncovered it today. Full of bodies. Very upsetting.'

'I guess it would have been,' said the soldier. 'He killed a lot of people, Saddam Hussein, that's for sure.'

'He did,' said Julian. 'So have you guys.'

The Journey To Fallujah

It was the end of April, and Baghdad sounded pretty much the same as it had every other morning for the past few weeks. Early mornings were always the same – the blaring of car horns as Baghdadis joined the mile-long queues for petrol or attempted, in a few cases, to go to work. The usual demonstrators were gathering outside the hotel: locals demanding fuel, electricity, for the Americans to go home, for the Americans to stay, for more work, for more freedom, for less freedom, for money, for Saddam to hang – even, occasionally for Saddam to be returned to power. It was democracy at its most embryonic, chaotic stage: I honestly think most of them just turned up every morning not really knowing what they wanted.

The atmosphere was generally unthreatening early on in the day, despite the growing racket. The rebels, kidnapping gangs and other gunmen who filled the Baghdad night air with the shattering sound of fire fights were usually still asleep, tired from their night's work.

We hadn't got too much planned. Three or four days before, Piers had suddenly remembered 'Comical Ali' and our job – in the absence of finding Saddam or his nerve gas – was to try and track him down.

Comical Ali was the cheeky little chappie from Iraq's Ministry of Information who had bravely insisted Iraq was winning the war, even as American armour parked up a few hundred metres away and Coalition troops took control of the city. 'They will burn in their tanks,' he had told TV news crews, as the Stars and Stripes was hoisted across the street. 'We are killing them everywhere. They are dying in their thousands.'

His wild claims, complete with eccentric rhetorical flourishes and delivered in an heroic lisp in defiance of the obvious truth, had made an unlikely star of this odd little man, whose real name was Mohammed Saeed al-Sahaf. Amidst all the talk of crazed dictators, chemical weapons and 'shock and awe', he had cut a strangely charming figure; with Iraq's deputy Prime Minister Tariq Aziz, Ali was one of the more acceptable faces of the regime and most journalists had a soft spot for him, as did some Iraqis. There had been something almost noble in his continuing to do his job when it no longer really existed.

He'd gone to ground once even he had realised the game was up and people had imagined he would turn up somewhere. But he hadn't and for some reason he'd popped back into Piers' head.

'Can we get a chat with this bloke?' our head of news Andy Lines had asked me earlier in the week. 'And… er… when you get him, get a picture of yourself talking to him.'

It made a refreshing change from mass graves and torture implements so Julian and I had been only too pleased to get the brief. We could both see straight away that an exclusive interview with this bespectacled loon would make a good read – for all his comedy value, Ali had been Saddam's spokesman in his final days and his insights and inside knowledge of the Iraqi administration would be explosive. I did wonder whether the idea of being photographed chatting to the mouthpiece of perhaps the world's most tyrannical regime was the right way forward, but we could cross that bridge when we came to it. It sounded like a good laugh.

How wrong we were. The trouble lay in locating the guy. One morning he had given his usual barmy briefing, the next he had vanished along with the rest of Saddam's Ba'ath party hierarchy. Those who hadn't been killed or arrested were in hiding, fearful of the unofficial Iraqi death squads that were hunting them down and taking revenge for years of oppression. The rumour was that he was still alive, holed up somewhere in Baghdad. He wasn't exactly advertising his whereabouts so the only way to find him was to spend all day trawling through huge swathes of the suburbs asking if anyone had seen him. What had started out as a pleasant and diverting change had become a nightmare task, and hugely frustrating. Each day, we wasted hours chasing up leads that led to nothing. Occasionally, things went beyond frustration: the previous day we'd been chased away from one house by three armed men in leather jackets. Nibras had really stepped on it as they set out after us in a blue car, and had managed to lose them after a few streets. It had been a highly unnerving experience.

The next morning, sat on the balcony, Julian and I agreed that we weren't going to find him after all. The problem was the Piers' one-track mind wasn't going to accept anything else: all he was interested in (apart from Saddam and the WMD) was Comical Bloody Ali.

As I rustled up a breakfast of bananas, Nibras's flat breads (which he brought as gifts every few days) and Primula cheese paste squeezed from a tube, Julian turned on his laptop and began flicking through the news wires. 'Have a look at this, mate,' he said, and turned the screen to me. It was a Reuters story: two nights earlier, US troops had killed a number of students in a place called Fallujah and had been forced to move to a more secure base.

Fallujah: I doubt all that many people had heard of it before then. I certainly knew very little about it. To the outside world, it was a place of little importance and even less interest – just an anonymous Sunni Muslim city of some 350,000 people, sitting on the great Euphrates river 40-odd miles to the west of Baghdad. Even the war hadn't brought notoriety: it had escaped the attention of the media – and any serious damage – during the invasion, because most of the Iraqi Army units stationed in the area had, sensibly, fled when they saw the Americans coming.

Inside Iraq, though, it was very well known.

There were three reasons for this.

Firstly, its hinterland was the site of one of Saddam's many follies, a Ba'athist holiday resort designed by Uday which he called 'Dreamland'. They had spent millions on creating a huge, artificial bathing lake in the middle of the desert outside the city, pumping water from the river and filling it with fish. Pomegranate orchards and date palms were laid in thick groves and a number of tasteless villas were built. Saddam, his sons and their favoured guests would adjourn here for occasional weekends spent drinking fine French wines and cavorting with whores. In a country where people were going hungry daily, and even dying for want of medicines and hospital care, it provided eloquent testimony to the vulgarity of the moustachioed clown at the top of the tree.

Secondly, and in stark contrast, it was also one of Sunni Islam's most famous and holy places, known as 'The City Of Mosques' for the 200 such places of worship found in and around the city.

Thirdly, it was known for its people. Iraqis, generally, are a hard, brave, warrior race – don't be fooled by their defeats at the hands of the Americans in the two Gulf Wars, which were much more about the vast superiority of US tactics and hardware, and the lunatic bravado of Saddam, than anything else.

Among Iraqis themselves, the Fallujans were regarded as the warrior's warrior – the most dangerous, vengeful and blood-soaked of them all. No-one ever crossed a Fallujan.

The Reuters story told how a crowd of several hundred locals had defied a curfew which had been imposed on them by the American troops occupying the city, gathering outside a local secondary school being used as a base by the 82nd Airborne. They wanted Coalition forces to leave the city and they wanted the school reopened.

Some demonstrators are said to have shot into the air; soldiers stationed on the roof of the building opened fire in response.

They killed 13 civilians.

It was a bad move.

Julian leaned over. 'Chris,' he said. 'I reckon we should take a trip down there. I can't see them taking that lying down, can you?'

Prophetic words.

It was 7am local time. The Mirror news and picture desks wouldn't clock on for another four or five hours. Fallujah was only 40 miles away along a good, quick road: we could forget looking for Al-Sahaf for the morning and just head over there to take a look around – and chat to witnesses, survivors and families – without even having to run it by the desk. If we got nothing out of it, we'd just get back to the capital around lunchtime and carry on our fruitless search. And if there *was* something worth filing, we could explain our presence in Fallujah by telling the desks we'd been following up a tip that 'Comical Ali' was in the area.

Fifty per cent of the skill of dealing with news desks lies in not burdening them with the truth. Some might call it lying; I see it as more of a grey area.

We didn't have long to wait before an out-of-breath Nibras burst into our room. He was almost bent double under the weight of more flat breads. Shortly afterwards, Adil arrived and we told them our job for the day: to drive to Fallujah and track down people who had seen what happened the previous night.

Adil beamed at the thought of not having to trawl through the suburbs looking for Comical Ali again. 'No Sahaf today? Very good.'

Neither of them enjoyed chasing the ex-regime man. With Saddam and his sons Uday and Qusay still at large, there was always that fear that the old dictator might rise again; understandably, few wanted to put their heads too far above the parapet.

The four of us took the terrifying lift to the ground floor of the Palestine. It groaned and creaked like it was about to break free of its chains and plummet to the ground. Occasionally, it would stop and various TV news crews would pile in. We'd listen out for possible story ideas and tips, but we never heard a single one. They were bored stiff, with their ex-military minders stopping them from going to the more violent and dangerous areas; all you got was gossip on who was having it off with who in the TV world. Sadly none of them were famous.

At the bottom, we made our way through the military cordon and the crowds to Nibras's BMW. This morning he was particularly pleased with himself, grinning proudly as we reached the car. He had visited his friends in the local body shop and had them plaster the word 'PRESS' down the side of the vehicle in bold black letters. The same word was painted on the roof. There'd been more stories, lately, of civilian cars being shot up by the Yanks and he was obviously taking no chances.

Julian and I looked at each other, and then at Adil. No-one wanted to be shredded by some twitchy-fingered gunner on one of the American assault helicopters that constantly whirled through the sky. But, on the other hand, there were only two ways to operate in Iraq. One was in armoured Land Rovers, tooled-up to the hilt and surrounded by bodyguards. The other was as low-key and incognito as possible. Now, our wheels thoroughly pimped, we were neither tooled-up nor low-key. How was this going to look parked up outside one of Fallujah's 200 mosques or cruising the streets looking for the angry parents of the teenaged victims?

It wasn't a great start.

It took us an hour to get out of Baghdad and onto the western road towards Ramadi and Fallujah. Adil and Nibras kept a weather eye out for Americans and militia, ready to turn off if they saw a checkpoint. The militia was a rag bag of former soldiers, policemen and concerned citizens who had taken it upon themselves – in the absence of any proper law and order – to try to restore some control to the streets. Dressed in an assortment of worn uniforms and with no real command structure, they patrolled their neighbourhoods looking for looters and other undesirables and set up roadblocks to search cars and trucks. But they were notoriously corrupt and you stood a very good chance of being stripped and robbed, and maybe even killed, if you came into contact with them.

Despite the danger, Julian and I were easily bored and, as we drove, we passed the time in a juvenile *Blackhawk Down* game. This involved wrapping your hands over your mouth and making the crackling noise of a radio, rasping out: '*We have a situation! We have a Blackhawk Down! We have a Blackhawk Down!*' Neither Adil nor Nibras had seen the film we were mimicking – about a disastrous US operation in Somalia – but they loved joining in with us. They liked the idea of being cheeky to the people who had invaded their country and were now running the show. To be fair to them, a few of the Yanks had started getting involved, too. The week before, we had approached an American checkpoint in full *Blackhawk Down* mode and a Marine Sergeant had overheard us. Instead of giving us a hard time, he'd joined in, copying us in a Texan twang and roping his men in too. Both Nibras and Adil were almost weeping with laughter and, from then on, whenever we went through that particular checkpoint the soldiers would launch into their own '*Blackhawk Down... we have a situation!*' routine.

The atmosphere in the car became much more tense as soon as we got onto the highway. The marauding gangs of thieves and insurgents were growing ever bolder in this no man's land and my thoughts turned to my Jordanian driver, Mohammed, who'd died out here just two or three weeks earlier. There was no doubt his killers would love to get their hands on a couple of Western journalists. The night before, we had been at a party in The Palestine with other reporters and the conversation had turned to our plan to drive down to Fallujah. A South African ex-Special Forces man had sidled up to us.

'If you want, boss,' he'd said, 'me and my guys will come down with you. We'll get rid of the problem for the right price.'

'What would you do?' I said.

'Well, if anyone comes near us we'll just kill them,' he said, looking at me as though I was slightly simple.

It was a sobering moment and we withdrew from that particular social event shortly afterwards. I felt, somehow, that I had stumbled into somewhere I didn't belong, that I'd crossed some sort of boundary. It didn't do to dwell too much on conversations like that and Julian and I tried to keep our heads down to avoid attracting unwanted attention; cars without Westerners inside were less likely to be attacked. Though, as I say, having the word 'PRESS' plastered all over the car in jazzy three-foot letters didn't help.

As we drove, Adil and Nibras both went quiet in the front. Every now and then Nibras, would whistle ominously, shake his head and say 'Faaaaaallujaaaah'. We asked Adil what was wrong.

'Nibras knows the city well,' he said. 'I told him about what happened there and he says only bad things can come of it. He says the people there will want retribution for what happened to their sons.'

Because of the potential for trouble, we had taken our cumbersome blue 'Press' body armour and helmets with us. These dirt-encrusted flak jackets made us both feel self-conscious and overdressed, especially when you were talking to Iraqis wearing nothing but the traditional *thaub* robes. I rubbed my hand nervously over the Kevlar. 'Look,' I said. 'If you think this is too dangerous, we can always turn back. It's only a bloody story. I don't want to get us all killed over it.'

Adil put his head on one side, thinking. Then he and Nibras spoke for a few moments. Finally, Adil said: 'No, I think it is OK. I think we can go there, just to see. But we must be able to leave quickly if necessary.'

Eventually, the city came into view in the distance and five or ten minutes later we reached its outer boundary, and a sign that said 'Fallujah' in English by the side of the motorway. Adil started playing with his worry beads. A common sight all over the Middle East, these are very like Roman Catholic Rosary beads; men pass the beads between their fingers and count through Koranic prayers in their heads. Adil did it when he was worried – hence their name – though he never admitted he was frightened, even when it was obvious he was (at which times I was in mortal terror). (Adil was a very tough man; he had served in Saddam's Republican Guard during the Iran-Iraq war, and had been shot during the fighting. He had dispelled for me one of the major myths of both Gulf Wars. These troops were always described as being "the fiercely-loyal Republican Guard" but in fact many of them were Shia from Saddam City – exactly the people who hated Saddam most. They were most definitely not loyal to him. They fought against the Iranians because they were forced to do so, for fear of being shot in the head by one of the regime's thugs, who were never far away.)

Nibras drove on and put an Iraqi folk music tape on, a woman's voice filling the car. The two men looked at each other, and burst out laughing. Nibras, his hands off the steering wheel and driving with his knees, cupped his palms against his chest, sending Adil into squealing fits of giggles. When they'd calmed down, he turned round. 'This singer, she is beautiful, with very big chests,' he said, grinning. 'She is a favourite of Nibras's.'

Nibras, next to him, nodded solemnly. 'She very big,' he said, cupping his hands again, and dissolving back into laughter.

Julian and I couldn't help joining in; for a moment, we could have been on the outskirts of Falmouth, not Fallujah.

But the mood soon sobered again and I watched Adil: his head was constantly in motion, twitching from side to side, looking for trouble.

'Do you think we should have told the office where we were going?' I asked Julian. 'Hardly anyone knows we're out here.'

'Would it make any difference?' said Julian. 'What could they do if it all goes pear-shaped anyway? Call the cops?' He grinned. 'Relax, mate, it's going to be fine.'

He was probably right. We'd do a few interviews, get some shots of the injured and the bereaved relatives, and be back in Baghdad by lunchtime, looking for Comical Ali again.

We drove over a bridge that spanned the Euphrates, the lazy, dirty-looking twin of the Tigris, which takes its time meandering 1,700 miles down through Turkey, Syria and Iraq before emptying into the Persian Gulf.

And then we were in Fallujah.

Massacre

As we pulled into Fallujah, an American Apache helicopter thudded over us from behind and screamed off to the right, towards a plume of oily black smoke rising up from the other side of the city. Another chopper, a Blackhawk this time, zoomed over, heading towards us just a couple of hundred feet up. Gunners leaned out of each side, their faces hidden by Darth Vader-like full-face helmets, their .50 calibre weapons pointed downwards at our car. I silently hoped they'd seen the 'PRESS' sign on our roof; these guys looked very serious. Maybe Nibras was onto something, after all.

Along the main drag, he pulled over. Dogs lay in the dust, already made lazy by the mid-morning heat, ignoring the noise of the helicopters overhead. Old men squatted by the side of the road, sipping tea in silence and looking over at us, swatting flies away and shielding their eyes against the sun. One or two nodded in our direction. Most looked suspicious, guarded.

Adil got out of the car and swaggered towards a group of men sitting on a street corner, to ask the way to the school where the shooting had taken place two nights before.

We watched uneasily from the relative safety of the car. The mere fact that we were not Americans had been a big plus, so far, with more and more Iraqis becoming vehemently anti-US by the day. But I'd read up about Fallujah, and the British had plenty of history of our own in the city. In 1920, when our armies had ranged across the Middle East, we'd had trouble subduing the place, even then known as the most unruly corner of the old Mesopotamia. We'd sent a senior colonial officer, a Lieutenant-Colonel Gerard Leachman, to take control of the town and Leachman had been killed in a fight with a local leader. His death had led to a savage war that had cost the lives of 10,000 Iraqis and more than 1,000 British and Indian troops. We had fought them again near here in the Anglo-Iraqi war of 1941 and, even more recently, and even worse, a British jet had accidentally bombed Fallujah's main market during the first Gulf War. As many as 150 civilians had died and many more had been injured. Given that these people were still thirsty for vengeance after the excesses of Richard the Lionheart's Crusades more than 600 years ago, it seemed unlikely they would have forgotten this more recent bloodletting.

I kept my head down, my default position in the back of that BMW, trying to look as inconspicuous as possible.

Twenty yards away, I could see Adil, still in animated conversation. He was nodding and smiling as the locals crowded round him, holding their heads in their hands or making rifle-shooting gestures, as if acting out the tragedy. Iraqis are an expressive, emotional people: if you approach a crowd of them, they surround you, all shouting and talking at the same time. Eventually, one man dominates, the others give ground and a proper conversation can develop. This group was following that pattern and I watched as a middle-aged man emerged from a shop doorway and approached the throng. The gathering crowd fell silent and the man nodded to Adil in respect. They spoke for a few moments and then the man pointed Adil in the direction of the school. He walked back to the car, grinning, and clambered in, and we drove off down a few streets until we entered a pleasant-looking, tree-lined boulevard with another crowd milling at the far end. This was middle-class Fallujah, the heart of what would become, later, the Sunni-led insurgency.

As we drew up to the crowd, we saw it was mostly made up of young men, hundreds of them, waving their fists and chanting 'Down with America' and 'Death to America'. They looked angry, agitated, and a robed man – the Imam – was standing on a wall in front of them, arms outstretched with the palms downwards, trying to calm them down.

We got out of the car and a man ushered us straight away, without introductions, into the school. The US forces had left it soon after the shooting, heading for the city's former Ba'ath Party HQ compound, which they felt would be more secure and more defendable. Inside was an elderly man, whom we approached. He did not speak to me or Julian, or acknowledge us, and addressed Adil as if we weren't even there. They talked in quiet, serious tones for a few minutes, wandering around the room as they did so. Occasionally, they would stop to pick up a battered book or kick a magazine across the floor.

Julian and I left them alone, wandering into another classroom. What I saw on the blackboard staggered me. Some idiot soldier had chalked 'I love pork' on the blackboard, alongside other anti-Muslim slogans. 'Have a look at that,' said Julian, in disgust. 'What kind of morons are these people?'

He was right. I struggled to comprehend the mindset of the American who had scrawled those calculated insults on the board. I imagined him, giggling, probably calling over a few mates to see what he'd written. What did he think he was going to achieve? They were supposedly here as liberators.

In another classroom, we found a US flag drawn on the blackboard; a small boy stood staring up at the image.

We made our way back to Adil and the Imam. They were just saying their goodbyes so we made our own exaggerated gestures of respect and followed Adil back outside.

Outside, Adil told us what had been said. 'The Americans have been using the school as a base for themselves for a few weeks,' he said. 'It is not good – the students and the teachers are wanting to get back to school. There is a curfew, so no-one is allowed to be on the streets after dark, but a group of the students broke the curfew and gathered here. The Imam says that they were demanding that the Americans leave the school and suddenly the soldiers opened fire on them. He says no-one fired at the Americans. You saw me walking around the room inside with him? He was showing me that there were no bullet-holes in the school walls, so there were no incoming bullets.'

I hadn't seen any damage to the inside of the building, that was true. The Americans had claimed they were returning fire aimed at them from the roofs and top floor windows of the houses opposite. I looked at those houses: there were no pock marks or broken windows there either, which seemed to mitigate against that explanation. Instead, all the fire had been concentrated downwards – you could see blood stains in the dust of the narrow streets and bullet holes at four, five and six feet high in the walls.

'What were those books he was picking up?' I asked.

'Those were copies of the Holy Koran with boot prints upon the pages where the American soldiers had trodden on them,' said Adil, his face dark with anger. 'And the magazines were pornography that the soldiers left around the building.'

I'd looked at one of those magazines: it was some sort of biker publication, with topless women in hot pants sitting astride motorcycles in the centre pages. It wasn't exactly what I would call pornography, but it was still offensive to Muslim sensibilities and the Americans must have known that. If they hadn't, they ought to have done. It all spoke of a casual disdain, an arrogant belief in their innate superiority. Hearts and minds? Not exactly.

Above us, the helicopters were still screaming away. The Apache had joined the Blackhawk and both were circling, their blades smashing through the air with that familiar 'whop-whop-whop' noise as they banked in tight turns over the streets below.

On the ground, audible over the roaring of their turbines, the crowd was whipping itself into a frenzy, with people waving fists at the choppers and chanting anti-American slogans. They were becoming more and more fevered by the minute and their numbers, already 1,000-strong by my estimate, were swelling.

Suddenly, a live bullet was pressed into my hand. I looked down, and a little boy of around eight was looking up at me. He was unsmiling and held my gaze unflinchingly. Then he nodded and walked off into the crowd.

Three or four people started herding us towards a tiny courtyard attached to one of the houses opposite the school. Once we were inside the yard, someone closed the wrought-iron gate behind us and a thin man with hollow cheeks handed me a glass of tea, nodding politely. He wore a tight smile, but had tears in his eyes and we followed him through the dusty, yellow-earth yard into his house. We entered a white-walled kitchen, with a large sink against one wall and a terracotta-tiled floor, dotted with Koranic mosaic patterns. Speaking through Adil, the man told us that American soldiers had shot his son dead during the events of two nights previously. The teenager had been inside his house and, as the troops had hosed down the crowd, several rounds – whether stray or aimed – had come through the family's windows. At least one of them had hit the boy, taking the top of his head off and killing him on the spot. Shortly afterwards, he went on, US troops had kicked in the door and had stolen money and some chickens, before leaving and racing back to the safety of the school.

Adil shot me a sceptical look as he translated, indicating he was unsure about the man's story.

'Is he telling the truth or not?' I said.

'Oh, I am sure that the man's son is dead,' replied Adil. 'This I was told by others earlier on. They buried him yesterday. I am also sure that he was shot by Americans. I am not sure that I believe that they also stole chickens and money. They have plenty of food of their own and Iraqi money is worth nothing to them, so that part does not make sense.'

It was critically important that we went as far as possible to confirm the man's story. I didn't want to fill the *Mirror* with this if it turned out to be lies.

'How about asking him to swear on the Koran?' I said. Even as I spoke, I winced, reflecting on my insensitivity. If a group of Middle Eastern soldiers had shot dead a youth in Liverpool, how would the father take it if a foreign journalist doubted his word? But no-one was insulted, and a Koran was fetched. We watched as the man swore that the Americans had shot dead his son the previous night. But he would not swear to the thefts.

Adil shrugged his shoulders. 'It is as I told you, Chris,' he said.

It is, to us, a curious mindset that would lead a man to embellish the murder of his son in this way. But, seeing death all around them, Iraqis have a matter-of-fact attitude to life. In a country where food is scarce, the allegation that the soldiers responsible had also stolen the family's chickens made it all much, much worse. A local caught in this way would certainly be dealt with harshly; at the very least, he would be stripped naked, the word 'thief' would be scrawled on his body and he would be driven through the streets, baying crowds beating him as he went to complete the humiliation. At worst, he might be summarily executed.

Whatever, there could be no doubt that the most serious allegations were true. The man disappeared further inside the building, shaking his head as he went, and Adil, looking sheepish, led us after him. We came to the family's sitting room, which was also tiled, and the man pointed at a black, gooey mess, about the size of a dinner plate, lying on the floor. It looked curious, like a pool of tar mixed in with matted hair and what looked the smashed remains of a broken china dish.

The man was now crying softly, rocking backward and forward on his heels, his eyes closed.

Adil touched him lightly on the elbow and asked him what it was.

The man opened his eyes and said something, almost inaudible, to Adil, who recoiled in horror and backed away towards the wall.

Then he looked at me and said, 'That is what is left of our friend's son's head.'

I turned my head away though, strangely, I didn't feel anything. Then I said the most crass and insensitive thing imaginable. I asked Adil why the man had not cleaned it up. The translator spoke to the man in whispers. Through his sobs the man replied in Arabic. With that, Adil bade the man farewell and walked us out of the house. As we got back out into the street, I asked him what the man had said.

'He said, "Why don't you clean it up, Englishman?"' Adil told me, before looking away and waving at Nibras, who was leaning against his car, the engine running, and looking increasingly nervous at the angry mob.

We had our story. We had confirmed the Reuters piece and added human interest to it with our interview with the distraught father; together with a 'From Fallujah' by-line and an atmospheric photograph, we'd probably get a page lead out of it. We could have headed back to Baghdad. But we decided to stick with the demonstration to see what would happen. The crowd started pulling away from the quiet street, with the Imam at its head; he was happy to talk to us, as were many of the demonstrators, all male and mostly students. They were intent on marching to the hospital where the surviving casualties were being cared for to make their feelings known. We walked with them for about ten minutes. It was baking hot and my mouth filled with dust whipped up by the rotors of the helicopters above; they were clearly shadowing the crowd, and the noise from their engines was deafening as they followed us in a slow hover. As we surged along the narrow streets, shopkeepers began boarding up their stores and mothers dragged their toddlers back inside their houses. But despite the febrile atmosphere, I didn't feel particularly threatened; I didn't see a single gun, and the mood, while angry, even aggressive, seemed under control.

Then we rounded a corner, and the marchers seemed to hesitate for a moment. We could either turn left, towards Fallujah's General Hospital, or turn right. That way led back to the main drag through the town, and the former local Ba'ath Party HQ, now commandeered by the Americans and full of US Marines. Turning right meant we would be heading for their guns.

There are lots of theories about human nature and the behaviour of crowds, about how at times of stress or anger a group of people can behave as one. Something like that happened now: somehow, all thoughts of marching to the hospital vanished in an instant, and everyone turned right.

The air suddenly became tense. The students were no longer answering my questions and Adil began to look nervous. Shouting to make himself heard above the noise, he told me to pull Julian, who was engrossed in taking his pictures, out of the crowd. The students were becoming more vocal the closer we got to the US troops. Two hundred yards ahead of us, I could see Humvees and armoured Jeeps reversing quickly into their new compound and the Marines who had been patrolling nearby, or who had been on sentry duty outside, were all doubling back through the gates, NCOs and officers yelling at them. On the roof of the building, 30 feet up, I could see dozens of men taking up firing positions behind sandbags and more running to join them. At the sight of this, the students became even more aggressive; now they were screaming at the tops of their voices and waving placards reading 'Americans go home' as though they were spears, stabbing at the air in front of them.

All the time, we got closer and closer and the feeling of foreboding grew and grew.

Nibras had been slowly following the march, and we peeled away and jumped into his BMW, driving past the Americans who were now locked inside their HQ. Several tanks, their turrets visible behind the thick outer walls, were swivelling their guns towards the advancing students. Although I knew they were unarmed, I could understand the Americans' fear: the mob looked and sounded terrifying.

Nibras parked up in an abandoned petrol station a few hundred yards further down the road and we got out, putting on our blue body armour and helmets and ignoring a gaggle of young kids. They were swarming all around us, shouting 'Hello mister!' and pointing excitedly towards the drama unfolding down the road. A few older boys in their teens looked less happy to see us, but Adil calmed them down and they seemed to relax, enjoying a joke at the sight of our ludicrous body armour and eyeing the sunglasses around our necks.

We walked tentatively back towards the crowd, keeping a weather eye on the Marines on the roof and hoping they could see the 'PRESS' stickers on our flak jackets; they all seemed to be pointing their assault rifles at us. (Later, when I was embedded with the British Army in the south of Iraq, I watched our own troops do the same thing. They explained that they were using their gun sights to check people out. Had I known this at the time, I might have been less scared. Since I didn't, I was expecting some trigger-happy grunt to blow me away any second.)

Julian started snapping away, as several Imams tried to hold back the students. Many of them were now goading the Americans by hurling sandals at them; some began to slip past their elders and started throwing themselves at the wall. They weren't armed, and had no chance of getting over it, but I could see the American officers inside growing ever more nervous and barking orders at the Marines. They were constantly scanning the crowd, looking for AK47s and rocket-propelled grenades through the sights of their M16s.

The tension was enormous and things were almost out of control; I got the strong sense that whatever was going to happen here today would no longer be about the conscious decisions of anyone, American or Iraqi. It was like pub violence, the mood hurtling towards an inevitable clash; all that was needed was a spark.

And then it came.

To our right, we saw a convoy of about six vehicles coming towards us at speed from the direction of the northern outskirts of Fallujah; they were obviously heading back toward the US HQ but had been beaten to it by the marchers. Julian and I jumped out of the way, towards the walls of the compound and just beneath the line of fire of the soldiers inside. One Humvee roared past us, Julian clicking away with his camera. Then a Jeep drove by and the student line broke. Everybody ran towards the speeding vehicles, hurling their sandals at the armoured sides. A soldier on the back of a Jeep ducked to avoid a flip-flop and, as he did so, he pushed the stock of his swivel-mounted .50 calibre machine gun upwards and opened fire on the screaming crowd.

Immediately, dozens of M16s opened up from the roof and, for 20 seconds, there was a deafening clack-clack-clack of bullets smashing into concrete and bodies and ricocheting into other people. I got as low as I could, crouched in a heap beneath the wall, hands covering my head, swearing to myself and watching the mayhem unfold. Then the sound of shooting stopped, giving way to the noise of angry shouts, moaning and screaming.

The smell of cordite filled the dusty air; bodies lay everywhere and the groans of the injured rang around. Ten yards away, a man in a white robe lay flat on his face, not moving. Slowly, I got to my feet. Julian had disappeared into the melee and I could see him over on the other side of the road, crouched over another dead or injured man, taking photographs of him. Within a minute, a line of battered cars had appeared from nowhere, lining up like mini-cabs touting for trade outside a nightclub at chucking-out time, and young men were pulling their wounded friends towards these vehicles, screaming and waving for help. It was as though this was normal, as though there was a system that worked every time a crowd got mowed down – you just got the local drivers to form a line and they took it in turns to dash to the hospital with the wounded and the dead. In the middle of the chaos, a man even stood and directed the traffic.

As one car moved off towards the hospital, another moved forward to take its place.

On top of the former Ba'ath Party building the Marines looked down at the scene of devastation. Julian emerged from within the crowd and waved me over. Behind him, a young man lay dead, the top half of his head missing and a pool of blood spreading around him. Julian had been very brave. While I had been cowering, he had stood in the crowd as the bullets flew. He'd captured the soldier ducking to open fire and had followed the whole thing to this: a teenager, dying in the dust. He had taken close-up pictures of him, egged on by the boy's friends who were eager to spread the story of what the Americans had done.

I started to become aware that we were in a kind of no-man's land: an easy target if the Iraqis needed to take it out on someone Western. The Marines looked pretty unapproachable if we needed to get away and the crowd, unsurprisingly, was turning very nasty.

We started walking slowly back to the car, feeling guilty and voyeuristic. I was convinced we would be attacked but it was as though nobody in the crowd could see us: we were totally ignored. Up in front, an Egyptian TV crew, the only other journalists I'd seen, was less lucky. We watched as they were pulled out of their van and badly beaten. There was nothing we could do to help, though, and as we walked away a small group of Iraqis began to chase after us. We considered running but as we dithered they reached us. One of them handed me some batteries from a TV camera that had been smashed up, together with the end of a microphone. They felt bad because someone else had stolen them from the crew, whose van had been looted. They insisted I take the battered remnants, and became aggressive when I at first refused. They were desperate to return the looted property, even if it was to someone from a different country, and company, to the original owner.

We reached Nibras's car and quickly collected our thoughts. We could leave now or follow the bodies to the hospital. We chose the latter: it was as though we were on auto-pilot, back in England reporting on a disaster, where the standard procedure would be to confirm the numbers of casualties and then to try to find relatives of the victims for follow-up interviews. As we made the three-mile journey, Nibras weaving his way through the throng of people, Julian scrolled through his pictures on the camera display. They were unbelievably dramatic.

We used our Thuraya satellite phones to call our desks back at the *Mirror*. The news desk were very excited – I'd called in time for them to list our story as a spread for the next day during that morning's editor's conference. They didn't even bother to ask whether we had found Comical Ali.

Nibras eased the car into the hospital grounds and we parked up about 30 yards from the entrance to the main building. As we stepped out of the car, a large crowd spilled out of the hospital, carrying coffins and brandishing banners. Several of the men had AK47s slung over their shoulders and a woman, dressed all in black, turned and saw us. Her eyes dark with fury, she began to scream that we were 'Jews' who should go back to where we came from. Others in the crowd started shouting that we were spies and jostling towards us with contorted faces.

'Chris, Julian,' said Adil. 'We need to get back into the car immediately. Now!'

We didn't waste any time, piling in as quickly as we could, the furious Iraqis surging towards us, their faces contorted in rage. Nibras stood on the throttle and sped towards the gate as a group of men began to push it shut. Skidding and sliding on the grass in front of the hospital, we only just made it through the gap, with mourners hurling stones at us as we made our getaway.

Looking back through the rear window, I could see men waving their fists and guns at us and my stomach lurched with nerves and fear. I realised how lucky we had been. If those men had managed to close that gate, Nibras would have had to have run them over to escape, and he would never have done that. We would have been dragged from the car, beaten and probably killed. Two minutes earlier, I'd been on the phone to someone sat in an ergonomically-designed chair in an air conditioned office in London.

All the way back to Baghdad, the car was silent except for Nibras whistling through his teeth, shaking his head slowly and saying 'Fallujahhhh.' It was as if he was saying 'I told you so.'

Two young men had been killed and eighteen others injured, some dreadfully, in those 20 seconds of fire. I had seen it happen, and I was amazed the death toll was so low. I didn't know what to feel; weirdly, I felt nothing except relief, relief that I was alive and unhurt, and would soon be going home.

The *Mirror* carried our piece as a double-page spread.

I was pleased with my day's work, as Julian was with his. And I think we had every right to be so. It sounds callous, but that's the way of journalism. Our job was to record events like these and to be doing so in the face of death… well, I didn't like it, but I felt almost proud of myself.

The ex-Special Forces team looking after ITN and Channel 4 came up to our room to see Julian's pictures then we got back.

'You are lucky, lucky boys,' said one of them, shaking his head. 'Those rounds could have gone anywhere. And you were bloody lucky not to have been properly sorted out at the hospital, too. You really shouldn't be going to places like that, with two Iraqis and no armed back-up. It'll all end in tears.'

Later, the US forces in Fallujah spoke to the media. There was no admission of fault, and no real apology. They claimed that troops had opened fire after being shot at first by someone using an AK47 from within the crowd. I'd heard that one before.

I think that's a highly unlikely explanation, to put it mildly. In all our time with the demonstrators that day, I didn't see a single weapon, and I was looking out for them. I didn't hear any shots, either. I did see the soldier on the Jeep open fire with his .50 cal after a flip flop was thrown at him. It's possible he meant to duck, and not open fire. Perhaps he thought it was a grenade or maybe a petrol bomb; I appreciate the stress and pressure the troops must have been under, partly because I felt some of it myself. But a *flip flop*?

The incident I had witnessed – and Julian and I were the only Western journalists to do so – was the second of Fallujah's two 'Bloody Sundays', and a dreadful turning point in the occupation of Iraq. The initial damage had been done two days earlier, with the first shooting. But the subsequent protests had been non-violent. In opening fire the second time, the Americans had fanned the flames of the insurgency in the region, intensifying and solidifying Fallujan hatred of the invaders. The following day, May 1, 2003, Reuters revisited the city. Their reporters interviewed local people and one, a retired soldier called Ibrahim Hamad, summed up the mood. 'Everyone here was happy at first that the Americans threw out Saddam,' he said. 'But these killings will make all our children go off with bin Laden.'

From then on, Fallujah, with its history of blood feuds and revenge, became the centre of the rebellion in the Sunni heartlands. Less than a year later, the bridge we had crossed to enter the city was to become sickeningly infamous following the murders of four US security contractors from the company Blackwater. They were pulled from their car, beaten and shot to death, their dismembered bodies dragged through the streets and burned before the butchered, smouldering remains were slung from that bridge. It has become one of the most horrific images of the entire conflict.

Several US operations, with names like Operation Vigilant Resolve, Operation Plymouth Rock and Operation Phantom Fury have followed. Thousands of people have been killed, and dozens of the city's mosques destroyed.

The Americans say they're rooting out extremists and insurgents. I'm sure many of the dead might be described in those terms. But I'm equally sure that many will have been women, children and innocent men.

And they have long, long memories in Fallujah.

Saddam's Palace

I'd been in Baghdad for five or six weeks, Julian longer still. Any day now, we were expecting the call to pull out. We'd done mass graves, we'd done instruments of torture and we'd done religious flagellation. We'd done people killed by abandoned weapons, people killed by insurgents and people killed by US troops. We'd filed several papers-worth of colour pieces, atmospheric pictures and general stories. Pretty much everything I'd written would have made the splash – the front page lead – if it had happened in Bath or Bangor, but Baghdad was a different matter. Piers' legendarily short attention span and the general tabloid urge to move on was working against us. Lately, most of my stuff had gone straight to the spike.

We hadn't found Comical Ali – the little PR man was dodging the Yanks, the Shia death squads and the *Daily Mirror* alike with a hitherto unsuspected cunning – and there was only really one other big story in town… Saddam himself.

Obviously, the wily old tyrant was going to be nabbed eventually, but no-one knew when. Effectively, they were only keeping me out there now on the basis that it would be someday soon, so they could run the story by-lined '*From Chris Hughes in Iraq*', thus giving it an additional veneer of on-the-spot credibility.

To be honest, I wanted to come home. I needed a break from low level fear with occasional surges of sheer, wild, 24-carat terror. I'd had enough of breathing in burnt faeces, eating tinned food and listening to all-night gun fights. Most of all, I'd had enough of the paranoia that goes with drawing a reasonable salary and getting less and less in the paper in return for it.

I think Julian had just had enough of me.

The paranoia – every tabloid journalist knows it – was exacerbated by my daily phone calls to the desk.

'Hughesy, *please*… no more torture stories,' someone would say. 'And Piers isn't interested in people being shot by insurgents any more, either. Come on, there must be something new.'

But there wasn't, in red-top terms anyway. It was getting to the point where I was dreading ringing in.

To make matters worse, I was fighting blind half of the time. The news desk, sitting at the top of Canary Wharf surrounded by a billion megabytes of computing power and the world's news agencies battering their doors down with stories, were much better informed about the bigger picture out here than we were on the ground. Our satellite links were increasingly unreliable, as the kit started to malfunction with the combination of heat, sand and warm Amstel it was being subjected to, so I spent most of my time pretending to know more than I did about what was going on in the country.

The *Mirror*'s Foreign Editor, Mark 'Gonzo' Ellis, called me one day, mid-morning Iraq time, ahead of the 11am editor's conference.

'Please, mate,' he said. 'Have you got a story that doesn't involve Saddam driving round in a cab? The boss is getting bored.'

'Er, I've got this tale about one of Saddam's generals…'

'Yawn, yawn, yeah, whatever… Hughesy, don't be a wanker.'

Phone down.

In newspapers, we don't tend to talk to each other like members of the WI, but it's usually meant in the right spirit. I knew he'd be getting worse from the editor, that was for sure.

Gonzo is a really good bloke, despite his way with words, but we did have a minor disagreement over emails. Most days, he would send over some wire copy for me to rewrite with a local perspective. That was fine, except that none of the emails arrived.

Hours of arguments and complaints to the IT department back in London finally uncovered the problem. The reason that Gonzo's emails were not making it to Baghdad was that he kept signing off with the expression, 'Get on with it, you idle cunt'.

The Mirror Group's cyber police had installed a filter which automatically meant emails containing abusive language were dumped. The next day, the wire copy came through, together with an apology from the Foreign Desk editor in which he signed off with the phrase 'Get on with it, you idle kunt'. There's always a way around these little communication problems.

My fruitless daily search for new news was helped, slightly, by Nibras and Adil, who were now competing with each other to come up with ideas for stories. We'd really grown close to them by now, much more quickly than you would with guys you'd only known for a month or two back home. We'd seen them in tears, we'd shared a lot of laughs and I don't think it's an exaggeration to say we'd faced death together; it had all bonded us tightly. Adil was the brighter of the two but Nibras, ever-smiling, wasn't far behind. His English was poor but it was way better than my Arabic and his BMW was a second home to us all. We were paying them well – hundreds of dollars a week, cash, in instalments every three days – with bonuses if we got good 'shows' in the paper. Julian and I had agreed the bonus plan between us after the Fallujah incident. When we handed them an extra hundred bucks or so they'd looked at it and then nodded at each other in approval of this new system. There was definitely a capitalist edge to them both, and they enjoyed getting paid – both had families to feed, after all. But they had also caught the news bug. I loved watching them winding each other up, claiming the credit for stories which both deserved in equal measure. At this point, Adil was on the back foot because of the bogus combine harvester torture job that had cost us an entire wasted day in the company of the fat, sleazy, bad breath man. Nibras loved to make sarcastic little cracks about this if he thought Adil was getting too big for his boots.

'Combine harvest today, Adil?' he'd say, a wide-eyed, butter-wouldn't-melt look of innocence on his face.

Every few days, the four of us would go to the local version of KFC, a backstreet restaurant not too far from the hotel, for the *Daily Mirror* Baghdad office's working lunch. In London, the environmental health people would have had it closed down within about ninety seconds: every fly-ridden surface was a filthy, greasy, sticky brown colour and I hate to think what the kitchens were like. But the hot, charcoal-grilled chicken tasted great – it made a fantastic change from tinned spam – the water was bottled and the clientele, all male and busily shovelling food into their mouths with their hands, left us alone, even if they were not exactly welcoming. Julian and I would be stared at throughout the meal, often with less than friendly faces, but Nibras and Adil just stared back and barked at anyone who said anything or appeared too aggressive. They insisted on taking the money off us before we went in; they would then pay, telling the waiter we were guests of theirs. This meant we paid Iraqi prices; Adil and Nibras thought it was hilarious that they were effectively ripping off the restaurant, though the proprietor was less amused. It was an education, to Westerners who had never known hunger, or even its threat, to watch Adil. As the poorer of the two, dining out – even in this culinary hell-hole – was an experience to him. He would eat very carefully and stare at any left-overs, tutting over the waste.

On this particular day, something was on Nibras's mind. 'Saddam's Palace...' he said. 'We might go today? No?'

Most of Saddam's Palaces had been done to death – every nook and cranny had been explored, every ounce of news value sucked out and regurgitated onto acres of newsprint after the end of the war. All three of us gave him a withering look, but he held his ground, eventually giving up trying to speak in English and rattling off an Iraqi explanation to Adil, whose eyes lit up as Nibras spoke.

'Chris,' he said, 'Nibras is talking about another palace which he thinks no-one has been to yet. It is in Owja.'

Owja was the little village where Saddam had been born and dragged up. It was just outside the city of Tikrit, a hundred miles north-west of the Baghdad. Julian and I looked at each other. Our desks weren't likely to be that interested, but then our trip to Fallujah had produced a brilliant story. Who knew what we might find this time?

'Is correct,' said Nibras, beaming with pride. 'Also is Saddam house there, where he live as little boy.'

'OK,' I said. 'Sounds alright to me.'

Julian nodded. 'Let's give it a bash tomorrow. We could do Saddam's childhood house too, as Nibras says. That might make something.'

Adil and Nibras grinned and started doing a familiar impression of their deposed leader.

Shrugging their shoulders repeatedly, they started guffawing, coughing out a 'Huh, huh, huh' sound.

Saddam had been famed throughout the country for this rather creepy laugh and it had been a pan-Iraq mickey-take in his days of power, strictly to be brought out only when the torture police weren't around.

As soon as they started, men at other tables around the restaurant began chuckling and doing the same thing. Before long, the place was like some sort of slightly odd Tommy Cooper convention.

* * * * *

We set off early next day so that we could get back before dark, as the route was crawling with kidnapping gangs and robbers after sunset. They were particularly dangerous around Tikrit, where many people still supported Saddam. Many of his inner-circle had come from the area, brandishing their tribal name – al-Tikriti, *from Tikrit* – with bullish pride. It was heavily policed by American Marines, who had based themselves in one of his larger palaces in Tikrit, but still we'd need to be watchful.

Nibras and Adil were a little tense, watching cars carefully as they overtook us, but the road was just one long convoy of US troops, so we felt relatively safe, and we'd not been going for very long before we all relaxed. We made good progress on the wide, straight highway. Transport is often a high priority for homicidal megalomaniacs: the Nazis made the trains run on time and Saddam's motorways were works of Tarmac art. He'd had them constructed to facilitate the transportation of troops and ordnance quickly to the various battlefronts he had opened. Sadly for him, he'd not factored in the possibility that one day the tanks and troop carriers racing along them might not be his.

Overhead, the ubiquitous Blackhawks and Apaches wheeled away, ferrying troops and materiel or zooming towards some tell-tale pillar of black smoke on the horizon.

It took three or four hours to get to Owja, stopping to ask passers-by for directions several times, but eventually we turned off the main drag a few miles south of Tikrit, after passing through several checkpoints full of bored-looking Marines.

We found ourselves on a country lane that reminded me, bizarrely, of a Cornish B-road, narrow and winding and with high hedges on either side. After four or five miles, we came out into the open, overlooking a lush green valley, and Nibras slowed the car down and stopped so we could take in the gorgeous view. There were trees and meadows as far as the eye could see, rising to rolling hills in the far distance, and a river cutting through the red earth, glistening as it snaked its way south. It looked, I imagined, as though it must have looked since biblical times; you half expected Three Wise Men to come wandering over the horizon.

Two other thoughts occurred to me.

How could so evil a man have sprung from so beautiful and tranquil a place?

And why was it so quiet? The only sound was the 'tick, tick, tick' of the car's engine cooling down and a gentle, whispering breeze rustling up from the valley floor. No birds twittering, no dogs barking or cows lowing, not even any gunfire in the distance. It freaked us all out completely. We'd left the last US troops a way behind and we all felt slightly exposed. Nibras hurriedly started the motor and drove on.

I'd had that weird, trashy novel feeling that I was being watched, even though there wasn't another soul in sight, and it had sent the hairs on the back of my neck up. Later, the other three said they'd had the same uncomfortable sensation; it was probably just the knowledge that we were in Saddam's heartland, that he owned this place, that he must have travelled this road countless times, that even now his spies were everywhere. But wherever it came from, the feeling was real.

We descended into the village, a place of about 3,000 people, and started seeking directions to the palace Nibras had in mind, one of many in the area. Pro-Saddam graffiti was everywhere, and one man insisted on us taking his photograph as he kissed a picture of the former leader before pointing us towards the palace. It wasn't hard to find, and within minutes we pulled up outside and got out. Again, the silence was eerie. Adil and Nibras reached into the boot and took out their body armour, strapping it on. This was an interesting hint as to the tension they were feeling; I hardly ever saw them wear their jackets. After a moment's thought, Nibras got back into the car and turned it around, parking up so that it was facing back out of the complex. He was obviously concerned that we might have to leave quickly.

I looked around. The palace was little, in Saddam's terms, and, unusually for him, it was rather tasteful – a beautiful, whitewashed, four-storey building overlooking the valley. This was a building Saddam had built for himself and his family, a country retreat, and a lot of thought had gone into it. A wooden, one-roomed gazebo with a dome-like wooden roof offered panoramic views of the countryside. There were tiled footpaths winding through well-manicured lawns and flower gardens, now slightly overgrown in some places and under-watered in others.

Littered on the concrete driveway were discarded US military 'MRE' packs. These brown, plastic 'meal ready to eat' bags were about three times the size of a packet of crisps; you opened them, poured in water and, when it hit a chemical at the bottom it rapidly heated up, giving you a hot meal and about 4,000 calories in three minutes flat. They were to be found lying around everywhere you went. In the litany of bad US behaviour in Iraq, littering was not the most serious offence, I know. But I always felt it indicated a deep-running lack of respect among the troops for the country and its people, and a failure of command among officers who ought to have known better. Once again, the 'hearts and minds' boast came back to me: how did the Americans think that leaving their rubbish everywhere, and empty food wrappers at that, was going to endear them to the hungry people they had conquered? So what if Iraqis themselves were just as bad? The Americans wouldn't do it in their national parks, or on Wall Street, or on Daytona beach... so why here? How difficult can it be to pick up your unsightly plastic waste and take it home with you?

It seemed that only a small unit of Marines had been here; there were no more than 20 of these empty packs, and there were no discarded shell casings, so clearly there had not been a fight of any sort.

The exterior of the building was untouched but there was a charred smell, from some kind of fire, hanging in the air.

Inside, we discovered why: a massive bomb, possibly a bunker-buster, had come through the roof of the main hall and blitzed the place. The blackened interior still hinted at stunning grandeur, though, with a slow-winding staircase sweeping up to the first floor through the middle of the building. Nibras and I tried the first few steps but it started wobbling so we hurriedly came back down.

Adil shouted from a room nearby, laughing out loud, and we found him sitting in a wicker easy chair, beaming from ear-to-ear.

'I am in Saddam's chair,' he yelled, cackling in glee. 'Look at me... I am in his chair. Where are you now, monster? I am in your chair and you can do nothing.' He stopped, and looked at Julian, stripping off the Kevlar jacket. 'Julian, take a picture of me, please! I want to remember this moment forever! Wait until I tell my father!'

Nibras stood there doing the 'huh, huh, huh' Saddam-cum-Tommy Cooper impression.

Someone pushed open a door and discovered Saddam's indoor swimming pool. The water was still full to the brim, and crystal clear, and we took turns in posing for the camera on his diving board, sniggering uneasily.

It broke the tension, but there was something about the place, an atmosphere that made me want to leave. It was as though we had walked into a horror movie, where everything seems fine but the music tells you it's not. I'm no believer in the supernatural, but there was a strong sense of evil there. It churned my insides and, once again, lifted the hair on my neck, making me feel I was being watched by unseen eyes.

I went outside, not wanting to linger any longer in the smashed, burned-out wreckage. Julian followed me and we walked to the gardens. We waited for the two Iraqis, neither of us talking and both increasingly uncomfortable. And then we heard a squeaking noise from around the back of the house. It came from a child's swing, creaking as it moved back and forth in the wind, discarded toys lying nearby in the lengthening grass. Again, I had that 'horror movie' sensation.

Adil and Nibras joined us.

'They say that Saddam would come here with his grandchildren,' said Adil, sombrely. 'Many parties here for them.'

I looked at the play area, clearly designed for youngsters. A rusting barbecue, around which the Hussein clan must have gathered to swap jokes, stood in one corner. Next to it were a pair of plastic, garishly-painted, eight-foot high statues of Mickey Mouse and Donald Duck, smiling down at us. It was utterly creepy. Saddam had obviously understood the things that children enjoy, had taken pleasure in the smiles and laughter of his own family. Somehow, that made his actions against his people worse still. Here was a man who could fondly push his grandson on a creaking swing one minute, and the next could order dozens of executions which would leave other children fatherless or grandfatherless. Here was a man, indeed, who could happily sanction the deaths of children themselves, as the Kurds of Halabja had found in 1988, when he'd had his military carry out a chemical gas attack on their town which had left 5,000 people, including many infants, dead.

I looked at the Disney characters again. They were so desperately out-of-place here. I wondered what the Iraqi people would have thought if they had been able to see these icons of American childhood standing there as Saddam rallied his Fedayeen to march through towns throughout the land, screaming death threats to the 'crusaders'. It was almost comical; for all Saddam's roaring about his hatred of the United States, he was as in thrall to its pop culture as everyone else. But it wasn't funny – it was horrible.

'Come on,' said Julian. 'Let's get out of here.'

We hurried back to the car, not looking back.

Once Nibras started heading away, I shuddered. 'God, that was a depressing place,' I said. 'Not scary, really, just weird. The kids' toys lying around, that big Mickey Mouse. It felt like there were ghosts there, or something.'

Julian nodded. 'Not sure what it was about it,' he said. 'But I didn't like it at all either.'

'Don't think we got anything out of it story-wise, either,' I said. 'Still, we might get something from his childhood house I suppose.'

Adil turned round. 'Oh, Chris,' he said, a slight grin on his face. 'I hear that that house was destroyed many years ago.' He looked at Nibras, who was sinking slightly in his seat as he drove. That had evened up the combine harvester score between them; Adil chuckled to himself the whole way back.

The trip had been a waste of time, though. Gonzo wasn't interested in the least when I called him on the satellite phone. I think he actually put the phone down mid-explanation.

That evening, we joined Phil Coburn and one or two of the other British print journalists at the Sheraton opposite our hotel. It was a farewell party for one of the broadsheet reporters who was being replaced. I got chatting to another of them who had just come back to Baghdad after a couple of weeks' holiday.

'It's good to be back,' he said, looking around the shabby and thoroughly unpleasant room. 'Life back home just doesn't hold the same meaning for me anymore. I'm getting kinda addicted to all this.'

'Really?' I said, mildly sceptical.

'Yes,' he replied, staring wistfully into the middle distance. 'I dunno why we do it, Chris. Maybe it's the excitement. Maybe it's the bang-bang.'

Maybe it's the bang-bang? Who would actually say that with a straight face? There are those reporters who revel in the drama, the danger, the blood and guts. Then there are the rest of us. The expression became an instant mickey-take; even today, friends from other papers will call and say, in a pseudo-posh, slightly Transatlantic drawl, 'Fancy a spot of bang-bang old boy?' It means there's the chance of going to Iraq or Afghanistan with the troops. The standard reply is, 'Yah... but of course, old thing.'

'Personally, I can't wait to get out of here,' I said. 'I want to get back to Jordan and then fly home.'

'Hey!' he said. 'Guess who I saw in Jordan? Your mate Dr Amin, the old Ambassador who you had all that trouble with when you were trying to get into Iraq first time round, just after 9/11.'

'Blimey,' I said. 'I thought he'd be dead by now.' He'd been unceremoniously thrown out of Britain once the war had started, with his wife and children due to follow him after they finished that term's schooling. Ba'athists were being assassinated in broad daylight by vengeful Iraqis and most of Saddam's government was either behind bars, dead or on the run. I hadn't held out much hope for Amin.

'No, it was definitely him,' the reporter said. 'I bumped into him in a lift in the Intercontinental Hotel in Amman. He'd grown a beard and dyed his hair, and he wouldn't answer me. I kept going 'Hello Dr Amin!' but he just kept his head down and looked away.'

I wonder why, you idiot, I thought. Well, it was cheering news that Amin was still with us, even if he wouldn't be for long if his cover kept being blown by British newspapermen.

Fried With Fear

For all its filth and stench and danger, and for all that I wanted to go home, Baghdad could be a beautiful place.

Every day, around dawn, I would wake in my room at the Palestine, go out onto our precarious balcony, light up the little cooker and watch the city wake up.

Palls of black smoke would break the pink-blue sky-line, US helicopters already screaming overhead every five minutes, and that smell of burning rubbish would be rising to meet me on the cool, humid, morning air. But the lilting, melodic calling to prayer, echoing from the loudspeakers of the mosques nearby through the movie-set streets of decaying Arab and French colonial buildings, and the mist rising from the lazy Tigris just a hundred yards away from where I stood, had an exotic and unearthly appeal. Soon, the log-jammed traffic down below would be beeping away and the street vendors' barbecues would be lit for the morning's trade; then the sweet, smoky scent of cooking lamb and chicken would waft up, masking the other less pleasant aromas.

On this particular May morning, though, the streets were very quiet, with very few cars and no food sellers to be seen.

Nibras always arrived first, always pleased with himself for having beaten Adil, who had to cadge a lift to the hotel. Today, he arrived even earlier than usual and, as he walked into the room, he looked worried. In his broken English, he explained. 'Road not busy in this morning,' he said. 'No car – something very bad.'

Julian came in and they said their *Salaam Aleikums* before I pushed Nibras to elaborate. But he couldn't explain anything, other than that he felt uneasy.

148

Adil arrived shortly afterwards, swaggering into the room with a nod and a sheepish grin as he pointed towards a shiny new pair of black shoes he must have bought on the way home the night before. I winced: the previous day, I had made some ludicrous, and light-hearted, crack about the fact that he always wore sandals, and always had dirty feet. I'd meant absolutely nothing by it – I was hardly spotless myself – but the poor guy had taken it to heart, thinking it was a criticism.

'Mate, I wasn't being serious,' I said. 'You didn't need to buy those. So, anyway… are they looted or non-looted?'

I hoped the obvious joke would show I was sorry to have embarrassed him.

It worked. He raised his eyes to the heavens, grinned and swore at me in Iraqi, before wandering out onto the balcony to make some tea. He was limping slightly from the rub of the new shoes on his heels, and I caught him looking back to see if we had noticed. I laughed at him and he laughed back, the minor cultural misunderstanding forgotten.

Over breakfast of coffee, Nibras's warm flat breads and strawberry jam, we asked Adil if had knew why the streets were so quiet.

'Lots of rumours,' he said, chewing his bread and sipping his sweet tea. 'There was a story that Saddam is back in power. I don't think it, but many people do. Also, there were lot of kidnappings in last few days. About 10 people murdered I think. The insurgents…' He pulled a face to show his distaste. 'Is not very safe right now.'

Nibras nodded in agreement. 'Not safe,' he said.

Adil looked at me and Julian, suddenly very serious. 'I heard that the gangs are really trying hard to find western journalists,' he said. 'They want to kill someone to make a big news.' He pulled his finger across his throat, in the time-honoured, international gesture. 'We must be very, very careful where we go now.'

It wasn't a pleasant thought. It was more than a year since Islamic extremists had beheaded the American journalist Daniel Pearl in Pakistan and, now I came to think of it, it seemed at least reasonable to assume that others of their ilk might try the same thing in Iraq. We'd travelled around the country, unarmed and relatively unconcerned, for weeks now and, although we'd had the odd close shave, we'd been fine. But what if we'd just been lucky? And what if our luck ran out? The trickle of foreign TV companies pulling out of Baghdad was turning into a flood, and more and more print journalists would only leave the safety of their hotels to go out on breaking news stories. Although we hadn't yet reached that stage, I didn't blame them in the slightest. The days of bumbling round, trawling, hoping to come across something newsworthy, were disappearing fast. Adil certainly seemed to be saying that the rules had changed.

'You're right,' I said.' There's no point in taking any risks any more. It's just not worth it.'

Julian nodded. I'd never really seen him show any fear; at Karbala, for instance, he'd refused to remove his earring, despite Adil telling him that some worshippers would find it odd that a man would wear an earring, and that some might actually take offence to it. 'I'm sorry Adil but no, bollocks to that,' he'd said, succinctly. 'No-one tells me to take my earrings out. I wouldn't do it for The Queen, I'm sorry, I'm not taking it out here.' He also regularly wore military clothing – multi-pocketed US combat trousers, ideal for stashing bits and pieces of his kit – despite the fact that it increased the likelihood of someone taking a pot shot and hitting him (or me, come to think of it – they weren't exactly good shots).

But even he was getting more careful. 'I agree,' he said. 'Let's wise up a bit in future.'

Everyone nodded, digesting this thought. Then we put it to one side.

We had been asked by our desks to visit the site of the old British Embassy in the capital. It had been occupied a few days previously by a small unit of 50 soldiers from the First Battalion of the Parachute Regiment (1 Para). They had been the first Brits to use the building since it had been abandoned in 1991, just before the first Gulf War. The detachment was commanded by a Captain Tom McDade, an Irishman so legendarily tough that even the ex-SAS guys floating around the hotel spoke of him in hushed tones.

The TV security guy B had worked with McDade in Northern Ireland. He'd warned me the previous day, 'He's a great bloke Tom, but one hard bastard so don't piss him off under any circumstances. Do that, and you'll have us all after you. A lot of the lads are very loyal to him.'

Armed with that warning, we knew we had to follow through with a promise we had made to McDade the day before. We had visited the embassy and asked for permission to have a look around inside and interview some of his troops.

'I probably shouldn't let you do that, boys' he'd said. 'But if you promise not to take pictures unless I say you can, and you don't tell any of the locals what kind of tools we've got lying around, I guess you can have a peep.'

'Great,' I said. 'Tell you what, we'll bring you all some ice cold beers.'

'Oooh,' he winced. 'Shouldn't really – this place is meant to be dry. But, well…' He grinned, and winked.

So we sent Nibras to get the ale and a couple of large bags of ice from somewhere. Before long he'd succeeded, like the scrounger in *The Great Escape*, and was back with the booze and ice. Quickly, before it all melted in the boot of his car, we sped round to the embassy, just a few miles along the river from where we were. It was a splendid 19th century colonial building which had once been the home of General Stanley Maude, a legend amongst British soldiers in Iraq. He had captured Baghdad in 1917 and had then made a conciliatory speech to the locals which resonates even today.

'Your palaces have fallen into ruins,' he had told the Iraqis. *'Your sons have been carried off to wars not of your own seeking, your wealth has been stripped from you by unjust men and squandered in distant places. I am commanded to invite you, through your nobles and elders and representatives, to participate in the management of your own civil affairs in collaboration with the political representatives of Great Britain who accompany the British Army, so you may be united with your kinsmen in the north, east, south and west, in realising the aspirations of your race.'*

A fine speech, and one that had applied just as well during Saddam's reign.

We stopped outside the building and staggered up to the front gate, lager in our arms, to be met by the Iraqi caretaker, Mahdi Alwan. His was another amazing story; unpaid, Mr Alwan and his son had tended the building and its grounds since the day our ambassador had left. He'd kept everything spotless and had even protected the royal crest which had hung above the main entrance. He'd recently been given back pay and a bonus, so was a pretty happy chap, and he greeted us with a wide grin. 'Welcome Misters,' he said. 'Welcome.'

We kicked at the main door, struggling under the weight of the dripping ice and 50 cans of lager, one can for each soldier inside.

A Geordie voice called from within: 'Who is it?'

'It's the *Daily Mirror*,' I replied.

There was a shooting of bolts and a rattling of the handle and the door swung open to reveal three sweating Paras. They eyed our beers like... well, like thirsty squaddies *would* eye a load of ice-cold beers in 100°F heat in May in Baghdad, and beckoned us inside. Leaving Adil and Nibras outside – no locals would be allowed in until the place was properly fortified – we stepped over the threshold and handed the amber nectar over. Cradling the boxes like babies, the three Paras carefully and conspiratorially carried them off to a darkened corner inside a mounted gun position nearby.

McDade came over with a big grin, shaking our hands vigorously and thanking us for the lager. I don't think he had believed for one minute that we'd be able to come up with the goods, but we had so he felt duty bound to show us around the place. We walked into a wood-panelled bar which was called The Oasis Club, where once embassy staff and diplomats had shed the heat of the day and lost themselves in a dry Martini or a gin and tonic. On one of the walls was the Winter 1990-91 fixture list for the Baghdad Darts League, which had been wrapped up rather suddenly because of the war a few hundred miles to the south. I wondered what had become of the players of the two teams – the Bent Arrows and the Double Bulls – which had been due to meet on February 23, 1991. Two glasses stood on the bar, with dusty mould growing inside them – the remnants of a couple of hastily-abandoned cocktails. McDade had touched nothing, wanting to keep it exactly as it was before the arrival of the acting ambassador, Christopher Segar, who had flown in earlier that day.

Outside, the embassy's small cricket field – I loved that, a cricket field... how ridiculously British – was filling up with temporary buildings. A wooden veranda overlooked The Tigris, which was heaving with river traffic.

The whole scene was very colonial; I could imagine the likes of TE Lawrence and Gertrude Bell, almost a century before, whiling their time away in the cooling shade, sipping long drinks and chatting about the issues of the day. I could have sat there for hours. But McDade reluctantly ushered us inside.

'It's a bit dangerous out here,' he said. 'They will insist on having a pop at us from the other side of the river. They're very poor shots, but every dog has his day.'

'Have you had any near misses?' I asked.

'Not really,' he said. 'A couple of AK rounds hit the wall next to me the other evening when I was having a cup of tea, but it was nothing serious. The lads had the fellow who was shooting at us in their sights, but I stopped them from slotting him. It causes too much trouble with the locals. I think the bloke was just letting us know he was there.'

I imagined how 'slotted' the Iraqi would have been had he been seen firing at an American embassy; he'd have been slotted into about a thousand pieces. It was so good to meet calm, unexcitable and unimpressed-by-their-surroundings British troops after so many weeks of watching the Yanks in action.

We wandered back into the building and I grabbed a stack of Baghdad British Embassy letterheads, by way of a souvenir. McDade frowned, and I went to put them back. But then he shrugged. 'Not much use for them now, I suppose,' he said.

Then he smiled. 'Hey, you've got to see this.' He walked back out and towards a garage and flung the doors open with a flourish. 'Pretty amazing, eh?'

Sitting in the garage, beneath an inch of grey dust, were two cars, a Dodge and a Volvo. Their tyres had flattened over the years, but they were otherwise untouched. Saddam's lunatic son Uday was notoriously obsessed with cars. Imagine the fun the psychotic Freddie Mercury look-alike could have had playing stock cars with the British Ambassador's Volvo? Yet he hadn't even thought to have a look to see if they'd been left behind. That's just being a lazy despot, in my book.

We had a good couple of hours there, chatting to the Paras and reading old letters from the John Major days pinned to various notice boards. But then it was time to go. It had been an interesting, unusual visit but I knew we'd struggle to get anything into the paper. I love tabloid journalism for its hard-nosed simplicity but, just occasionally,

I wished I had the opportunity to write about things that were slightly tangential to the obvious angles.

The feeling of homesickness had grown, badly. Maybe it was mixing with a load of (non-journalist) Brits, maybe it was the tense discussions of that morning. I just I felt different about being there. I don't know whether Julian felt the same way. I do know that thinking about home made me take my eye off the ball.

On the way back to the hotel, Nibras raised the idea of visiting some caves about 60 miles east of Baghdad on the main highway heading for the Iranian border. He had been banging on for weeks about the place, probably with a little Brucie bonus in mind. He was convinced it was the kind of place that Comical Ali might have gone to hide out. It sounded just about plausible, and it was only lunchtime, so we decided to give it a whirl.

We arrived back at The Palestine, quickly filed some words and pictures from the embassy back to London – it made about two paragraphs the next day, by the way, stuck at the back of the paper, between the cartoon strips and the astrology – had our lunch and met the two Iraqis outside the hotel. Our ex-SAS pal Bob was standing there talking to B and another of their colleagues, the man who'd been shot in the arm protecting his TV crew. As we gathered around our car, the three of them walked over.

'Aye, aye, boys,' said Bob, all smiles and bonhomie. 'What's the plan for today, then?'

'We're thinking of heading out east, towards the Iranian border. There's some caves there and...'

'Hang on, hang on,' said Bob, raising his palm, his face suddenly serious. 'You're going *where*?'

'Towards the Iranian border,' I repeated. 'There's these caves...'

'I've been wondering about you lot for a while, now,' said B. 'No back-up, no guns. You can't stay lucky for ever, you know.'

I half thought about mentioning Nibras's pistol, but I wasn't sure if it actually worked and, if it did, I thought there was a fair chance he'd do more damage to us with it than anyone else.

'Ah, we'll be alright,' I said. 'It's only a little trip out. We'll be back before dark.'

'Yeah,' said Julian, with a grin. 'Don't worry. We'll be careful.'

Bob and B weren't happy, but there was little they could do to stop us.

B looked at Nibras's BMW and pulled out a notebook. He wrote down the make, colour and number plate. 'Right,' he said, staring very hard at our driver. 'I want to know the exact route you're taking, where you're going and when you'll be back. Show me. Now! On the map!'

Shaken by his aggression, Nibras pulled out a map and B made more notes.

'If you're not back within two hours, we're coming out looking for you,' he said. And, stony-faced, he turned on his heel and stalked away.

A minute or two later, sitting in the back of the car, Julian and I discussed the incident briefly.

'What the hell was all that about?' I said.

'Dunno,' he said. 'They weren't happy though, mate. Never seen them so protective of us.'

'Sorry they were rude to you guys,' I called to the two Iraqis. 'Totally unnecessary.'

'It is not a problem,' came the answer from Adil.

We drove through the streets of Baghdad. They were still unusually empty, and even the Americans seemed to be staying at home. There were no troops walking the streets, just the occasional tank or a convoy of armoured Humvees steaming by.

I did notice that their top gunners seemed unusually tense; normally they would wave you by to overtake them, but today they were holding their palms upright and ordering us to stay back with a pushing motion of the hand not holding the machine gun. We could have turned back but, for some reason, despite our breakfast-time chat about the increasing dangers, we didn't really talk about it.

Nibras negotiated his way towards the Eastern suburbs of Baghdad, a scruffy, dusty sprawl of dirty red, single-storey houses and shuttered-up shop fronts. Occasionally, we'd pass a gaggle of old men, sitting outside the odd cafe, chatting away. Soon, we reached the Eastern Road. This was busier, though by no means packed, a steady stream of pick-ups, trucks and cars bowling towards the Iranian border. This was a new route to us: a double-laned, smoothly Tarmac-d affair, with a three-foot high concrete central reservation.

We sped past occasional side streets, taking little notice of what was going on down them.

That was the second big mistake we made that day.

The first had been to leave the hotel in the first place.

The third was not checking our rear view mirror.

On the 'hostile environment' courses designed to give inexperienced journalists half a chance of staying alive in places like this, the instructors constantly impress on you the importance of knowing what is going on around you at all times. They stress, especially, the rear view and side streets. I don't *think* they mention chatting to your photographer mate about the girl you've been emailing back home, and how desperate you are…

I remember that we came to a stretch of open road, and that there was a group of men loitering on the hard shoulder, chatting and smoking and watching the cars as they drove by. I remember that they narrowed their eyes when they saw us, and I remember seeing them sort of dive into a people carrier parked there.

But then, where was I? Oh, that's it. There's this girl…

Nibras was driving along happily, eyes fixed on the road ahead, and Adil had his head down in the passenger seat, either asleep or just nodding off.

We'd driven on for another couple of miles or so when, suddenly, Nibras shouted something in Arabic that made us all sit up. It sounded like something was happening up ahead so Julian and I leaned into the middle of the car to look through the windscreen. A couple of teenage kids were standing on the central reservation, one holding an AK47 in the air, the other pointing a pistol at the cars heading towards him, including our own. I couldn't tell if either of them were firing but they were obviously trying to get a car to stop. Nibras swerved right into the overtaking lane, putting the car in front of us between us and the youths, and we sped on. Julian and I turned to look at each other, speechless. *Had* they been firing at us?

We had no choice but to press on. Everyone was wide awake and looking around, now, Adil too. We started looking behind us, at last.

Then we saw them.

To my right were two white, open-backed Toyota pick-ups. One had two men with bandanas drawn over their faces in the rear, the other just one man. All three were slightly off-balance, swaying on their feet and holding onto the cabins of the trucks as they raced to overtake us. As they drew level, we could see that each was carrying an AK47.

Whenever you read accounts of this sort of thing, people seem to say it all happened in slow motion. I think it's just a cliché, but even though these two vans were speeding past us, and now pulling in ahead to try to box us in, they seemed to take an awfully long time about it.

I distinctly recall screaming, 'Fucking slow down, Nibras! Let them get ahead... put some distance between us.'

Julian says this never happened, and that in fact it was he who shouted exactly those words.

Who knows? Maybe we both said it, maybe we both just thought it. It wasn't much of a solution anyway. They'd just have stopped as well. The pick-up containing the lone gunman was closest now, about ten yards in front of us. The other was ahead of it and pulling over to the left, perhaps to get a better shot at us.

There was silence in our car, Nibras desperately looking for a way out but with houses to our right and the damned concrete central reservation to our left we had nowhere to go but forwards.

The man on the back of the pick-up in front was now lowering his assault rifle and beginning to take aim at our front windscreen, briefly taking his spare hand off the cabin to steady the barrel as he fingered the trigger.

My brain was fried with fear at that point, blasted from a state of slight unease, which I always felt, to sheer horror. It was a hundred times more terrifying than anything else I had ever experienced. I was absolutely sure I was about to die. I recall glancing across at Julian, a far braver man than me, and I remember his eyes and mouth being very wide open; I guess I must have been the same. I was very aware of my hands being clenched tight, as you might do at the dentist as you try to concentrate on something other than the drill or the needle, and I reeled between feeling utterly out of control, to deflated, to utterly resigned to death, to bracing myself for what was about to happen.

There was no thought of trying to grab Nibras's gun, or pull the steering wheel to make him ram one of the pick-ups, or do something, anything, to try to influence the situation. Later, I would recall the words of B, after his unarmed colleague had disarmed and 'got rid of' the insurgents who were attacking his TV crew: *Some people get it wrong, back off, do nothing. You need the bottle and the brains to be aggressive and have a go at them and take them by surprise. Do what they're not expecting.* Well, we just backed off, doing nothing, that's for sure. But then we weren't former SAS troopers; we were just four utterly terrified blokes. Rabbits in the headlights. Useless.

Out of the corner of my eye, I saw a third vehicle coming up at speed on our right and settling in behind us. I turned: it was the people carrier from five minutes back along the road, and the men inside were staring at us and waving at us to stop.

I looked back, at the gunman in front of us; his finger was on the trigger of the AK and he was squinting along the barrel at us.

Suddenly, he lifted the rifle into the air and waved in anger as a big shape came between us. It was the people carrier; it had driven up alongside us, probably intending to force Nibras off the road, and was now between us and all three armed men.

Their mistake saved our lives, I'm absolutely sure of it.

At the same moment that the masked Iraqi was waving to his accomplices to get back out of his way, I felt our own car lurch, violently and at speed, to the left. I was thrown hard against the right-hand window as Nibras hurled the car through a 20 foot gap in the central reservation and handbrake-turned so we were facing back the other way on the other carriageway. It was a brilliant piece of driving. We swerved crazily for a second or two – thankfully the traffic on the other side missed us – and then started accelerating away, engine screaming and gravel and dust spraying everywhere. I looked in the rear view mirror; the three vehicles were already in the distance, speeding towards Iran, the bandana-wearing shooter waving, in fury now, at the people carrier.

We were all dumbstruck.

A minute or so later, Nibras muttered: 'It is important to be calm.'

I felt anything but calm. My entire body was soaked with sweat. I sat there, my head in my hands, looking at the floor of the car. I was shaking, shuddering like I had hold of a jackhammer. I glanced at Julian. He was the same. I don't believe either of us spoke a word.

A little further down the road, Nibras swore again, the same oath he had uttered earlier.

Looking up through the windscreen, I could see a group of five or six Iraqi teenagers in the central reservation, a couple of others running across the road. They were openly firing at cars and lorries coming the other way, and drivers were careering all over the carriageway to avoid being hit. Nibras pulled us alongside a large lorry, putting that between us and these new maniacs, and as he did so I could see people leaning out of the oncoming vehicles and firing back.

What unbelievable, lunatic anarchy had been unleashed here?

I'm not a religious person, but I was praying to see The Palestine again, unable to look any more, as Nibras flung the car from left to right, doing a hell of a speed and overtaking everyone in our way to get us out of this Wild East. I was in a daze of permanent fear; I remember a sense of amazement, of disbelief, that this had actually happened to us. I had seen rotting corpses dragged out of shallow graves, I had watched people being killed and horribly wounded close-up, I had interviewed the victims of the war. But none of it had really touched me; I'd been a journalist, a spectator, a voyeur, call it what you like, just doing my job. Today, that had all changed. Today I had become the target, with my friends, and we were incredibly lucky to be alive to tell the tale.

We arrived back at the hotel within 40 minutes, I guess. To be honest it's hard to tell. Nibras stayed outside to check his car for bullet holes or other damage and the three of us went to report what had happened to Bob and B. They compiled daily bulletins about what happened where and they needed to know that the Eastern Road to Iran was strictly off limits.

They were chatting in Bob's room. As we walked in, they saw our pale faces and shaking hands.

'Come on then,' said B. 'What happened?'

We told them.

'Fuck me,' he said. 'Well, at least you got out alive. You're just a walking cashpoint to them. Still. You lived to tell the tale eh lads?'

'You're very lucky,' said Bob. 'Classic *modus operandi*. Box you in, make you stop, force you out of the car, strip you, rob you, shoot you in the nut by the side of the road and someone from the people carrier fucks off in your motor.'

We nodded, like schoolboys in front of the headmaster.

'I'm running a convoy back to Jordan in a couple of days,' said Bob. 'No problem if you want to join up with us. You ought to think about it.'

We caught the dodgy lift back to our room and looked out of the window. Several of the tanks which had been parked nearby had gone, diverted to deal with the growing unrest in the city. We'd just had the biggest let-off of our lives, and the urge to get out wasn't just about homesickness, or boredom, or lack of stories in the paper any more.

Back at the room Adil was quiet. We asked how he felt.

'Nibras and I both agree with those men,' he said. 'We think you should go home. It is not safe for you here anymore. It is too dangerous for you. We want to work with you very much. You are our friends. But you have to go. We are not worried for ourselves. We are Iraqi and we are from tribes so we have protection. But you are not safe and if this happens again we might not be able to help you.'

This hit home even harder than the words of the experts. We were paying Adil and Nibras a small fortune. They needed the money, to put aside to help their families through the lean, hard times that were surely coming for them and their country. Adil was waving goodbye to that, for us. It was very moving.

Just then, Nibras walked into the room. He was shaking and his skin blanched almost to the colour of his white shirt.

He spoke rapidly in Iraqi to Adil, whose face turned grim. Both men sat on the floor, their heads in their hands.

Eventually, Adil looked up.

'Nibras just saw a woman taken from her car and shot to death, maybe five minutes from the hotel,' he told us. 'Four men dragged her from her car and emptied their guns into her while people watched. No-one helped her. Then they just drove off in her car and left her in the road.'

Tears were streaming down Nibras's face now. He looked at us, nodded and then shook his head and got up, walking out onto the balcony. I could see his shoulders heaving as he stood there.

'She was a member of the regime,' said Adil. 'Either she was married to somebody, or she was somebody. I don't know. What is happening to my country, when they can do this in daylight so near to Americans?'

I hoped it was a rhetorical question. I certainly didn't have an answer for him.

Shortly afterwards, they both left and I started writing my account of what had just happened. I filed it without calling the desk, and checked in half an hour later.

The news editor Conor Hanna was just reading it.

'Are you OK, the pair of you?' he asked.

Conor comes from Belfast and cut his journalistic teeth covering the troubles there before coming to London. It takes a lot to impress him, but he sounded almost worried.

'Fine, thanks,' I said. 'Just a bit shaken up.'

'Piers has read the story and he wants you to get out of Baghdad as soon as possible,' he said. 'Come back to me and let me know how you're going to do it. Whatever you need, let me know.'

It had been Conor who had interrupted my cold beers on a beach in Doha during my CentCom all those weeks earlier. The order to get out of the city was as abrupt as the order to get in had been. I told Julian we were headed home.

Next morning, we settled our bill with the hotel staff and said our goodbyes to our two Iraqi friends.

First there was a lot of stuff that we didn't need to take with us – a couple of hundred pounds-worth of food, some medical packs, dozens of bottles of clean water, 20 or 30 litres of petrol and our cooking gear. Nibras and Adil divided everything between them. Our small stove went to Adil, whose family was the poorer of the two, and a spare flak jacket that we had picked up along the way went to Nibras.

Adil shrugged and grinned as he handed it over to the driver. 'Nibras likes this sort of thing,' he said. 'He loves any gadgets and these military things.'

There were dozens of bars of chocolate for their kids and their eyes lit up like children when we handed them over.

'My daughter very pleased,' said Nibras, laughing.

Adil picked up a couple of dehydrated meals we had bartered from US troops and threw one at Nibras. 'What will your father say when he sees this?' he asked, chuckling. 'That we cannot spare the water?'

Clean water was so scarce in the country that the head of the family was the only one allowed to distribute it.

After the division of the spoils, we sat and talked for a while. I told Adil about my family, about my flat in London and my job. As I spoke, my eyes fell on his worry beads. 'I must remember to get some of those as a souvenir,' I said, half to myself.

Without a moment's hesitation Adil handed me his.

'I can't accept those, Adil,' I said. 'I shouldn't have said anything. I was just thinking out loud.'

He looked at me, hurt and upset. 'You insult me, Chris, when you say you will not take this thing,' he said, pressing them into my hand. 'Please, take them. Maybe they will bring you and Julian luck as you drive to Jordan. It is very dangerous in the desert now.'

Reluctantly, and apologetically, I accepted the beads. 'Thanks, Adil,' I said. 'You didn't need to give me them but I'm very grateful.'

They're now hanging in my living room at home.

Some time in the afternoon, Adil raised his eyes at Nibras. It was time for them to leave and they both stood.

'No kissing!' said Julian, jokingly.

'But, really, fellas – no kissing,' I said.

Middle Eastern men are a lot more demonstrative in their affection for each other than buttoned-up Englishmen like us. Adil and Nibras both grinned and hugged us in turn. We finished with a nice, firm, manly handshake and they were gone, weighed down with chocolate and other goodies.

That night, we had a beer down in the ITN room with the security guys.

We stood out on the balcony, the TV guys staying inside.

'Fair play to you guys after today,' said B. 'You've certainly seen the sights.'

'Very stupid, I think,' I said. 'I won't be doing that again.'

I stared into my drink, feeling very low.

Suddenly, Julian shook himself. 'Shit!' he yelled. 'The balcony's collapsing.'

He staggered towards the safety of the room.

B took his arm. 'No, mate, it isn't,' he said. 'You're just in shock.'

We looked at each other, starting to realise just how much the day's events had affected us. (Even now, when Julian and I occasionally talk about the experience it is fresh in my mind and I can still feel the fear of what happened.)

We carried on getting drunk with ITN, but we listened to them, not really joining in.

Our journey out of Baghdad started at dawn the next day, a six-car convoy, led by the armoured Land Rover that Bob drove all the way back to Amman.

We saw the odd people carrier and a few pick-ups, an unnerving sight despite the fact that, for once, we were travelling with a group of men who were armed to the teeth and knew what they were doing. But we were both absolutely exhausted – you don't realise how tiring it is to live under permanent stress and fear until you start to leave it behind – and before long we were sparked out, sleeping most of the eight hour journey to the border and, finally, the Intercontinental Hotel in Amman.

We checked in and I called my family to tell them I was out and all was well. Standing in my room, an air-conditioned paradise of fresh white sheets, hot running water and a gold-embossed room service menu, I looked at myself in the mirror. I'd lost half a stone in weight, my face was haggard, dirty and drawn and my clothes were ingrained with filth and streaky white salt stains. But I was alive and safe, and Baghdad seemed a very long way away.

For weeks, I'd dreamed about lying in a hot, sweet-smelling bath for hours. But there were beer and women downstairs. I hopped in the shower, scrubbed up and was in the bar in about three minutes. Julian was already there. We had more than a few beers, no luck at all with the women and spent the night listening to the chatter of excited American civilian contractors heading over the border to rebuild the country their government had wrecked.

We watched these guys chucking back Jack Daniels like it was going out of fashion and laughing raucously; it was another world.

One of them, a big, white lumberjack-looking man, turned to us at the bar.

'So what brings you here, fellas?' he asked.

We told him.

'I'm heading into Iraq' – he pronounced it Eye-rak, as they all seem to – 'tomorrow. Part of Halliburton. Working on a major construction project.'

'Whatever,' said Julian, contemptuously.

'Nice of Bush to smash the place to bits for you,' I said. 'Gives you something to do.'

I feel bad about that, now. He was making money out of the war and I thought that was wrong, still do. But he was being friendly enough and he hadn't started the damn thing. There was no need for me to be so rude. It was a sign of how anti-American we'd become in our time over the border.

The office gave us a few days in Amman to calm down and get drunk before heading home.

The first Fallujah incident was sparked after American soldiers shot at demonstrators who wanted them to leave a school they had taken over as a base. Here, after the school has been vacated, a schoolboy looks at a US flag drawn on a blackboard. In another classroom, the words 'I love pork' had been scrawled. It's hard to imagine a more pointed – and pointless – insult.

Picture: Julian Andrews

The father of one young man shot dead in the first incident swears on the Koran that he is telling us the truth about the shooting.

Picture: Julian Andrews

The man's son had been hit by a bullet fired through the window; here, the dead boy's skull and brain matter lie in a pool of blood on the floor.
Picture: Julian Andrews

Angry marchers descend on the Americans' new base in Fallujah; many waved banners or the Koran, but we saw no guns.
Picture: Julian Andrews

A flip flop is thrown and this soldier ducks and opens fire as protestors run for cover.
Picture: Julian Andrews

Seconds later, dead and injured people lie everywhere; this man has been shot in the head and killed instantly.
Picture: Julian Andrews

The pool inside one of Saddam's palaces at Tikrit.
Picture: Julian Andrews

Adil relaxes in one of the dictator's wicker chairs in a bedroom in the devastated palace; as a Shia from Al Sadr, this gave him a tremendous thrill.
Picture: Julian Andrews

A Saddam loyalist openly kisses a portrait of his deposed leader in the streets near the palace.
Picture: Julian Andrews

Inset: Months later I was back in the region and exploring Saddam's last hiding place.
Picture: Ian Vogler / Daily Mirror

This great picture by James Vellacott (Daily Mirror), taken leaning over the back of a Chinook's

A British soldier patrols in Iraq. The berets have gone but the approach is still softly-softly, non-confrontational and highly professional.

Picture: James Vellacott / Daily Mirror

Meanwhile, the American forces employ more aggressive tactics – a young boy stands-off a US soldier at the gun market in Baghdad, while a grunt towers over a terrified man caught looting. We accidentally re-armed one of the looters later.

Pictures: Julian Andrews

Dozing in a Warrior as the Welsh Guards prepare to provide security during the elections. The *Daily Mail's* **Nick Craven** is to my right.
Picture: James Vellacott / Daily Mirror

Suddenly, thousands of voters appear as the elections get underway.
Inset: One voter proudly shows off his inked finger.

A golden sunset over Baghdad captures the contradictions of the city; horror was all around and yet there was beauty too.

Picture: Julian Andrews

Adil, left, and Nibras: two of the best and bravest men I've ever met. Without them, working in Iraq would have been impossible for me. We've obscured their faces because of the risk of reprisals from insurgents angry that they have worked with the British media.

Picture: Julian Andrews

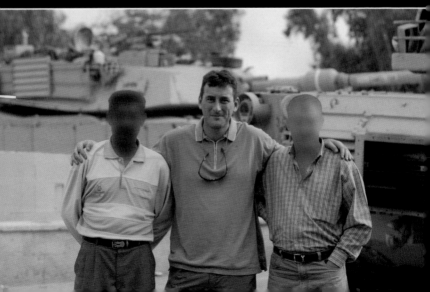

Saddam's Hole

It was December 13, 2003, and most of the Western world was settling down for its annual orgy of gift-wrapped plastic tat, Rennies and endless screenings of *Back to the Future*, when George Bush and Tony Blair finally got the Christmas present they had been waiting for.

Saddam had been found, alive, cowering in a six-foot-deep pit close to the palace at Owja we had visited six months before.

Around 600 soldiers of the 1st Brigade, 4th Infantry Division, and special operations forces of Task Force 121 had been searching for the former dictator after a tip-off that he was hiding out near Tikrit. One of them had moved some dirt near a two-room mud shack and found a board covering the entry hole. Inside they discovered their quarry, dressed in filthy rags and sporting a bushy salt-and-pepper beard.

'I am Saddam Hussein, I am the President of Iraq, and I'm willing to negotiate,' he apparently told them. He must have practising that proud line for months and it demonstrated, finally, his endless capacity for self-delusion. He wouldn't be negotiating anything with anyone, ever again. Disorientated and blinking against the light, and looking more like the sort of fellow you see pushing his belongings in a shopping trolley and arguing with himself than the all-powerful leader he'd once been, he was dragged out of his hiding place and hauled onto TV screens around the world.

The Americans didn't waste any time with their press conference.

'Ladies and gentlemen, we got him!' US administrator Paul Bremer told journalists in Baghdad, as Iraqis in the audience cheered. They showed humiliating film of Saddam having his teeth inspected as part of a general health check and made much of the fact that he'd been arrested without a fight.

'Here was a man who was photographed hundreds of times shooting off rifles and showing how tough he was,' said Donald Rumsfeld. 'And in fact, he wasn't very tough. He was cowering in a hole in the ground. He had a pistol but he didn't use it and he certainly did not put up any fight at all. In the last analysis, he seemed not terribly brave.'

The prevailing theory was that once Saddam was caught the growing insurgency, much of which was being propagated by Ba'athists, would tail away. His sons, Uday and Qusay, had been killed in a shoot-out with troops in July and many other senior members of the Hussein regime were either dead or behind bars. This, surely, was the beginning of the end.

So the capture was great news for Tony, George, the Coalition, most of Iraq and probably the rest of the world. But it was terribly inconvenient for me. I was relaxing at home when my phone rang.

It was Conor.

'Chris?'

'Yes?'

'Get yourself to Heathrow,' he said. 'We need you in Iraq ASAP and you're booked onto a flight to Jordan this evening. Saddam's been caught. It turns out he was hiding in a hole not far from that place called Owja. That's where he's from, right?'

'Yes,' I said, a chill rippling through my guts. That horrible feeling we'd all had at the Owja palace, and in the surrounding hills, the feeling that we were being watched... maybe we *had* been.

'OK, get there as soon as possible. We want some general reaction from the Iraqis but the main thing is Piers wants you to be the first tabloid reporter in the hole. Don't let *The Sun* beat you.'

Click.

Great.

Get yourself to Heathrow. We need you in Iraq. That would be the Iraq where I had a fighting chance of being kidnapped and beheaded, randomly shot or, at best, beaten and robbed. The Iraq where the beer was warm, the hotels stank and the food came out of the tins you carried in with you. The Iraq, in short, that I'd been so delighted to get out of a few months earlier. Worst of all, I'd miss the newsroom's Christmas party. These are always shabby, drunken affairs, where all the disgraces, cock-ups and indiscretions of the previous year are raked over in public in speeches by news executives. Everyone gets utterly hammered, a few sporadic fights break out and the odd marriage collapses. Fantastic fun. Still, at least they'd all toast me sincerely and wish me *bon voyage in absentia*. Yeah, right. I'd be ripped apart behind my back and I'd have to listen to it all down a satellite link-up a day or two later, as kindly colleagues passed on all the bile and mickey-taking.

I sat and collected my thoughts for a few minutes.

On paper, the job itself didn't seem all that difficult a task. The road to Baghdad from Amman was probably dodgier than ever, but once I got to the capital the trip north would be fine. But being the first tabloid into the hole was going to be tough. At the moment I was in Fulham, after all. I had to get to the hole before *The Sun* did. They're our main rivals, though to a lesser extent we will worry about what the *Daily Star*, the *Daily Express* and the *Daily Mail* are running. Like all papers, the *Mirror* is locked in a fierce battle for circulation; we all have our loyal readers so we're all fighting for the 'floating voters', people who will buy the paper on a whim because they like the look of the front page on the news stand. A picture of the *Daily Mirror*'s own man in Saddam's bolthole might make the front and it might pick up a few readers. If *The Sun* got there before me… well, it wasn't necessarily a sacking offence but it wouldn't do me any favours at all.

I made a few calls to contacts on other papers and people out in Basra and Baghdad, trying to find out how the land lay, who was out there, media-wise, and where they were.

They told me what I already suspected; reporters from *The Times*, *The Daily Telegraph* and *The Guardian* were in Iraq. They were probably visiting the spot as I sat there, but that actually wasn't too much of a problem. Firstly, they were broadsheet guys, and not our immediate rivals, so they didn't really count. Secondly, I doubted they would actually be allowed into the hole anyway. In the first few days, the US intelligence people would be crawling all over it, looking for clues and, well, intelligence.

The last call I made, to a friend at Wapping, was less encouraging. *The Sun*'s senior foreign correspondent, Nick Parker, was in Iraq already.

'He's in Basra, mate, doing some sort of stunt with our soldiers out there,' said my mole. 'There's some big job on, though... I've heard them shouting about getting into Saddam's hole or something?'

This was a huge problem. Competing tabloids actually work together in a war zone from time to time, putting aside rivalries to scratch each others' backs, but Nick was hardly going to wait for me to get there. If he got a move on he could be in Owja in 12 hours, way quicker than me. I thought about ringing Conor with the bad news, but decided against it. Executives don't tend to like being called with reasons why you can't achieve something. I mentally filed it; it would be a reasonable defence if the worst happened.

My phone went. It was a *Daily Mirror* staff photographer, Ian Vogler.

'Chris,' he said. 'I'm going to Iraq with you. Are you on your way?'

Ian's a good bloke, an excellent photographer with a great sense of humour and a lot of guts. If I had to go with anyone, he was fine.

'I'm just getting my bags together, mate,' I said. 'I'll meet you at the airport.'

I chucked my passport and a few clothes into a bag and called Bob Graham, a veteran freelance Fleet Street hand working for *The Daily Mail* and a few other papers in Baghdad. Bob very helpfully agreed to book us a couple of rooms next to his in the Al Hamra hotel – The Palestine was no longer regarded as safe, and the Al Hamra was now protected within a ring of concrete and Iraqi security men. And then I rang a cab.

* * * * *

A dozen hours later, Ian and I emerged into the chaotic arrivals lounge at Amman airport. Dozens of the airport's official porters immediately descended on us, like wolves on the fold, clamouring to collect our bags for a few dollars. It's the same at any Middle Eastern airport I've ever been to; they quickly work out that you're journalists, and often even recognise you from previous trips. Thus, they know they you're on expenses, they know that you have lots of cases full of expensive equipment and they know that you're knackered, or idle, or hungover, or all three. Vogler and I were made of sterner stuff than the average

British journalist, though; impervious, we batted away all-comers and, eventually, they got the message, slinking across to the carousels and eyeing us sullenly as we hunted for our own bags. Three hours later, sullen looks had turned to gleeful mockery as we finally accepted the awful truth, delivered by the smiling head of airport baggage control.

'I'm very sorry, sirs,' he said, not actually looking sorry at all. 'But some of your luggage has gone to Damascus. I really am most awfully apologetic about this.' He was almost tittering. We'd got Ian's camera gear, and our laptops and satellite phones. We'd also got our clothes and personal bits and pieces. But our helmets and body armour were several hundred miles away in Syria, probably closer to Saddam's hole than we were. For some reason, I couldn't see the funny side.

I started pacing up and down while Ian, being far more pragmatic, called a contact in Israel who might be able to sell us replacement gear. It would mean an eight-hour drive to Jerusalem in the opposite direction, but it was better than the alternative, driving across the bandit country of the Western Desert without protective kit. It was all academic, though; Ian's call drew a blank. While I sat smoking and chewing my fingernails, wondering what the hell to do, he went back to see the head of baggage. Then he walked back over to me.

'It's alright Chris,' he said. 'He says the airline are flying the cases back to us tomorrow. It just means we'll have to spend a night in Jordan. There's worse places to be.'

I looked over at the grinning baggage bloke. Could we trust him? Was this just an elaborate wind-up? Were *The Sun* even now clambering down into Saddam's hiding place? There was only one way to find out. I called Nick Parker on his satellite phone.

'Hi Nick, it's Chris Hughes.'

'Hello, mate, how's things?' said Parker, his Brummie voice bouncing up and down through space.

'Good, mate, thanks,' I said. 'Look… are you in Baghdad yet?'

There was a pause.

'No, I'm not,' he said. 'I'm still in bloody Basra, handing out sodding Christmas puddings to the troops. The desk won't let me go till I've dished out the last of the puds. I think I'm on my way up there tomorrow.' He sounded pretty fed up.

'Thanks mate… maybe see you there.'

The line went dead.

This was good news, as long as Parker was telling the truth. It may surprise readers to know that tabloid journalists are not always paragons of honesty. I had no way of knowing for sure but, on balance, I trusted him. Nick is an utterly ruthless reporter, totally dedicated to his job, and it looked like he was champing at the bit to get going while his desk messed around.

'At least *The Sun* aren't there yet,' I said to Ian. 'That gives us a bit of breathing space.'

'What are our options?' he said.

I thought for a minute.

'Well, we could just start driving tonight, without the body armour. But it's a hell of a risk along that road. I'd rather not, to be honest.'

'Fair enough,' said Ian.

'Or we can trust that shifty git over there and assume our gear will be back here in the morning like he says, and get linked up with a convoy as soon as we collect it.'

'That's what we'll do then,' said Ian. 'Let's book in at the Intercontinental. You never know, someone there might sell us some replacement gear so we can get going earlier.'

That sounded like a plan and, for the first time, I started to feel optimistic about the job.

Just then, my sat-phone rang. It was a hassled news desk executive.

'Are you there yet?'

'What, in Baghdad?' I said.

'No. Are you at Saddam's hole yet?'

'Bloody hell,' I said. 'We're still in Jordan.' What did they think? That you could just hop on a bus, or catch the train? Did they actually *follow* the news?

'How come?' he said.

'Er… problem with the flights.'

It was technically true. There was no point telling the desk that our luggage had gone astray. News desks only want to hear good news, because editors only want to hear good news, and if you've got bad news it had better either be very bad ('I've been shot' would buy you some time) or very vague and unfixable. In their world, lost luggage isn't a problem that war zone journalists suffer and, if they do, they should be able to sort it.

'Oh, bloody hell. OK, mate, get there as quick as you can. Piers is all over this one.' He hung up.

By now, the office would have made their own enquiries and would know that Parker and *The Sun* were poised to go, and that Bob Graham, of the *Daily Mail*, was in Baghdad. I knew the pressure from the editor would be mounting. I knew, too, that they'd be telling him white lies and half truths in the same way I was them.

I could hear the conversation now.

'Where's Hughes and Vogler, then? Are they there yet?'

'Er, they're on their way Piers, but there were problems with the line and they kept breaking up. Somewhere close to Baghdad, I think, but then I lost the connection.'

We headed for the Intercontinental, a luxurious hotel full of ornate furniture, obsequious bell hops and drunken journalists. We checked in and set about finding ourselves a driver for the next day's journey, and lining up a convoy with other travellers, before hitting the bar for a few nerve-calming drinks.

Next morning, our driver ferried us back to the airport to pick up the missing gear – thankfully, it had arrived – and then back to the hard-standing in front of the hotel where several other GMC people carriers were waiting. I'd rather have been in a battered old Toyota, because these GMCs were prized and targeted by the robbers out in the badlands. But there were several other vehicles with us and there was a chance this would mean any potential sand pirates would be intimidated and keep away, assuming we might have military or armed security people on board. Which we didn't. Our fellow travellers were a couple of French journalists, a TV crew from Scandinavia and some holier-than-thou people from some kind of charity who looked snottily at us as we loaded our gear up. Thankfully we had our truck to ourselves. We spoke once more to Bob Graham, just to assess the latest reports of trouble on the Western approach to the capital.

'There hasn't been much going on of late,' he said. 'It's a bit iffy, obviously, but you ought to be OK. The Yanks have helicopters up a lot of the time, watching out for that sort of thing.'

That was good news, not that it would have made all that much difference if he'd said the odds of dying were fifty-fifty. It was day three of our journey, and we were 24 hours behind news desk expectations. Somehow, a one-in-two chance of death is less frightening than the stone-cold certainty of a major bollocking.

We stepped into the GMC and got ready for the journey, wrapping scarves around our heads to try and look less Western, as if any self-respecting Iraqi traveller would get into one of these bandit magnets. To make matters worse, Ian's scarf kept falling off his head, and bright blond tufts of hair were poking out everywhere. I don't think we were fooling anyone.

By now there were no requests for visas at the border and the bored US Marine threw a *'Good morning, sirs!'* at us and waved us through. A few hundred yards inside Iraq, we were stopped once again by men in Parkas waving AK47s. They were obviously forming a rudimentary border police force, with American approval. We were ordered from the vehicle by one of the men – I recognised him from an earlier trip – who opened his mouth to go through the old AEEEEDS test spiel. Some things never change. Before he could speak, I handed him $50.

'Is that OK?' I said. 'I still haven't got AIDS. Neither of us has AIDS, as far as I know.'

He nodded and gave us a broken-toothed grin. 'Shukran desira,' he said, waving us on.

A few miles inside the border, we called our desks to tell them we were on our way.

As I spoke to the news executive who answered the phone, I could hear Conor shouting, 'Is he in fucking Iraq yet, or what?'

He sounded – even at a distance of several thousand miles and however many feet from the phone mouthpiece in Canary Wharf – very stressed.

The exec placed his hand over the phone and a muffled conversation took place. Then he came back on. 'Look, Chris,' he said. 'Just to put you in the picture. Piers wants you in that hole.'

'I know,' I said.

'No, he *really* wants you in it. There's no way we can be beaten by *The Sun* on this. No way at all.'

'Er… well…'

Click.

I turned to Ian but I didn't need to say anything. He'd obviously just had exactly the same conversation with the picture desk, and he looked just as annoyed as I was. It's one of the downsides of working for national tabloid newspapers: you get to do some amazing things – OK, I was terrified at being back in Iraq, but what an experience – but you're always under massive pressure, there's very little room for error and it seems, at times, that there's little understanding at the top about what the troops at the bottom are going through.

I thought, briefly, about phoning Nick Parker again to see if he was still in Basra but then I realised there was no point in panicking and doing that. So I panicked and phoned Bob Graham in Baghdad instead.

'Bob, it's Chris… I just wondered… do you know what Parker's movements are?'

'Yes, he's down in Basra and I think he's coming here tomorrow,' said Bob. 'Why?

'Nothing. Thanks Bob.'

Well, that was some good news at least.

I settled back into my seat, watching the yellow-grey desert blur past at the customary 95mph. The hulls of the burned-out tanks and the wrecked cars I'd seen on my first post-war drive this way were rusting now, and sand, blown by the whipping winds, was piling up against them. My eyes were always on the horizon, looking for robbers or insurgents, but the land remained empty and sterile. The occasional Blackhawk or Apache would swoop down, have a look at us, and pull away to head north, always north, into the Anbar Province, where the insurgency was gaining momentum in Fallujah and its surrounding towns and villages.

Despite our protestations, the drivers made the utterly stupid decision to stop at a café halfway. We were there an hour, and it was one of the most uncomfortable hours of my life. Ian – who really is very blond indeed – and I stayed inside the vehicle, sliding nervously lower and lower as dozens of local travellers ate kebabs, drank *chai* and regarded us with cold, blank eyes. We were on the point of stealing the car and getting out of there when our bloke came back, grinning, without a care in the world.

'Is OK?' he said.

'Yes. Can we go now?' said Ian.

To my surprise, the journey passed uneventfully and soon we reached the outskirts of Baghdad. The city had changed radically in the few months since I had last been there. People looked more nervous, scurrying along with their heads down, and the place was scarred by 15ft high concrete blast walls which had sprouted everywhere. Suicide car bombings had become a daily occurrence and these walls were designed to contain the explosion. But they obscured the pretty houses, with their green courtyards and wrought-iron gates, and gave Baghdad a Cold War, Eastern European feel. Watch-towers and gun emplacements were dotted along the tops of the walls like grotesque flower-heads. I didn't like the look of it at all and even our Jordanian driver looked uncomfortable, shaking his head and muttering to himself, occasionally touching the worry beads that hung from the rear view mirror. This was a different Baghdad entirely from the one I'd left, I realised, and the one I'd left had been getting frightening enough. Much of the city was in a state of murderous anarchy, ruled by the bomb, the bullet and the beheaders, with occasional American army patrols providing merely a thin veneer of security and stability. Warring militia, different groups of insurgents and terrorists held sway and murders were in double figures most days. We stuck out like sore thumbs, too, in our shiny, soft-skinned GMCs, but there was nothing to be done about it; you just had to keep your head down and hope the wrong kind of people didn't take an interest in you.

An hour of nose to tail weaving later, we passed The Palestine. Many of its windows were shot out, and it looked a far more forlorn place than I remembered. But still I felt vaguely nostalgic, and spent a few minutes boring Ian about some of our adventures. A few miles on, but still close to the centre of Baghdad, we slowed down and, gratefully, we realised we had arrived at our destination. It was a good thing, too, as it was getting dark and very bad things happened after dark. A group of intense-looking Iraqi guards gave the car a good going over, searching the boot and the engine, running mirrors on sticks underneath and checking our passports and bags. There was none of the usual *laissez faire* Iraqi half-heartedness about any of this; it reminded me of Northern Ireland during the worst of the Troubles, and these men were clearly very, very serious. It took at least 10 minutes before they allowed us to continue, waving us on through a chicane of blast walls, with more guards looking down at us from above and following our progress with the muzzles of their assault rifles. Although the Al Hamra was in a middle-class area of Baghdad, Karradah, it was far from safe. The rebels knew it was now the hotel of choice for journalists. (In November 2005 it would be attacked with two car bombs which exploded within seconds of each other, killing several Iraqi guards and injuring 43 other people. *The Independent*'s Kim Sengupta was very lucky; his room was all but destroyed, though he escaped with cuts and bruises. Journalists' hotels became regular targets: a huge lorry bomb hit The Palestine, for instance, killing more than 20 people, injuring dozens more. It developed into an occupational hazard.)

'Is a bad place, now,' said our driver, and I realised that the long stop in the desert had been as much about delaying our arrival in Baghdad, about putting off the evil hour, as getting something to eat. The poor guy had to go back the same way in an hour or two, and tomorrow, or the day after, he'd be repeating the same journey.

'Very bad,' he continued. 'These gangs, they look for Westerners. They want kill Westerners.' He shook his head, and whistled through his teeth.

Ian and I looked at each other, glumly.

In the hotel, eager porters grabbed our bags and scuttled off into the interior. It was winter, and the cold was already setting in for the evening. But it wasn't a fresh cold, it was a Baghdad, dirty-air cold, one that would give us both that familiar and ubiquitous Baghdad flu within hours, a horrible sweaty and shivery illness that you could only get rid of by staying in bed for two days. We didn't have time for that.

I'd called Nibras on his satellite phone from the airport, and told him I'd be in Baghdad if he wanted to meet up. I wasn't sure whether I'd need his services, but it would be good to see him (I had no way of contacting Adil, and was just hoping I'd bump into him as I was sure he'd be floating around the journalists' hotels. As it turned out, I wouldn't see him at all on this trip.). As I checked in, the receptionist told me Nibras had visited the hotel looking for me twice the previous day and would return the following morning. That was good news: I was knackered and stressed, but I was looking forward to seeing him.

We went to our adjoining rooms and discovered that we had been allocated the generator suite – the spot right next to a lorry-sized, petrol-guzzling monster outside which pumped electricity into the hotel, and smoke and vibrating noise into us. To be honest, we were past caring: it seemed reasonably safe and the beds were relatively clean. No-one expected the Savoy.

Ian and I went up to Bob Graham's room, where a few of the Fleet Street contingent were gathered, including Bob, his photographer and the immaculately coiffeured Ross Benson, a legendary *Mail* and *Express* foreign correspondent. Ross was the sort of reporter you wished you'd been yourself: a brilliant writer and a self-deprecating storyteller, who had been shot at on several continents and had particularly distinguished himself in Afghanistan during the Russian occupation, when he had spent days dressed as a native trekking through the hills covering the war and its aftermath. He was renowned as a snappy-dressing dandy; that night, in this shabby Baghdad hotel, while everyone else was slumming it in worn jeans and scruffy fleeces, Ross wore a smart, Jermyn Street blazer, a pressed shirt with the cufflinks just visible and a dazzling pair of cream slacks. I wondered if he'd worn that get-up as a young man reporting from Vietnam. (Tragically, Ross would die of a heart attack a little more than a year later, aged just 56.)

Bob showed us to the roof where Ian could set up his satellite dish and all that other complex stuff photographers use to send their pictures back to London. I've lost count of the times abroad when various snappers, Ian included, have elbowed me impatiently out of the way to sort out some technical issue that's preventing me from sending my copy. They just type in a few codes onto the laptop, stick a disk in somewhere, upload something or other and the problem is resolved. It all seems so easy but, at the same time, so difficult. They usually finish by slamming the laptop shut, looking at me with no attempt to disguise their contempt and saying, 'Anything else? Would you like me to actually write the rubbish for you as well, perhaps?'

I usually respond with some remark about chimps and digital cameras.

But I digress.

Bob had sent out for beer that day and one of his coterie of Iraqi helpers, a swarthy chap with a 9mm pistol tucked into the back of his trousers, arrived with the tray of tins as we returned to the room. We got stuck into these, swapping stories, before walking over to a restaurant over the road.

As we ate, Nick Parker called my satellite phone.

'Alright, Chris?' he said, sounding glum down the echoey, time-delayed phone line. 'I'm getting to Baghdad tomorrow morning... I suppose you're already on your way to Tikrit?'

'No,' I said. 'You can relax, mate. We're in Baghdad for the night ourselves. We're going tomorrow.'

Finally, I could relax a little, too. This meant we'd be travelling together. It was too late to travel now as it was dark, and further north it was very dangerous. I wouldn't be getting an exclusive, but Parker wouldn't be scooping me, either, and that was my main worry.

After dinner, we scurried back to the Al Hamra and to our rooms. I took cover in my sleeping bag under a pile of blankets to try and sweat out this dreadful flu thing, the throbbing of the generator masking the traditional Baghdad night time sounds of gunfire and explosions and even the rumble of Vogler's oblivious snoring from next door.

Next thing I knew there was a knock at my door, barely audible over the rumble of the generator. I staggered to my feet, bleary-eyed, my mouth dry and rank and my eyes squinting against the wintry morning sunshine coming in through the curtains. I opened the door, and there stood Nibras.

I was shocked. He'd aged a decade in the last six months, looking much skinnier and baggy-eyed, with a grey pallor to his skin and flecks of silver in his hair.

'Bloody hell, Nibras,' I said. 'How are you? It's great to see you.'

He came into the room and we shook hands and hugged, a little embarrassed, before we sat down and started talking like the old friends we had become. His English was much better than it had been when we'd first met.

'So what's new, then?' I asked.

'Chris, I have very bad news,' he said, looking downwards and rubbing his forehead. 'I am OK but my daughter, she is killed some weeks ago. There was a big battle between Americans and Iraqis and she died. She was killed by the Americans.'

I felt like someone had slapped me across the face. I just sat there, staring at him.

'She is dead? Your daughter?'

He nodded, an ocean of pain in his eyes. 'She is dead. My daughter.'

Haltingly, he told me what had happened. The little girl, who had been just three years old, had been in a car driven by other family members up in Kirkuk, where Nibras had relatives and to where the whole family had gone to escape the murderous chaos of Baghdad. A group of American soldiers had been caught in a fire fight with some Iraqis and the family car had been hit in the cross fire.

'It is a very bad time,' he said. 'So I want to say that I cannot work for you now, Chris, because I must be with my family.'

I was literally speechless. He had driven perhaps 400 miles through some of the most hazardous terrain in the world, terrain teeming with insurgents, militia checkpoints, robbers, terrorists and trigger-happy US troops, just to see me to tell me he could not work for me.

He was clearly struggling with his emotions. He was a proud man who obviously didn't want to break down in front of me, so I waited for him to speak again as we sat there, that damned generator banging away a few feet away from us.

At length, he smiled weakly and said: 'This is not The Palestine.'

'No, Nibras, it's not The Palestine,' I replied. 'Things have changed since then.'

He nodded and for an hour or so we talked about our times with Adil and Julian, even raising a laugh occasionally. Eventually, with a weary smile, he got up to leave.

'Thank you very much for coming,' I said. 'I'm so sorry to hear about what happened to your daughter and I hope you start to feel better soon.' It was a thoroughly inadequate thing to say, but I was hard-pressed to find anything better.

'It is the will of Allah,' he said. 'Please, if you see Adil, tell him I was asking about him?'

I nodded, and pushed a few hundred dollars into his hand as I did so.

He shook his head, staring at the money, with tears in his eyes. 'Not always money, Chris,' he said. 'Not always money. You are my friend.'

I knew it was a clumsy, Western gesture. How could money

compensate for what had happened to his country, his life and his family? But, at the same time, I knew that the money would be useful.

'Please, Nibras,' I said. 'This is just something that will help you. It's not for your daughter.'

He nodded, wiped his eyes and hugged me, and then opened the door to go.

As we stepped outside, and walked to where he had parked his beloved BMW, I saw that Nibras had scraped the 'PRESS' lettering off the paintwork. That was probably for the best. I waved goodbye to him and he set off for Kirkuk.

I felt as low as I had in a long time. I thought back to Tghreed, the little girl who'd been wounded in the eye in similar circumstances months earlier. I thought about the man with the car full of dead bodies from the ammo dump on the edge of Baghdad, about the people at the mass graves, about Mohammed, my old Jordanian driver who'd been killed in the western desert. I'd known Mohammed but I hadn't been close to him. The death of Nibras's daughter brought home, more than ever, how awful this mad war was.

As I wandered back into the hotel reception, I was jarred out of the black cloud that was settling on me by the sight of a group of men striding through, festooned with guns and carrying clinking bags and boxes of ammunition. They were British mercenaries, and I watched them take the stairs, two at a time despite their heavy loads. As I walked up I saw they had taken rooms opposite ours. Ian was standing in his doorway, coughing from the smoke that had now filled our suite, and raising an eyebrow at these blokes. Through the open doors, we could see them checking their weapons and stowing kit in a very businesslike way. A few of them nodded at us, as travelling sales reps might acknowledge each other in the corridor of a Travel Inn in Derby. I have no idea what they were doing there, but they weren't selling radiator fittings.

Then *The Sun* arrived, Nick Parker and photographer Terry Richards with their driver.

They'd had a nightmare journey, bravely travelling through the night from Basra. It had taken them eight or nine hours, stopping constantly at army checkpoints and all the time fearing attack. They'd been OK, but the stress of driving in the dark had taken its toll and they looked exhausted.

We shook hands.

'What are you doing, then?' said Nick.

'I've spoken to a couple of the hotel's drivers and they're happy to take us up toward Tikrit for a few hundred dollars later on,' I said. 'There's an American base near there and we reckon we should be able to get permission there to go to the hole.'

It was our best hope.

'What about the *Mail* and the *Express*?' said Nick.

'They're not going up,' I said. 'Everyone else reckons it's a waste of time and the Yanks will never let us go there. It's just us and you.'

The drivers weren't going to be ready for us until late morning, so we went up to join Bob Graham upstairs.

We sat there for an hour or two, drinking Heineken and plotting our route to Saddam's hole. Suddenly, the door flew open and Ross Benson burst in looking flustered.

'Chaps,' he said. 'I'm working on a colour piece about life in Baghdad and I need to know which of Shakespeare's characters said this, and how the quote finishes.'

He rattled off a few lines of medieval verse. Nobody but Ross could have got away with asking that question without having a beer can thrown at him. Heaven only knows what flowery metaphor he was trying to pull off.

I hadn't got the faintest idea. 'I think you're out of luck with the likes of us lot, Ross,' I said.

But as I finished, Parker swigged from his can of warm lager and belched. Sighing, he rattled off the answer in his broad Birmingham accent, making a faux poetic gesture with the hand that wasn't clutching a can of ale.

Ross looked at him in surprise. 'Thank you kindly, Nick,' he said.

Parker coolly then reeled off the rest of the quote – it was something from Richard III – as we all applauded. Somehow, you don't expect the *Sun*'s man in Baghdad (or anywhere else, to be honest) to have an intimate knowledge of Shakespeare.

* * * * *

The journey to Owja and the area around Saddam's hiding place was a nail-biting affair, full of stops by shabbily-uniformed, balaclava-wearing Iraqi Police Service men, Iraqi Army or US troops. There were strong rumours that the police had been infiltrated by insurgents and the possibility of being kidnapped, and worse, was always in our minds.

Once again, the deterioration in the situation in the country since my last visit was brought home to me. American armoured convoys were everywhere, the top-cover men on the Humvees and Bradley fighting vehicles keeping their thumbs close to the triggers of their .50 cal machine guns. Their attitude was much more hostile; where before, more often than not, they would have chewed their gum and waved you past, now they were all raised palms, aggression and shouts of 'Stay back!' On the previous trip, Julian and I would have sworn at them and urged Nibras on; now we didn't dare try any of that nonsense. These soldiers were wired, totally on edge.

So was I, all the way to our destination.

Ian was a lot more relaxed. He sat there, his blond hair sticking out from the folds of his head scarf, poking fun at me and gossiping about our colleagues back in the office.

Eventually, I cracked. 'Will you put that fucking scarf on properly and shut the fuck up?' I shouted. 'At least stop taking the piss around here.'

He kept laughing. 'Shut up, Hughesy! Lighten up.'

I shut up but I didn't lighten up. I didn't blame Ian; he'd never been to Iraq before, so he wasn't so aware of the little nuances that, at their extremes, might mean the difference between life and death. But the last time I'd been in a car in this place I'd almost been carjacked, and that was when things had been a lot safer than they were now.

Eventually, and much to my relief, we arrived at the US base in Tikrit. They had taken over Saddam's Salah-Al-Din palace in the town, a humble little pad which had cost the thick end of $500 million to build. It was named after the Arab hero Saladin, who had led the fight against the Crusaders in the 12th century. Like Saddam, Saladin was supposedly from Tikrit, and the dictator had modestly taken the ancient warrior as his role model. This was ever so slightly cheeky of him: Saladin was a military genius who was renowned for his humility and mercy and who gave away every penny he amassed, to the point where there wasn't enough left to pay for his funeral when he died. Saddam, on the other hand, was a military blunderer renowned for his conceit and cruelty who amassed huge fortunes while his people starved. But these are mere details.

We pulled up at the front blast wall and I got out under the suspicious and hostile gaze of the guards. To my right, a thick-walled lane, overlooked by machine gun nests, chicaned through to the heart of the base.

Cautiously, I approached a sergeant.

'We're from the UK press,' I said. 'Is it possible to meet one of your officers?'

He nodded with his head to a small gathering of four or five four-story blocks of flats.

'Wait over there please, sir,' he said, curtly. 'I'll see what I can do.'

We all got out and wandered over to the buildings, where we stood in the shade and watched the curious local kids wander by, smiling at us and making the odd remark. We felt, as the Special Forces guys say, very much 'on offer' to any passing rebels or robbers.

An hour or so later, a US Army Major ambled over to us, chomping an unlit cigar like some sort of movie cliché.

'I'm Major Gordon Tate,' he drawled. 'How can I help you, gentlemen?' As he spoke, he rolled the cigar around his mouth, finally clamping it in his back teeth.

'We were wondering if it would be possible for us to go up and take a look at where you found Saddam?' I said.

'Obviously it would be a great piece of PR for the US Army and the way the war's going,' added Nick.

Tate thought for a moment and then nodded. 'Follow me, gentlemen,' he said. 'Maybe I can help.' He looked at our drivers. 'But those two gentlemen will have to stay outside.'

We shrugged and followed him through a gap in the blast wall and into the palace grounds beyond. He insisted on giving us a brief guided tour of the palace – the usual tacky gold-trimmed chairs, the sub-Athena poster art and the lavish marble everywhere – and we tagged along behind, dragging our feet slightly. Apart from Ian, we'd all seen all of this elsewhere and the effect had long worn off us; we wanted to be 10 miles away in Saddam's final, slightly less grand, home. But we tried not to let on to the Major. This was a means to an end; if we sucked up enough, and nodded in agreement at everything he said, he might be persuaded to take us to Ab Dawr.

After wandering through the fifteenth ornate bedroom and admiring yet another dusty chandelier, the Major stopped. 'Say, I could use some lunch,' he said. 'How about you guys?'

More delays. But we were hungry – it was late afternoon, now – and we didn't have much choice anyway. We all agreed quickly. He took us down to the canteen, a huge room deep within the palace's interior where army chefs were working on cooking lunch for the fighting men and women of whatever unit this was. The menu was an unbelievable reflection of the huge difference in wealth between the invaders and invaded. Outside, people were getting by on flat breads, goat meat and tins of stuff saved up from before the war. In this chow hall, a little piece of America transported across the world, the troops were filling their faces with pizza, steak and French fries, huge bowls of salad... even lobster, shipped in from I have no idea where.

Major Tate waved his hand expansively at the groaning food servery. 'You folks just choose what you want,' he said, a proud grin on his face.

I didn't blame the US Army for feeding its soldiers well. But I did feel guilty as I ate my chilli and rice and glugged back an ice-cold Coke. I could see from the looks on the faces of Ian and the *Sun* guys that they felt the same way. We assuaged our guilt, slightly, by stuffing bread, cheese and apples into our jackets for our drivers and the kids outside, despite the sign that read 'Don't feed the locals.' I could see why they didn't want locals begging outside the gates – they needed to be able to get in and out at speed and didn't want to be mashing hungry six-year-olds into the ground as they did so, for Public Relations reasons as well as humanitarian ones. But this time... well, stuff them.

As we ate, Major Tate went to make enquiries from his superiors about our request. Fifteen minutes later, he returned. 'Gentlemen,' he said. 'I'm sorry, it's not possible for you to go to the place you want at this time. I'm afraid you'll have to come back tomorrow. If you've finished your chow, come with me please.'

We had, so we did, tramping slightly dejectedly in the squeaky footsteps of his sand-coloured desert boots and out to a jeep that would dump us back outside the base.

Standing as close to the US guards as possible without being overheard, we assessed our options.

'What about trying to get out there ourselves?' said Ian. 'It wouldn't be that hard to find it. The Yanks will still be all over the place like a rash.'

A few months earlier, I would have done it without thinking twice. Now I didn't fancy it at all, and Nick was even less keen.

'I just don't particularly want to be winding the window down and asking locals if they know where Saddam's secret hole is,' I said. 'I've been up near there before, it was spooky as hell then and I don't think they'll be too friendly towards us now.'

It turned out to be an academic argument anyway. We broached the subject with our drivers and they flatly refused to go anywhere near the place without American support. So that was that. 'We'll just have to come back tomorrow like the guy told us,' I said.

Disconsolate, we chucked apples and cans of fizzy drinks to the waiting Iraqi kids and headed back to Baghdad. We'd get up at the crack of dawn next day, beat the checkpoints and be doorstepping the US base first thing.

On the way, the office called and I briefly considered telling them we'd been really close but had not quite made it to the finish line. But then I realised what a schoolboy error this would have been – if you get 'really close', you *have* to get to the finish line, no excuses.

'Er, we've made contact with the Americans,' I said, 'and we're trying to arrange to go there tomorrow.'

The journey back was uneventful and back at the hotel a few of the other reporters who had told us we were wasting our time looked relieved. We missed out the bit about going back for another go the following day, of course. One or two of them had been mildly conde-scending about our chances and we felt we owed them nothing. And the more I thought about it, the more I had a feeling in my bones that the Americans would give us the go-ahead tomorrow.

I was right. Early start, no checkpoints, and, within 15 minutes, there was Major Tate, grinning all over his face.

'Gentlemen, I have good news for you,' he beamed. 'We're going to get you to where you want to be. If you drive to that piece of waste ground' – he indicated a nearby patch of scrub – 'and wait there, I'm going to come out in a convoy of Humvees in ten minutes. We'll all move out to another RV point and wait there for a convoy of tanks. We'll all set off together from there. You just make sure you're tailgating my Humvees.'

It wasn't perfect. If a fire fight started between the Americans and the locals, we'd be caught up in it in soft-skin cars, and we had heard plenty about crossfire recently. But we had come so far and we couldn't back out.

We followed the instructions and tail-gated the five Humvees that came out of the base, the top-cover gunner waving at us, for once, to stay close. At the second rendezvous point, five or so miles away, we all waited for the heavy armour and then the bigger convoy trundled up to Ab Dawr.

On the outskirts, we came to an outer cordon manned by balaclava-wearing Iraqi security men who waved us through. It was a typically shabby Iraqi village, with all the shops shut up and very few people on the streets. Occasionally, we passed gangs of youths, and I got a taste of what it must feel like to be an American soldier in Iraq; without exception, these young men spat at the dusty ground and shot murderous looks of pure hate at us. It wasn't lost on our drivers, either. They shook their heads and whistled nervously as we wound our way after the Americans. I slunk down into my seat, nervously fingering the body armour which lay uselessly at my feet and wondering why I'd not bothered to put it on. One lucky gunman, hiding in a doorway or down an alley, and we could be dead.

After a few hundred yards, the armoured convoy turned right off the road, down a dirt track that had been churned to slurry by count-less other tanks and trucks. To the right, US sappers were searching for mines in a large cornfield. We passed dozens of armoured vehicles, with troops with their hands on their guns watching us closely, before the convoy stopped and we stepped out of our cars. Major Tate, still chomping that now forlorn-looking cigar, strode over to us.

'Follow me, please!' he barked, turning on his heel and heading off down the dirt track. He rounded a corner, past a farm building to the left and into the edge of a palm grove. And there, in the shadow of a shabby little hut, was the hole.

I'm not sure exactly what I expected – probably forensic scientists and the like, still poring over the spot, perhaps with a protective tent over it and some brightly-coloured barrier tape to keep people back. But all there was was a group of US soldiers standing around the opening, laughing and posing up for their own pictures to send home. Even uncovered and in daylight, it would have been easy to miss.

'If you just wait in line, gentlemen,' said Major Tate. 'Just take your turn.'

We stood, slightly self-consciously, in this thin queue of soldiers and, eventually, a young private emerged, chuckling. 'We called him the Ace of Spades,' he said, referring to Bush's pack of regime cards. 'Hell, he musta knowed how to use a spade to dig that mother out.'

And then it was my turn.

I stepped forward and had got one foot in the hole when I was barged out of the way by Nick Parker, who jumped straight in, cackling. I had to laugh at his insane competitiveness. It didn't matter which one of us was *actually* the first British reporter into the hole, we were both going to claim it. But by about two minutes, and by failing to observe that most British of conventions, queuing, Parker did beat me. Though I got my foot in first.

I waited my turn and before long he emerged, beaming at having got his pictures. I squeezed down through the two-square-foot hole in the dirt and half-slid down the six or seven feet of earthen steps into the place where the world's most wanted man had hidden for months. I looked around, using a torch Major Tate had lent me.

I found myself in a chamber perhaps 8ft by 6ft with a ceiling so low that, at 6ft 1in tall, I could barely stand. I flashed the torch around. There was an air vent and a small strip light hanging by a wire from the ceiling. With its dirt walls, filthy plaster ceiling and uneven earthen floor, the cramped little space was more like a medieval *oubliette* than anything else. I couldn't help thinking that Saddam was probably better off in American hands, even with a noose waiting for him at the end of it all.

It stank, too; Saddam had been sweating literally as well as metaphorically down here.

A huge cockroach scuttled past me, making me jump. This place was more like a coffin than anything else: a very cramped space, with no natural light to speak of. I'm smaller than Saddam's 6ft 4in, and I couldn't have spent more than five minutes in this tiny dungeon. Feeling increasingly claustrophobic, I stooped back towards those rough-cut steps. Ian rattled a couple of frames off, of the *Mirror*'s man in Saddam's hole, before I scuttled back out into the fresh air.

A grinning soldier pointed out a pair of Saddam's undies lying on the ground. They were a shabby, grimy pair of long-legged black and yellow boxer shorts. I pounced on them gleefully and posed up for more pictures. I should probably have stuck them in my pocket and eBayed them, but some inner sense of morality – or an aversion to carrying around pairs of tyrant's used pants – stopped me, and I replaced them where they'd been lying.

Nearby, an outside kitchen had been built, a lean-to with a corrugated roof. He hadn't been eating too well, though; as far as I could tell from the litter, his diet had recently been consisting of Bounty bars. A rainfall pipe caught water, filling a nearby tank from which Saddam presumably drank for weeks. There was an Arabic style, porcelain hole-in-the-floor loo slotted into the ground. Good taste forbade me from mentioning it in my subsequent *Daily Mirror* piece, but the evidence of Saddam's most recent bowel movement was there for all to see, and we all guffawed and pointed at it like overgrown kids.

The immediate area was a dense, date palm orchard, a quiet, pleasant place with enough cover for him to have gone for an evening walk without being seen from the air. The Tigris river flowed gently by a hundred yards away and, from the far edge of the cornfield, he would have been able to see his biggest Tikrit palace. He'd have seen the Americans parked up outside it, too. And then he'd have sloped off back to his hole, amid the filth and cockroaches, to eat a Bounty and ask himself why, oh why, he hadn't let those bloody weapons inspectors go wherever they wanted. The irony would have been hard to bear; I stood for a moment and tried to imagine the savage bitterness he must have felt. And I have to admit, I laughed.

Major Tate stood nearby, still chomping that cigar, occasionally spitting out shreds of wet tobacco and smiling from ear to ear. 'He lived like a lion and was captured like a rat,' he said, as the nearby soldiers nodded and grinned.

Next to Tate stood Colonel James Hickey, the officer who had given the order to search the area a few days earlier.

'We received information that Saddam was in a hide-out here and we sought to identify the location of that objective,' he said. (Why they have to speak like that, I don't know.) 'I had Special Forces soldiers with listening devices at the scene and they heard noises which appeared to be coming from underground. One of the team located a Styrofoam lid, camouflaged to look like an innocent patch of earth. When he lifted it and shone his torch inside, he found a man. That man was Saddam Hussein.'

'What was said?' I asked.

'Not a great deal,' he replied. 'He was offering to negotiate with us.'

Major Tate laughed. 'A little too late,' he said.

And we were done.

Feeling very pleased with ourselves, we drove back without the cover of the Americans. We had all felt far more vulnerable in that convoy than out of it but, as with so many things in Iraq, the grass was always greener on the other side. It was a distinctly uncomfortable couple of hours. There was just the occasional gaggle of US trucks hurtling past, with the rear gunners ordering us to back off, and, when they weren't around, you started missing them. Now and then, we were passed by cars full of Iraqi men, some clearly carrying guns, who clocked us as they drove by. I thought about our journey out towards the Iranian border. This looked ominously similar to me. If these boys were planning to run us off the road a few miles later, there wouldn't be much we could do about it. The *Sun* driver – a skinny but tough-looking man from Basra – had a knackered old car which topped out at about 60mph, which meant we were very vulnerable. Maybe Ian and I should have told our driver to zip ahead and leave them but we felt, perhaps illogically, that we ought to stick with Nick and Terry. Our driver was nervous, too. A quiet, podgy little man with the usual moustache, he had been – if anything – too smiley and relaxed earlier. Now he'd stopped smiling altogether and was tapping the driving wheel and nervously eyeing his rear view, shaking his head every time a Toyota load of gunmen zoomed by.

To make matters worse, we had to stop for petrol half way to Baghdad. This was not as simple as it sounds. If you called at a proper filling station, you would wait for two hours in a half-mile queue before you got to the pump, and there was no doubt we'd have been snatched or killed, and probably snatched *and* killed, before our turn ever came. So we had to buy it from one of the many punters selling black-market fuel from barrels at the side of the road. There were dozens of these men, always accompanied by lots of kids who would run about being clipped round the ear and madly waving siphon tubes by way of advertising their dads' wares. This dodgy petrol came in several grades, from acceptable to useless. Most of it was in-between – it would work but it was adulterated with various chemicals to make it go further (the petrol, not your car). It would just about get you from A to B, but it would be a lurching sort of journey, with your engine coughing and spluttering like a man on 80 woodbines a day.

Our driver assessed a few of these shysters, before pulling over next to one he thought looked slightly more trustworthy than the rest and hopping out of the car. The *Sun* car pulled in behind us and the two Iraqis started haggling with the vendor. A curious group of locals began to gather, and we sat there wondering how long it would be before some men with tea towels on their heads bundled us away with AK47s in our backs. Well, *I* wondered. Ian was far too busy not appreciating the potential gravity of our position and watching the two drivers.

'Look at them!' he suddenly yelled. 'Have you seen this? They're tasting the stuff! Have they gone totally mental?'

I'd slid almost into the footwell so I had to crane my neck to see what he was on about. Nick and Terry were hunched low in their seats but I could see they were wetting themselves laughing in the back of their car too. I watched our guy. He took another sip of the petrol, gargled it around his mouth and then spat it onto the road with an approving nod. He looked like a man appreciating a particularly fine Chateau Margaux.

It was a strangely amusing sight and I was so engrossed in watching that I didn't notice Ian get out of the car. Suddenly, my mobile rang. It was Parker.

'Tell Vogler to get back in the fucking car!' he shouted, panic unmistakable in his voice. 'He's going to get us all killed!'

I turned to see Vogler strolling up the hard shoulder, all blond hair and Western clothes, idly kicking a pebble through the grit and dust as he chatted to the picture desk on his sat-phone – a piece of equipment which everyone in Iraq knew was worth thousands of dollars. He looked a picture of unconcern, like a chap out for a stroll along the Thames at Henley. If he'd also been carrying a neon sign saying *'Please rob me and kill me'* it wouldn't have been much of a surprise.

I leaned out of the window. 'Ian!' I screamed. 'For fuck's sake, get back in the car!'

He shot me an angry look, wandered back and climbed in.

Ian has been to trouble spots all round the world – places like the Balkans and Afghanistan – so he knows what's what. But he didn't know Iraq; out here, the place was crawling with gunmen. All it would take is for one of them to have a pop and get lucky.

The drivers had finished filling up and, thank God, we were soon on our lurching, coughing way.

We didn't speak all the way back.

Nick and I filed our pieces from our cars on those Thuraya satellite phones and we all got utterly slaughtered in the hotel that night. It was pretty empty, too. Our tabloid colleagues had left for Amman that morning, confident we were out on a fool's errand (I later learned that another journalist who had not bothered going to Tikrit – I won't name him – had been bollocked by his desk when our piece appeared. He'd tried to laugh it off at first, saying that the *Mirror* and *Sun* desks had been conned, and that Nick and I hadn't really gone to Saddam's hole at all. At that point, he didn't realise there were pictures of us in the hole, and interviews with US officers conducted at the site. Oops!).

My piece didn't make the front page but it was run as a spread across two pages, which is the next best thing.

The news desk were delighted.

'Well done, Chris,' said Conor. 'Piers is really pleased.'

It was a good result: we'd had a job, a tough job, too, and we'd achieved it. It's a satisfying feeling which was made all the more enjoyable by the scepticism of some of our colleagues in Baghdad. All journalists are praise-junkies – it's pathetic really. But it was great to hear something positive, to have my efforts appreciated.

'Oh… and your name was shite at the Christmas party.' He chuckled. 'Absolute shite.'

Click.

We joined a convoy for Jordan the next day, and I was back in London in time for *The Great Escape* and some lukewarm turkey.

2004

The Accidental Gun Runner

Back home, things were pretty quiet for a few months. Every day, I'd rewrite foreign agency copy about the rising death toll from suicide bombings across Iraq, and the ever-bloodier insurgency. The broadsheets had a constant presence in Baghdad but this wasn't serious tabloid fodder: Saddam was awaiting trial and there wasn't an awful lot new coming out of it until then.

I started thinking about new ways to tackle Iraq. What about the growing private security industry? British former soldiers were earning a fortune out there. I started bashing the phones and talking to contacts and, after a few dinners with the right people, *Mirror* photographer Chris Grieve and I were invited to spend a couple of weeks as guests of one of the largest outfits, Erinys.

The last time I had flown into Baghdad had been on that illegal Iraqi Airways flight from Basra shortly after 9/11, with an American F18 threatening to blow us out of the sky if we didn't turn back. Since then, every time I'd gone in it had been via that nightmare drive across the Western Desert from Jordan, dodging AEEEDS tests and murderous gangs of brigands, and hoping a Blackhawk pilot didn't decide to hose you down with his 30mm cannon (10 shells a second, give or take).

It felt so much more *executive* to be taking a little hop over the desert with a load of security contractors in the Jordanian Airways plane from Amman. It was much quicker, too – but that was where the good news ended. It had started fine, but I'd noticed the tough-looking blokes all around me fidgeting and looking decidedly uncomfortable as we got closer to Baghdad. One or two looked as though they were praying, which I didn't find all that reassuring.

The cabin intercom crackled into life. 'Good afternoon, this is your senior steward speaking,' said the nasal, electronic voice. 'We are now at 10,000ft and we are shortly commencing our spiral dive. Please ensure that all your tray tables…'

I missed the rest of it, just two words banging around in my brain.

'Spiral dive?' I said to the man next to me, a Scottish ex-Para called Ken, who looked like he was made of scrap iron and granite. 'What did he mean by that?'

'Exactly what he said,' replied Ken, with an attempt at a grin. 'We can't fly in and land normally, along a nice, 15-mile glide path, because we'd be shot down. So they basically dive at the ground, turning as they do, and just level out at the last second.'

It was April 30, 2004.

Every time George Bush or Tony Blair appeared on the telly, it was all rictus grins and claims that everything was going well and the 'war on terror' was being won in Iraq. Every single person you spoke to who'd recently been there told a quite different story. It was degenerating into an unbelievable nightmare, with many different religious, political and criminal factions fighting amongst themselves and, when they got the chance, having a pop at the British and the Americans too. Horrible acts of butchery were being carried out daily; the last month had been, as each month seemed to be, the worst-yet, and anarchy reigned. Planes were the number one target for serious insurgents. A DHL jet had been hit by surface-to-air missiles not that long before – it had lost a lot of one wing but no-one had died – and pilots had had to reassess the way they approached Baghdad airport after that.

'Bloody hell,' I said to Ken. 'What's it like?'

'Well,' he said, choosing his words with care. 'It's not a lot of fun. In fact, it's bloody terrifying. I would take the steward's advice and brace yourself for the next few minutes. And grab that sick bag, just in case.'

Ken was a man whose whole life was dangerous. He'd HALO-d across the English Channel, for instance. High-Altitude-Low-Opening parachute jumping is the sort of thing only advanced military lunatics get to do. If he was scared, I was scared.

All around, these stone-faced private security contractors were taking deep breaths. I'm not sure, but I think I went green. The plane suddenly dropped its right hand wing and began a series of very tight turns. I was hurled at the window face first, staring straight at the ground which was hurtling up at me and spinning wildly as it did so. We corkscrewed at impossible angles for several minutes, like a high-speed, aluminium sycamore seed. It was literally terrifying, and all the worse because I felt I ought to adopt as nonchalant an attitude as possible. Every nut and bolt in the bodywork of the plane screamed and creaked and groaned as the dizzying, vertical-circular descent continued.

Then, with little time or room to spare, the pilot pulled the machine level and we belly-flopped hard on to the tarmac at Baghdad International Airport.

Breathless, queasy and sweating, I turned to Ken. 'I bet you've had a few horrible flights in your time,' I said. 'Where does that one come in your league table?'

Ken winced, looking almost mortal for a second or two. 'It's the second worst I've had in my life,' he said. 'Bloody awful.'

I didn't ask what the worst was.

Chris and I staggered off the plane, bags in hand, following Ken and the others to a welcoming party of Erinys staff. There were eight of them: shaven-headed Rambos with ear pieces, M4 assault rifles and side-arms strapped to their legs. They whisked us through check-in and into two armoured BMW M5s for the high-speed drive to the firm's HQ in Mansour, the middle-class area of Baghdad that had been home to my driver friend Nibras and the remnants of Saddam's Sunni hierarchy.

Once again, Baghdad had deteriorated since my last visit four or five months earlier. Everyone looked yet more tense, the US troops we saw were even more aggressive-looking… the place looked like what it was, a city under siege from within.

Our drivers took no chances at all. I don't think the speedo ever dropped below 50mph, even on crowded streets, and it often touched double that. Speeding down a dusty, palm-lined road, we suddenly slewed side-ways into a pleasant residential street and the driver brought the car to an undignified halt. Two Iraqi guards, dressed in dark blue combat uniforms, approached us out of the dust and slid mirrors on wheels under the car, looking for bombs. We were waved through, and parked up 20 yards further on in front of a courtyard fronting a white, two-storey, flat-roofed house.

We got out and our driver curtly ordered us to follow him down the path to the door, indicating we should dump our bags outside.

Chris and I looked at each other. 'What's his problem?' hissed Chris. I shook my head, mystified.

The guy pushed open the door and strode in, with us close behind. Inside, 30 former Marines, Paras and Guardsmen sat and stood staring at a huge TV screen.

Sky News was on. And on Sky News was the *Daily Mirror*'s front page.

WORLD EXCLUSIVE! screamed a big red flash in the top right hand corner, over a picture of a soldier apparently urinating on a cowering, hooded man. *'VILE'*, said the headline. *'But this time it's a BRITISH soldier degrading an Iraqi.'*

I stared at the screen. I couldn't believe my eyes. I'd called to ask the desk if there was anything I needed to know before I set out that morning. It was a standard sort of call and I'd got the standard answer: 'Not really.' How on earth they'd thought that I didn't need to know we were about to run a splash accusing British squaddies of mistreating prisoners, when I was going to be spending the next fortnight with a load of former British squaddies, I don't know. On the screen, they cut to a discussion between the newscaster and some sort of expert and then to library pictures showing US troops abusing prisoners at Abu Ghraib jail.

'Good afternoon gents,' said our driver, smirking now and pausing for dramatic effect while 30 very hard-looking guys turned round to eyeball us. 'These chaps are from the *Daily Mirror*.'

You could have heard a hand grenade pin drop.

I weighed up our options. There was no way any of these guys were going to believe me if I said I knew nothing about this story and wasn't involved. A tactical retreat seemed in order. I raised my eyebrows by way of a 'Hello', grinned sheepishly and walked back out side with Chris Grieve.

'Bloody hell,' said Chris. 'Did you know anything about this?'

'Not a thing, mate,' I said, scrabbling for a cigarette and trying to get my head straight. I didn't *think* we were going to get filled in, but you never know.

I was mentally planning a route back to Jordan when a former SAS Regimental Sergeant Major – a decent bloke, who was part of the firm and a bit of a legend in Baghdad – came out of the building.

He saw us standing there, looking shifty, and laughed. 'Don't worry lads,' he said. 'You'll be all right. This lot are just a bit pissed off about the story.'

'When will they become less pissed off?' I asked.

'How long you here?' he asked.

'Two weeks.'

'Well,' he said. 'They'll stop being pissed off in about a fortnight.' And off he went, cackling.

I called the office. I can't remember who answered.

'Why wasn't I warned about this bloody soldiers story?' I asked. 'You know where I am… it's embarrassing and awkward, to say the least.'

The executive at least had the decency to try to come up with an explanation. 'Sorry, mate,' he said. 'We just thought it was better you didn't know.'

I put the phone down and finished my cigarette, trying to look on the bright side. At least the story was making the TV news, keeping the *Mirror* in the spotlight. We'd have stuffed *The Sun*, whatever they had on their front, and Piers would be in a good mood for the next few days.

Little did I know how pyrrhic that front page victory was to be.

I stubbed out the fag and steeled myself to go back into the building and tell anyone who would listen that I hadn't known a thing about those sodding photos.

* * * * *

The arrival of the large-scale private security sector in the modern-day war-zone is a relatively new phenomenon, reflecting the asymmetrical nature of modern conflict under the permanent scrutiny of the media in a world of human rights, together with the ready availability of arms and former soldiers and the reluctance of democratic nations to accept large body counts among their service personnel.

What I'm trying to say, in English, is that regular squaddies aren't really equipped to fight wars in populated cities against unknown guerrillas when the world's media is watching out for civilian casualties. But private companies, armed to the teeth, highly trained and not fighting under the same rules of engagement, are a different matter. Best of all, if some South African mercenary gets killed it doesn't cause the same problems back home as it does if a 19-year-old PFC from Numbskull, Arizona is blown to bits and sent back in a bag. America, the theory goes, won't stand for casualties even at the relatively low Vietnam War level any more. Oh, and privateers are massively cheaper, too.

In 2004, there were around 25,000 private security contractors working in Iraq. By comparison, there were only 8,500 British Armed Forces personnel in the country and even the US forces numbered only 135,000. At the time of writing, it is believed there may be as many as 50,000 contractors in Iraq, of varying degrees of legitimacy.

Some, mainly little groups of freelance Americans in my experience, are cowboys, clearly high on machismo. Some get a kick out of driving around the place getting into fire fights. These were true mercenaries – guns for hire, who rented themselves and their weapons out to the highest bidder for specific operations, before moving on afterwards.

Others are far more reputable. Many of them are also from the US – companies like Armor Group, Blackwater and Custer Battles. From the UK, former Guards officer and Falklands veteran Colonel Tim Spicer brought Aegis Defence Services to Iraq. This was a fledgling company which turned over £554,000 in 2003; three years later, it had expanded more than 100-fold, announcing it had generated £62 million worth of business, most of it in Iraq and most of it paid for by The Pentagon.

Our hosts, Erinys, were also at the reputable end of the market. They had secured a £40 million contract to guard pipelines and installations the length and breadth of the country and also provided highly-trained close protection teams to look after senior American officers and British Embassy staff. They employed more than a thousand Iraqis alongside a crew comprising largely ex-Guardsmen, SAS troopers, Paras and Marines and Nepalese former Ghurkhas.

These were not your stereotypical unshaven, sweaty mercenaries in filthy, Vietnam-style bandanas; they were designer dogs of war, smartly-dressed, military versions of city slickers, in razor-creased Chinos, Oakley mirror-shades and polished boots. Their tools were M4 assault rifles and matt black body armour, instead of laptops and the *FT*.

The regular British Army troops, somewhat sneeringly, called them 'Fishermen' because they tended to finish off their outfits with light-coloured angling jackets – the many pockets come in handy. There's a little needle between the two groups, much of it driven by understandable jealousy: the contractors are earning £10,000 or more a month, whereas your average squaddie is paid between £18,000 and £28,000 a year, with overseas allowances.

Given the novelty of this sector of warfare, and the interesting things they got up to, spending some time with the firm had sounded like a really good idea.

It didn't sound quite as good a couple of nights later, as I huddled on the roof of the main building, trembling with fear and adrenalin and making myself as small as possible, as the roar of gunfire filled the air.

The *crack-crack-crack* of automatic rifles raged and echoed up and down the streets, mingling with the heavier rattle of machine guns, hundreds of rounds spitting and ricocheting around our little corner of Baghdad.

It had all started a few minutes earlier, just a few, sporadic shots breaking the calm of an otherwise relatively tranquil evening in our compound, a group of houses stuffed with Erinys personnel and guarded at the perimeter by Iraqi freelances. Quickly, it had escalated to what sounded like an all-out attack, with constant shooting and yelling.

As soon as the firing had begun, our hosts had hustled me and Chris quickly upstairs and out onto the flat roof. There wasn't a lot of time for explanations, but I gathered they felt that getting higher gave them a better chance of beating off the assault and staying alive. The building was tall and had a commanding view of the surrounding streets. They could pour fire down onto the insurgents below, when they finally showed themselves, and could also cover the doorway from the stairs if they got into the building, shooting anyone who came through. Engaging in room-to-room fighting downstairs, against a numerically superior force, was suicide.

The company's intelligence network, led by a calm and reassuring former MI5 man called Fred (I've withheld his surname at his request), were tirelessly working to pick up leads, trying to second guess the insurgents, liaising with US intelligence. They had picked up rumours of a possible attack the previous week and the camp had been fortified earlier that day. Several Iraqi guards had been busy in the workshop, fashioning poles with t-bar endings and rough metal ladders. The poles were designed so that people could lift the razor wire surrounding the walls and the ladders were to allow quicker access to the roof where I now found myself.

I poked my head, briefly, over the low parapet surrounding the roof. The picture was confused, but it seemed that rebel forces were trying to burst through the security cordon at the end of the street; the Iraqi guards were spraying their AK47s at someone or something but we couldn't make out what. Muzzle flashes and tracer rounds were visible all around in the gathering dusk and I expected to see rebels streaming towards our position at any moment. We'd been warned that if we were attacked we would have to hold out for an hour before the US military could get to us. I prayed they were on their way.

Men in Erinys uniforms were hurling themselves up the stairs, two at a time, hauling ammunition boxes, medical supplies and weaponry, grunting and sweating with the effort. Everyone was talking hurriedly into radios clipped to their shoulders, trying to work out what was happening.

In the street below, five ex-Ghurkhas were running at a crouch along the side of a wall, stooping to avoid the bullets, trying to get to their designated rooftop on a separate building, from where they could make their own stand. All along the road, people were scuttling up ladders and filling up the flat roofs, their heads popping up every few moments to try to work out what was going on below. I could hear the zip-zip-zip of rounds ripping through the air above me, and the whine of ricochets off in the streets nearby.

I looked around and saw 10 more men taking up positions on our rooftop; their faces grim, weapons at the ready, they peered over the parapet, watching and waiting for the gunmen to come pouring down the road and head for our house. Next to me knelt a young Scottish ex-Guardsman called Tam, calmly pointing his M4 assault rifle at the top of the stairs. There was a lull, and they took a quick head count. It seemed as though all were present and accounted for.

Then a South African ran up the stairs and burst through the doorway, breathless and panting, the last to get to safety.

'You *stupid* cunt,' said an English voice somewhere to my left.

'Next time shout 'friendly' as you come through, you twat,' said a Scotsman. 'I could have shot you.'

Nerves were running high and Tam nodded at another South African, a medic, asking him to stick close by in case he was shot.

By now it seemed the whole of Baghdad was involved in a deafening fire fight. Red and green tracer streamed across the darkening sky and heavy machine gun fire blasted away nearby. Every few seconds, loud explosions and blasts competed with the gunfire. They could have been grenades or bombs, we weren't sure. Flares went off somewhere across the city, lighting up the minarets of a huge unfinished mosque that dominated the skyline and briefly silhouetting dozens of men who were hurriedly taking up defensive positions on the tops of buildings all around us.

Amidst all the mayhem, Chris and I sat there, heads down, for an hour, clinging to our roof, 100 flat, concreted square metres of safety, wondering whether the rebels had burst in downstairs. They could be ransacking the place, preparing to charge up the stairs at any moment. Looking around the armed men alongside me, I felt reassured. They didn't look scared and occasionally they threw a reassuring nod our way. They knew what they were doing and just sat or knelt, guns at the ready, waiting patiently for the attack.

Clutching my hand-held satellite phone, I motioned to Chris with hand signals, debating whether we should phone in. It's the classic journalistic impulse: ring the news desk, tell them what's going on. The debate didn't last very long. It was a ludicrous idea. The noise was impossibly loud; you couldn't even shout and be heard by the nearest person to you, let alone on a time-delay call back to Canary Wharf. Anyway, I'd probably just get a bollocking for not phoning in earlier.

I was getting the feeling that some of the news desk staff didn't really appreciate what it was like out in Iraq, despite receiving reams of my finely-honed prose explaining the situation pretty much every day. A few hours earlier, before all this had kicked off, one of them had actually rung to ask if either Chris or I had a home telephone number for the nurse-turned-glamour model Abi Titmuss.

It was a mildly surreal request, under the circumstances. A couple of days before, a young South African guy working with this team had bled to death on the streets of Fallujah, shot through the neck by a rebel sniper. The love life of some D-list celebrity, racy as it might be, seemed somehow irrelevant in comparison.

'Are you joking?' I asked.

'Look, mate,' he replied, in a world-weary tone, 'I know you're in Bag-fucking-dad, alright, but have you got one or not?'

I hadn't.

The furious fire fight continued all around and still Tam and the other contractors looked as calm as it was possible to be, given the situation. They are trained to identify whether rounds are incoming or outgoing, and how close they are. An incoming bullet makes a cracking sound, followed by a high-pitched, drawn-out whine as it speeds past. Phonetically, it is like a very harsh 'pach-ooo'; the 'ooo' part is longer and louder the closer the bullet is to the person hearing it. But their training was useless now: in any built-up area, the echo effect can make an accurate assessment very difficult and here the sheer number of rounds being fired made it impossible. All Chris and I could really do was sit there, chewing gum and keeping our heads down.

Suddenly, the noise stopped. We waited. There was the odd, random shot, and a red flare soared into the sky, but as the minutes ticked by it became clear that it was definitely over.

My ears were ringing, still full of the metallic cracking noise, but I could just make out Tam, talking on his radio to the firm's control room, which was 40 yards away on the other side of the street.

'Yes, boss, we're all still here, all accounted for... what? You're having a laugh? You're bloody joking?' He was grinning. 'Have we got the all-clear to stand down now then? Many thanks – out.'

He turned to the rest of the men, laughing. 'It's a fucking celebration, not an attack,' he said. 'Iraq just beat Kuwait at football and that's why they're making the racket. What a bloody place. We can stand down – apparently it's tea-time now... that's why they've all stopped.'

From the shadows in a corner of the roof, an English voice shouted: 'Well, at least they'll have wasted all their ammunition, hopefully. We'll all be able to get some sleep.'

Everyone laughed and most of the tension on the roof dissolved. I lit a cigarette with shaking hands and Phil, one of the guys nearest to us, shouted over. 'Hey, Two Chris's' – (their catch-both name for me and Grieve) – 'chuck us a fag, and stop being so bloody tight with them.'

I threw him the packet. Slowly, my heart calmed down from around 300 beats per minute to a more leisurely 180 or so and I tried to stand up. My legs were cramped and shaking with adrenalin, but I managed it.

Tam clapped me on the back.

'Alright, mate?' he said. 'Wasn't too bad after all, was it?'

They all gathered up their ammunition and water bottles, and began trooping down the stairs, wary and alert, just in case.

They were – bizarrely to a civvie like me – disappointed not to have seen some action. They wanted revenge for their dead friend.

I got chatting to a burly, black Scouser called Cy, an ex-Royal Logistics Corps man, who had served in 5th Airborne Brigade in Northern Ireland and Germany.

'Shame it was all bollocks, really,' he said. 'It would have been good shooting at a few live bodies.'

'What if they'd got in?' I said.

'Nah,' he said, shaking his head dismissively. 'No way. Every shot would have counted. We'd have been all right.'

It won't be the last time the place goes bananas over a football match and my advice to anyone thinking of travelling to Iraq in the near future – apart from don't – is get inside and keep your head down if they win. Entire cities all over the country open fire, filling the air with lead and, as many people were painfully reminded each time, what goes up must come down. There's no point asking the Iraqis why they do it: you might ask well ask why we wear silly hats and pull crackers at Christmas. We just do. In the AK47 capital of the world, a country bursting with guns, a man will squeeze off a magazine of 30 rounds as casually as you'd blow your nose. It's natural.

It was the early summer, and al-Mansour was baking hot, all

parched gardens and the sound of croaking crickets in the still heat. It was a quiet, deceptively pretty suburb, of palm-lined avenues and sedate driveways leading to elegant, white-washed villas which had once been home to the wealthy middle classes and were now rented out to the private security companies. With so many Westerners housed there, the place was a magnet for the terrorists and rebels led by the fat and now very dead Jordanian lunatic Abu Mousab al-Zarqawi (just a few hundred yards away from our compound was where Ken Bigley, the British engineer, lived before he was kidnapped and beheaded). Its undoubted pre-war elegance was rudely marred by the 12ft concrete blast walls, the only real defence against suicide car bombers. More of these seemed to sprout in front of the buildings by the day. With the threat of kidnappings and assassinations, no-one walked anywhere. The leafy streets were deserted, except for the Iraqi guards. I marvelled at their nerve. Every day, police stations were being bombed, army patrols engaged and civilians kidnapped and yet these blokes happily lounged around on plastic seats, smoking cigarettes and chatting, occasionally standing up to allow a car through once they'd checked it over. They looked as though they hadn't a care in the world, and I didn't know whether to be reassured or terrified by this. I spent an afternoon one day, sitting with them at the end of the street. You didn't have to wait long before they would point at a car full of men, driving past slowly. They would shake their heads, whistle through their teeth and say, 'Kidnappers.' It reminded me of all those films set in places like South Central Los Angeles, where gangs of black kids or Latinos stuffed into pimped-up cars drive slowly by, casing an address before a hit.

One of the most senior men at Erinys was John Holmes, a former Major General with the Scots Guards and the UK's ex-Director of Special Forces. He was a disarming, laid-back man who wore a constant smile despite the danger and pressure of his job. I watched him trying out one of the new M4 assault rifles handed over by The Pentagon at the company's firing range in South Baghdad. He handled it with an easy familiarity, as though he had been given an old pair of gloves to slip on. With the weapon in his hands, he was quickly transformed; gone was the avuncular, well-spoken former public schoolboy and in his place was a dead-eyed killer, squinting in the sun as he blasted away at Coke cans, 'double-tapping' each one, the first round sending them jumping into the air, the second spinning them around before they had had time to hit the ground. It was a highly impressive piece of shooting.

We had been badgering him to be allowed to join one of the teams on an operation outside the compound. It sounded glamorous and it would provide more colour and pictures for the piece Chris and I were planning to produce.

One morning, Scouser Cy and his mate Tommy, a grey-haired, slender 45-year-old also from Liverpool, walked up to us at breakfast. We'd got on well with them; they were close mates, who'd known each other for years, and spent all day taking the mickey out of all and sundry and bickering and carping at each other constantly like an old married couple.

Tommy said: 'Be outside this building at midday – you're coming with us. Don't tell your office and don't use the phone.'

We asked where we were going and Cy laughed. 'You'll see,' he said.

Later that day, we turned up as arranged carrying our body armour and a day bag. The two blacked-out armoured BMW M5s slipped out of a nearby garage, a door opened (the windows don't) and Tommy told us to get in the back.

The plan was to 'hard-target' out of the compound and join a convoy heading off on a mission to a heavily-guarded warehouse in Al Sadr, a very dangerous place for us with no Adil to watch our backs and smooth the way. There we would load up crates of supplies into a truck and somehow ferry them back through the streets to a heliport within the city's safe Green Zone. From there, the supplies would be airlifted to Northern Iraq. What these 'supplies' were, and who they were destined for, no-one would say. It all sounded less glamorous and more scary now we came to it, but we'd got ourselves into this and we had to see it through. Hard-targeting – literally, making yourself a hard target to hit – is a speciality of the British Army, perfected over many years on the streets of Belfast and the winding roads of Armagh's bandit country. The idea is to avoid stopping, or even slowing down, where possible. The black BMs had been bought from Sicily, where they had been used to transport judges trying Mafia trials. They had run-flat tyres, were bullet proof and would even provide us with a degree of protection from an RPG strike or the bomb blast from a suicide attack. But despite that, and despite Cy's driving skills, I still felt very vulnerable as we slid out onto the streets. Tommy sat alongside him cradling his automatic rifle, all the Scouse wit and sparky banter gone from both men as they concentrated on keeping pace with the car in front and watched for potential threats.

As the car ahead of us came to a roundabout or a junction, its driver would slow and pull over into the oncoming traffic, blocking the way for us to roar past, hardly slowing from 60mph. Immediately, the guy behind would floor it and race up behind us until it was our turn to block the traffic for them and repeat the whole relay. All the time, Tommy kept up a constant commentary.

'Roundabout here, mate... slow... slow... OK! Go! Go! Go!'

'Him there, mate, he's on his phone... he could be calling ahead (to alert ambushers). Get a move on!'

'Watch this guy on the left... no, he's OK.'

'Head that guy off, there...'

For 20 or more minutes, we weaved through the traffic in narrow streets and broad dual carriageways, concentration etched into their faces. I think my own face was probably a mixture of fascination and terror. The roads outside were a blur of cars and carts and walking people, each one a potential threat. Every window could contain a man with a missile launcher or a heavy machine gun, every box by the roadside an improvised explosive device.

The atmosphere lightened slightly as we got to the edge of the city and found ourselves out in the open, where the traffic was lighter and there was more space to manoeuvre; by now, we were speeding along the flat, dirt tracks outside Al Sadr. We came to a dense grove of palm trees and then shot out into a piece of wasteland. In the middle of it, there was a huge warehouse, where a gang of scruffily-dressed Iraqis were already heaving crates into the back of a battered old lorry. Tommy and Cy were out in a flash, guns at the ready, eyes scanning the trees and distant houses for any signs of threat. Satisfied, Tommy called the team from the other BMW round him to brief them.

'Right, listen in. Once this lot have loaded up we're gonna steam through Al Sadr and back round Baghdad. At some stage, we'll RV with the American Marines. They'll escort us to the heliport within the Green Zone. Anything happens, like if we're attacked, you all know the score. We shoot the tyres of the lorry out, so the rebels can't move the goods away, and then we drive off, returning fire all the way. The Americans can send in the heavy mob to pick up the stuff afterwards. They know what's in the lorry and we don't want it getting into the wrong hands. Some of these lads' – he jerked a thumb at the Iraqis, who were almost finished – 'will sit on top of the lorry to make it look more innocent to nosey people. We'll keep our distance in the Beemers and hopefully no-one will put two and two together.'

RV-ing with the US Marines: I definitely liked the sound of that. I wasn't quite so keen on all the talk of tyres being shot out and fire being returned.

We watched as the last of the crates were loaded up.

'What *is* that stuff, Tommy?' I asked.

'Guns, mate,' he said.

Hundreds of guns, in fact, supplied by The Pentagon and destined for ex-pat-led security forces tasked with guarding the oil installations in the north of Iraq.

I swallowed nervously. This was going to be like walking through a crack den with a bag full of drugs. The grinning Iraqis closed up the truck and clambered up onto the roof, waving and laughing as though we were heading for a day at the seaside rather than back through the most murderous city on earth, where bands of armed fanatics were sharpening their knives and dreaming of beheading people like me.

The convoy pulled off and it was the same routine as before – speeding aggressively through Baghdad, until we reached the outskirts of the airport where we were met by the Marines – several Humvees-worth – who escorted the lorry back to the Green Zone. Once we were there, we waved goodbye to the PSD teams, who were returning to base in Mansour leaving us and our lorry load of hardware behind. We wandered off for a while, Chris and I wondering what was coming next. Information about this mission was coming our way in dribs and drabs. I shared a fag with Tommy. 'How did you get into this?' I asked him.

'I was in logistics in the Army and I left after a bit,' he said. 'I thought there was more to life than polishing boots. I went to

University and trained to become a social worker, actually. But after doing that for a bit, I started missing the Army. Too late to get back in, so I thought I'd have a go at this.' He grinned. 'Not much difference between this and social work, really. What we're doing here is what you might call community regeneration with an edge.'

Night fell and, after an hour or two, we were called over to a US forces Chinook helicopter and told to climb in. I could see the crates of guns tied down on board; it looked very much as though we were heading north, too. We walked along the rear ramp of the huge aircraft, the giant, twin rotors already screaming and whirling away above our heads, and strapped ourselves into seats facing each other near the front. It was very loud inside, and dark, and very hot from the huge engines; the smell of aviation fuel, oil and metal filled my nose as I watched the two side-gunners, based just behind the pilot's cockpit, loading up their huge calibre weapons with belts of brass-tipped rounds. A third gunner was strapping himself into a harness in the tail-end Charlie position at the back, legs dangling over the ramp entrance, which was left open. Suddenly, the engine notes increased, the blades accelerated and the machine started juddering, straining to get airborne. As we lifted off, I looked towards the back, watching us rise against lights on the buildings in the distance. In the foreground, Tail End Charlie was hunched over his gun, alert and ready. His was the most dangerous job on a Chinook, Cy had told me. Statistically, the man at the rear of the helicopter has almost no chance of survival in the event of a crash.

'Why's that?' I'd asked.

'Well, the counter forces of the two rotors literally tear the back end apart and anything inside it goes the same way,' Cy had said. He'd pursed his lips with an expression of distaste. 'They get splattered. Not a pretty sight.'

I looked away and tried not to think about that. Much as I was concerned for the gunner, my mind was occupied more with my own chances of survival. We were banking left now, the Chinook groaning and shuddering as the pilots wound it up to full revs for maximum speed. Once we left the Green Zone, every insurgent for the next fifty miles – and that was a lot of insurgents – would be trying to bring us down with everything from anti-aircraft missiles to pea-shooters. Chris and I were close to the safest part of the chopper, the armoured cockpit, but I had the uncomfortable feeling that surviving a crash over Baghdad might actually be worse than dying in one. There were a few people down there who would like to make my acquaintance, after all.

The chopper was zig-zagging painfully from side to side, like some sort of cumbersome, airborne lorry 100 feet up in the night sky. I looked at Cy and Tommy, strapped into their red seats opposite. Both had fallen asleep immediately, despite the noise, smell and danger.

Leaning forward, I could just make out the Baghdad rooftops, see-sawing up and down and left to right as the pilot threw the machine around.

I was trying to work out exactly where we were when, suddenly, there was a loud bang and the entire sky all around us lit up, as the helicopter's anti-rocket flares fired off. A split second later, there was a heavy *thud*, and the chopper shuddered and momentarily lost height, lurching down and rendering me temporarily weightless. It recovered, and the routine evasive action became almost panicked. The aircraft turned virtually on its side – I could see vegetation and what must have been the Tigris no more than 50 feet beneath us – and then flipped back the other way, engines screaming with four thousand horsepower of effort. Simultaneously, the tail gunner opened fire, spewing rounds into the night air. The front left and right gunners joined in, blazing away at unseen targets on the ground, sending hundreds of burning hot empty cartridges flying back into the cab and showering Chris Grieve in them. Chris was bolt upright in his seat opposite me, mouthing, *'What the fuck is going on?'* and frantically brushing the hot metal away.

Cy and Tommy were jarred awake by the noise and the light of the flares. They looked not terrified but irritated, as only former squaddies can be in situations like this. I remembered someone telling me that some people take off their body armour and sit on it when they are in helicopters; the idea is that rounds penetrating the thin-skinned floor don't take your testicles with them. Mine was firmly, uselessly, strapped to my chest, something I began to regret as the machine gunners carried on firing. After 15 or 20 seconds, though, they stopped and it seemed we'd passed over the worst, whatever it had been. The helicopter thrashed off to the left and soon we were being hurled along the river bank at ridiculous speed and height. One of the flight crew came back and looked us over, giving us a thumbs-up, checking we were all OK. I nodded, and grinned uncertainly. I *thought* I was.

The flight continued, straightish, levelish, and uneventful for the next half an hour until we came to a hover above the dim lights of a base out in the middle of the desert.

We landed in a huge cloud of dust, with US soldiers running towards us in that familiar helicopter crouch. The engines whined down as I unstrapped myself and staggered, wobbly-legged, down the ramp and out into the humid night air. I had no idea where we were but we'd been in the air for an hour at least and the Chinook had a cruising speed of around 200mph. I hazarded a guess that we were maybe 150 miles from the capital.

The crew, all Hawaiian Americans, were already on the ground and reloading ammunition belts and anti-missile flares as a ground crew drove to our position to refuel.

Chris and I walked over to the flight captain, a greying officer who had flown Hueys in Vietnam and had also served in the first Gulf War.

'Can you tell us where we are?' I asked.

'Not exactly,' he replied. 'That's classified. But we're about 35 miles from Baghdad.'

More than an hour in the air to cover 35 miles; that showed how much zig-zagging he had had to do.

'I thought we were headed further north?' I said.

'We are, but after what happened back there, we need to check the ship over.'

'Are you allowed to tell us what did happen back there?' I asked.

He grinned. 'Something travelled towards us at speed from the ground.'

'What, like a missile?' I said.

He smiled and nodded, watching as the flares were replaced. 'Yes,' he said. 'A surface to air missile was tracking us. The anti-missile flares drew it away but it exploded quite nearby.' I remembered the *thud*. 'We could have been hit by shrapnel... that's what these guys are looking for.'

I could see a group of ground staff, working by torchlight, undertaking a fingertip inspection of the craft and its engines.

'Bloody hell,' I said. 'How close was it to hitting us?'

'Close,' he said. 'Very close. And that would have been very bad news.'

I digested this uncomfortable thought for a few moments; as I did so, Cy burst in. I made a half-hearted attempt at an introduction, which he completely ignored.

'How far are we were from Kirkuk, mate?' he asked the pilot. This northern city, 150 miles north of Baghdad, was our final destination, it seemed.

'About another hour,' said the Captain. 'But we have to check her over very thoroughly first. We wouldn't want to be taking off with damage. Assuming everything's OK, I guess we'll be airborne in another half hour or so, at the most.'

He watched the fuel bowser back up to the helicopter and the hose being attached. Then he turned back to Cy. 'So what are you guys doing here? What are you... British Special Forces? MI6? Private contractors?'

It sounded like a polite enquiry to me, but Cy was having none of it.

'I'll tell what we're doing, mate,' he said, stabbing his finger at the pilot's chest. 'Looking after your fucking Generals and earning the kind of dough you lot could earn if you leave the services.'

The Hawaiian laughed. I suppose you tend not to take a little brusqueness too much to heart if you dodge surface-to-air missiles for a living.

I wandered away, leaving the pair of them chatting amiably, and had a nose around. We seemed to be in the Delta Force area of a larger base. In the low light, I could make out a perimeter fence and soldiers on guard. But there wasn't a lot to see so I headed back to the helicopter, where people were boarding up. They'd found no damage and, 10 or 15 minutes later, we were back in the air. With far less likelihood of being targeted in the open desert, the pilot was able to fly a fairly straight line and it wasn't long before we could see the huge arc of light that was the Kirkuk oil field coming into view. We put down somewhere in the desert, and an armoured protection team from the US Army, waiting nearby, drove over to meet us. Those crates of gleaming new AK47s were unloaded as the rotors turned: within 20 minutes, we were back in the air and heading south, our mission complete.

But our unscheduled night-time stop had cost us precious time, and the sun was starting to come up. If it is vulnerable by night, the slow, ponderous Chinook is a death trap by day. The pilot threw us into the same jarring evasive action as he raced towards Baghdad, skimming the earth and trying to get home before daybreak proper. But the sun beat us and we were forced into an emergency landing at another US base about 50 miles from the city. As we descended, a crew member came back and motioned to Chris that he was to take no photographs. Soon we realised why. Parked up on the runway, and stretching as far down it as the eye could see, was a seemingly endless line of Black-hawk troop carriers and Apache assault helicopters. There were hundreds of them. (Some time later, I recalled that line of choppers as President Bush explained that there were not enough helicopters in the southern US to help with the rescue and relief effort in flooded New Orleans following Hurricane Katrina).

We climbed out again, blinking in the now-bright sun and feeling the humidity of the early morning on our faces. And we just hung around, waiting for a lift. It's a strange contradiction, travelling with the US military in Iraq. Getting into the system in the first place can be a huge logistical conundrum – hours of filling out forms and making calls to gain clearance and book yourself onto flights. Once you're in, though, you just find a chopper going your way and get on it. No-one really asks who you are or what you're doing. It's quite odd.

Cy and Tommy headed off into the heart of the base to make enquiries while Chris and I sat in the shade of the Chinook. Eventually, they came back with good news. We had one minute's notice to get ourselves onto a Blackhawk that was heading back to the Green Zone. The Blackhawk is America's Huey of modern times, a threatening, burnt-black, insect-like machine bristling with weapons, electronics and power. There is nothing charming about it, no colour, no elegance and no concessions to comfort. It's an airborne stock car, with gunners wearing full-face helmets leaning out of the side and daring the enemy to come and have a go if they think they're hard enough.

None of us had ever travelled by Blackhawk before. An explanation as to how the various straps worked, and perhaps a pointer to the lack of doors, would have been nice. As it was, a couple of Darth Vaders pushed us in and lobbed our bags after us; seconds later, the *whop-*

whop-whop blades were beating at the soupy Iraqi air and we were airborne and hurtling towards Baghdad in a G-force blur of rushing fields, green hills and tiny hamlets north of the capital. I clung onto my bag and concentrated on not falling out as Chris pulled out his camera. The two Scousers tried to look as Vietnam as possible, pointing their guns at the ground and posing for pictures with gleeful grins that ruined the picture completely.

The pilot was hugging the terrain, zipping along dry river beds with the rotors seeming to shave the grass on either side, pulling up over hills at the very last minute, weaving this way and that to make his ship harder to hit.

Then we climbed slightly before swooping down over the flat Baghdad rooftops; a minute or so later, the chopper unceremoniously dumped itself, and us, back in the Green Zone.

I sat there for a moment. Whatever I thought about the war, and the actions of some Americans, I knew one thing: I'd spent a day being flown around by two of the best, and bravest, pilots imaginable.

Even the Scousers were silent for a few minutes.

'Phew,' said Tommy, eventually. 'That was some ride.'

We were met as we got off the flight by one of their colleagues – a former intelligence man – who was trying to find an American officer so he could get a death certificate for the South African guard who had been shot two weeks earlier.

We hard-targeted it back to Mansour and the Erinys HQ and, as we drove, my satphone went.

It was someone from the news desk. I ran through the story we'd picked up and he half-listened.

'Is there something on your mind, mate?' I asked.

'Piers is in a bit of bother,' he said.

'Oh?' I said. 'Why?'

'Those pictures of the troops pissing on the Iraqi prisoner... a lot of people think they were faked.'

'Faked?' I was incredulous. 'What – by Piers?'

'No, by the toe rag who sold them to us,' came the reply. 'We're sticking firm that they weren't but it's not looking good.' There was some noise in the background. 'Sorry, mate,' he said. 'Gotta go.'

Click.

Faked pictures. I wondered whether to mention this to the guys we were with. I quickly put that thought out of my mind. Best let sleeping dogs of war lie.

I filed my piece and spent the next few days keeping my head down, trying to avoid getting involved in any more near-death experiences. And then our fortnight was up.

I got back to London in the early hours of May 14. I had some days off in *lieu* following my latest Baghdad trip, so I got a few hours' kip in my flat and then nipped down the road to a local greasy spoon caff which does fantastic (very late) breakfasts for about a fiver. I was sitting there, nibbling my fried bread and sausage and enjoying the fact that the place wasn't crawling with psychopaths carrying guns – at least, they weren't carrying them openly – when my mobile started bleeping and ringing.

The call was from the office, so I ignored it and checked the texts instead.

The first of those was from a mate on *The Sun*.

'Hv u herd piers frd!!!!', it said.

That didn't make much sense, so I called up the next one. This was from a friend on *The Times*. *'Is it true Piers Morgan has been sacked?'* it read. You get a better class of text from the used-to-be broadsheets.

I dropped the fried bread in mid-nibble.

Bloody hell.

The phone rang. It was the office's number, again. This time I answered it.

'Hughesy,' gabbled the excited voice on the other end. 'Piers has been sacked. They just marched him out of the fucking office.'

I wittered something in reply and put the phone down.

Bloody hell!

The TV in the corner of the caff was tuned to Sky News and, sure enough, they were running the same pictures of the same front page I'd seen in Baghdad a couple of weeks earlier. Then some expert came on. He ran through the whole sorry story – how it became clear the photographs were set-ups, how the pressure had been building on Piers and how, eventually, it had blown that morning and he'd been dismissed after a board meeting.

I couldn't believe it. I'd known Piers for 15 years or more, since the days when we'd both worked on *The Sun* together. We'd been good friends in those early days, though we'd inevitably drifted apart as he shot through the hierarchy of various papers and I didn't. He'd been a good editor to work under, though: a popular and fair boss, with a good eye for a story and a willingness to go with his gut instinct. The public perception of him seemed to be that of a buffoon with a galloping ego but that wasn't fair: he was sharp and, while he did have plenty of self-belief, much of that ego and pomposity was put on for a laugh. He'd taken the *Mirror* into much more serious waters of late, particularly in our coverage of the war, and while circulation had dropped he'd held his nerve.

Clearly, no-one was untouchable.

But I wonder: if it's right for an editor to lose his job over some faked pictures, how come the Prime Minister keeps his? Dodgy dossiers, the non-existent 'Axis of Evil', imaginary WMDs, lies about missiles which could hit us in 45 minutes, thousands of civilian fatalities and deaths among our own servicemen and women running into three figures…

Maybe I was wrong?

Maybe some people *are* untouchable.

With The Black Watch

The British troops in Iraq had generally been far better received than their American counterparts.

They were primarily in the Saddam-hating Shia south, around Basra, which helped, as the most serious insurgency was further north among the Sunnis, around Fallujah and Ramadi and in Baghdad itself. They were also, frankly, far better at dealing with the Iraqi population. Where many of the US soldiers I'd seen seemed gung-ho, even bloodthirsty, the Brits adopted a much more softly-softly approach; they had 30 years' experience of patrolling the streets of Northern Ireland to call on and were using it.

That all started to change in late 2004. Those major US assaults on Fallujah had begun, and these operations had knock-on effects for the British forces further south. Though many of the insurgents stayed put to fight the Americans, others were fleeing. With nothing but desert to the west, US Marines to the north and occupied Baghdad to the east, their only option was to go south, and thousands of them did just that.

Five hundred and fifty troops from the Scottish Black Watch Regiment and a further 105 from the Queen's Dragoon Guards were sent up to Camp Dogwood, a British base 25 miles south of Baghdad. The idea was that they would cut off the insurgents as they tried to escape Fallujah and would also interrupt the supply of arms and ammunition to those who were staying behind. British military intelligence called it the 'Dogwood Trap' and it worked, to a degree. However, it did turn the British troops into a major target. As a bitter November chill swept across the camp – a scruffy cluster of Warrior armoured vehicles and old stone buildings behind 15ft high sand berms – they were like sitting ducks for rocket attacks and sniper fire.

Outside, on patrol, they faced roadside bombings orchestrated against them from the safety of the nearby rebel villages. Six Black Watch soldiers died in these bomb attacks that month alone.

As the Camp Dogwood story grew in interest and importance, the Ministry of Defence offered up places for print and broadcast journalists to become embedded at the base, one week at a time, via a lottery, on a pool basis. Being 'embedded' means being based with the Armed Forces and operating under their protection. It's a restricted, censored situation – you can't disclose your location, its defences, troop strengths or mission details (not that you'd want to anyway, if it meant compromising the safety of troops). 'Pooling' means – in print terms – that one journalist provides copy which is pooled and shared out with all newspapers via the Press Association, not just to his or her own desk. All in all, it's not an ideal situation, but it means the Army only has a few unfit, clueless, slightly parasitical hacks to worry about at a time, rather than dozens. There are upsides: uniformed squaddies with guns and tanks will be looking after you and if you happen to be unlucky you'll receive the full benefit of the field hospital. You also get access to combat areas that are pretty much inaccessible to most reporters. The broadsheets tend to be a little snotty about the inevitable compromise of editorial integrity involved in being embedded (though they still join up) and, to a degree, I suppose they're right. But they devote acres of newsprint to wars and so can justify independently keeping reporters out in theatre for years. Most tabloid newsrooms, where the cost versus space equation gets more ticklish as the war drags on, take a pragmatic view; it's access to a war zone, of a kind, and it's cheap, so it's worth going.

Conor Hanna – by now Deputy Editor, with Richard Wallace promoted to the top job, called me in to his office.

'Hughesy,' he said. 'We've got you into Camp Dogwood in a couple of weeks' time. If you don't want to go you don't have to.'

'Should be good,' I said.

'OK. See if you can get out to Basra with the Army for a week before you go to Dogwood,' he said. 'It's probably worth doing a bit of schmoozing with them, just to make sure we're properly on side.'

This was a clever call. Relations between the *Daily Mirror* and the

British Army and the MoD were icy to say the least in the aftermath of the fake photos scandal but they'd be only too keen to help us spend some time in Basra, showing us some of the good work the troops were doing there and which was being woefully under-reported by the red tops.

I called the MoD and then I rang Padraic Flanagan, a *Daily Express* journalist who'd been among the first reporters into Dogwood. So far, I'd travelled to Iraq on my own; Camp Dogwood would be my first embed and I had no idea what to expect. I was hoping Padraic could fill me in.

The call didn't fill me with joy. He'd had a terrible time – not that you'd have known it from the great copy he'd filed to the pool. It was freezing, there were no showers and the food was abysmal. The squaddies were bored, so they delighted in winding up journalists with ridiculous tales like the one about the ferocious camel spiders, bigger than your hand, which would jump onto your face in the night and bite huge chunks of flesh out of it while you were asleep. Ignore that one, he said, it's rubbish like all the rest.

Oh, and the camp was being rocketed around six times a day.

Other than that, it was great fun.

I thanked Padraic for his help and wondered whether I'd done the right thing in accepting this job. (By the way, when I was at Dogwood two weeks later I learned that one of those insurgent rockets had landed a matter of yards from Padraic, splattering him in mud but leaving him miraculously unharmed. He was unable to report it at the time, since it might have tipped off the rebels, who were firing from as far away as eight miles, that they were becoming accurate. The insurgents were known to follow world-wide news coverage on the internet and feasibly could see a *Daily Express* report. Though even they probably have standards.)

* * * * *

I caught a flight out to Kuwait the week before I was due in Dogwood and called the British Armed Forces press office at Basra airbase. They told me that a party from the 4th Armoured Brigade, better known as The Desert Rats, were heading back into Iraq the following day.

They'd pick me up from the Sheraton hotel at 5pm for the three-hour night-time drive across the border to Iraq's second city.

Dead on the appointed hour the following afternoon, a little convoy of British camouflaged Land Rovers, lightly armoured, covered in netting and more commonly known as 'Snatch wagons' (because they are used for driving into crowds and snatching trouble-makers), arrived outside the hotel.

A couple of red-faced, exhausted-looking Scots squaddies from 4th Armoured nodded a quick *'Hello'* and started heaving my bags into the back of one of the Land Rovers.

I stood there, waiting to get in. Then one of the Jocks pointed to a little blue mini-bus. 'Jump into the back o' that thing there,' he said.

I looked at it, doubtfully. It was pretty vulnerable-looking. In fact, the whole convoy wasn't quite what I'd been expecting. My mind's eye had conjured up a picture of a couple of heavily-armoured Warriors, with goggle-wearing, machine-gun waving heroes riding atop them, the breeze blowing in their lantern-jawed faces.

I climbed into the mini-bus. Several Desert Rats were slumped asleep in their seats, caps pulled down over their eyes. As I looked for a spare seat, a man's voice rang out, in very Cockney tones.

''Ere, mate!' it said. 'Oi! *Daily Mirror* man! Man from *The Daily Mirror*! Come on back here with the Royal.'

I looked. Another squaddie was beckoning me to the back seat. He grinned and nodded. 'That's right, son,' he said. 'Back 'ere. Don't hang around with that lot, mate... come and have a laaaarf with the Royal. Come on... come and join the Royal.'

I hadn't got the faintest idea what he was on about, but he seemed friendly enough and the rest were asleep, so I made my way to the seat next to him.

'That's better,' he said, as I sat down.

'I'm Chris,' I said, shaking his hand.

'Alright, Chris,' he said. 'Nice one. My name's Kev, mate. I'm a Royal Marine Commaaaarndo and somehow I've had the fackin' misfowchoooon to be linked up with this fackin' mob.'

He was part of the force protection unit at Basra and he was very pleased with himself for being a Marine. This, I learned, made him a cut above the rest. In fact Kev 'thanked the Lord every fackin' day' he'd joined the Royal Marines because it meant he wasn't in the fackin' Army.

His cheerful and loud banter started waking the squaddies up, and they turned towards us, sleepily. They eyed me without suspicion, nodding a quick greeting, before raising their eyebrows at the antics of the 'Royal' next to me. He was now in full swing, a 25-year-old Alf Garnett. 'You stick with Royal Marines, mate,' he would tell me. 'It's the *Royal* fackin' Navy and the *Royal* fackin' Marine fackin' Commaaaarndooes. It ain't the fackin' Royal *Army* is it?'

Then a young Fusilier would pipe up. 'Ah, but you do have the *Royal* Regiment Fusiliers, the *Queen's* Dragoons…'

But Kev had heard it all before. 'Yeeees, an' we 'ave the *Royal* Marine Commaaaarndoes in the *Royal* Navy. You, on the other hand, may well have the aforementioned Royal Regiment Fusiliers but they are part of the *ordinary* Army, the *very* fackin' *ordinary* Army.' He was hardly pausing for breath. 'Now arrrrrrsk yourself why that is, son? Shall I tell you? It's because, son, there *ain't* a Royal Army.'

All of these guys were good company for the next hour to the Kuwaiti desert even though the subject of the *Mirror*'s fake photo story was never too far away. They wound me up none stop about what was going to happen to me, my food and my bed when we got to Basra.

In desperation, the Army guys would try and shut the 'Royal' up by saying, 'Yeah, yeah – with your new mate from *The Daily Mirror*.'

'Speak as I find, mate,' said Kev. 'Speak as I find. Mind you, it ain't *The Royal* fackin' *Daily Mirror*, now is it?'

'I dunno,' I said. 'We always say we're part of Her Majesty's Press.' I thought it was an old joke, from the fictional Greg Kettle in the TV tabloid skit *Hot Metal*, but apparently not. Kev and the squaddies all laughed.

Suddenly, Kev's eyes narrowed and he pressed his earpiece deeper into his ear. Now he was all business. 'Right, lads,' he said. 'We're crossing the border into Iraq. Body armour on – that includes you, mate.' He pointed at me. 'And helmets on as well… that also includes Her Majesty's fackin' *Daily Mirror*.'

The vehicles pulled over into some waste ground and the squaddies started putting on their armour and webbing and checking their SA80 rifles. It was dark, now, but still humid, as the cold night air had not yet taken over. A senior officer ordered me to join in the 'huddle' as they all stood, out of earshot of the Kuwaiti drivers who were hanging around, and listened to his briefing. He rattled through it, telling everyone that if a vehicle was hit they would make a decision as to whether to destroy it and carry on or make a serious stand until a QRF – Quick Reaction Force – could get there. Medical kits were checked and they all went through their detailed maps of the area, covering every eventuality. Each of the soldier's faces was full of concentration. Whenever I'd been with British troops, serving or ex, I'd always been impressed by their calmness and discipline and it was no different now.

When the briefing was over, we headed back to our mini-bus. As we climbed in, Kev muttered an aside to me: 'Thank *fack* they never brought up the Royal Air Force, eh? That would have scuppered me, wouldn't it? Here, mate… draw that curtain shut, eh? Cor, dear Gawd, look at the state of your body armour.'

He stared at my filthy blue Kevlar vest and then prodded me in the chest where the 'PRESS' sticker was placed, before giggling like a kid. It was a squaddie joke I'd seen a hundred times before. Trust me, they all think it's hilarious.

Despite their obvious professionalism, I felt different – more vulnerable – with them than I had on previous visits to Iraq. I was safer, in a way, because I was surrounded by well-trained and disciplined men with guns, but the Snatch wagons screamed 'military convoy' and there was the ever-present danger of roadside bombs or random small arms fire. At the back, Kev had fitted a night-sight onto his rifle. He was our tail-end Charlie, guarding the rear of the convoy. If we were shot at, the troops in my vehicle would shoot out the windows of the bus and open fire on the ambushers. There was a tense atmosphere as we drove; everyone had his gun pointing towards the nearest window and there was little or no banter, just the occasional squawk of radio chatter.

I rarely looked out of the window but, through a crack in the curtains and with the aid of the moonlight, I could see we were driving through narrow lanes with built up banks on either side: a dangerous combination with few options for escape if we were attacked. Still, the squaddies in my bus seemed calm enough until Kev held his hand up and shouted out that he'd heard over the radio net that a lorry had pulled out in front of the convoy and was slowing down. Then Kev saw more danger behind.

'All call signs, all call signs,' he said, speaking into the microphone strapped to his throat. 'Be aware a white Merc has pulled up behind us and is closing in. That's a white Mercedes pulling up behind us and closing in. Over.'

We were boxed in.

Kev had pulled back the curtains covering the windows – there was no point trying to hide our identity now – and had his rifle trained on the car. Beads of sweat were forming on the forehead of the young fusilier in front of me and I slid lower in my seat next to the Royal Marine. He looked at me and winked, like a jellied eel salesman or a music hall comedian of old. 'Relax, son,' he said. 'We'll be fine.'

Another squaddie came up to the back to increase our fire power, kneeling on the back seat and covering the Mercedes.

I watched the driver edging closer to us. He was either a terrorist or a madman; he must have been able to see the rifles pointing at him and he must have heard of countless civilians being blown away, admittedly by American troops, in similar situations. The stand-off went on for five minutes as we drove on through the countryside before the Merc pulled off the road at a junction and headed west.

Slumping into his seat, still watching the road behind us, Kev whistled. 'Fack me,' he said. 'If we'd been Yanks back there that facker'd be dead now. What a dickhead... trying to cop on to the back of a military convoy and feel safe. Don't he read the fackin' newspapers? He's a lacky, lacky baaarrstard that I'm a *Royal* Marine, not a *US* fackin' Marine.'

The relief was palpable but the tension never quite went away and it was good to pull into the concrete blast wall chicanes that marked the entrance to Basra air base. Kev and the rest drove me to the Divisional HQ of the 4th Armoured, dropping me off with lots of handshakes and Cockney banter, and I went inside to get my *'must be escorted'* pass and to sign a load of papers about my blood group and how to contact my next-of-kin in the event of my death. Then a Fusilier from Scotland called Mick picked me up in an SUV and took me to where I would be staying for the next few days.

As we drove, I got my first look at the huge base. It was several miles across, with a perimeter marked by a wire fence and patrolled by helicopters, unmanned aerial surveillance drones and sentries with German Shepherd attack dogs which can snap your arm with one bite. Later, I'd meet the scariest of these; it was about the size of a small horse, with a mouth like a tiger shark and a foot long slab of tongue flapping as he ran. His handlers called him Snap, a fitting name for an animal with a bite pressure of 1,000 lb/sq in. We renamed him 'The Hound of Basraville', a name which, to the irritation of the handlers, stuck. The buildings were dotted around in small groups, all dug in and surrounded by five foot high sandbag walls and guarded by machine gun posts covered in camouflage netting. Warrior Fighting Vehicles were parked outside the living areas and there was the constant noise of generators pumping out electricity.

'That's the Pizza Hut over there... they do deliveries,' said Mick.

'Yeah, right,' I said. But I looked anyway, and saw a shack with a bright, *Pizza Hut* sign above it.

'Seriously, mate,' said Mick. 'I'll give you the number if you want a delivery. They'll bring you a pizza and Coke and it's proper stuff, mate. Really good pizza. Tell you what – you can come to the pub with us tonight if you like. There's a two can rule, as in you can't have any more than two cans, but I'll introduce you to a few of the lads.'

'That would be great, thanks,' I said. Thinking *What sort of reception is a* Mirror *reporter going to get in there?* At least they wouldn't be too rowdy after a couple of cans.

He dropped me off at my tent. These were canvas buildings, kept cool with air pumped in through huge, flexible pipes from ACs standing outside. There was electricity and flushing toilets and showers but, with water being precious, I'd been warned to observe the 'ships rule': wet yourself, switch off the shower, soap yourself up and then switch it back on for a quick rinse. Most of the tents held about 20 people at a stretch and they were bunched together in little groups in the interior of the base, with covered corridors joining them. Mine was a bigger affair, with about forty camp beds lined up on each side, but I was on my own. I stored my bags and had a wander outside. A 'lume' went off over the camp, a bright flare sent up from time to time to illuminate the base and its perimeter. A squaddie wandered by. 'Stay back in the shadows when those things go up, mate,' he said. 'If we can see them, they can see us.'

'Is there often much to see?' I asked.

'Not really,' he said. 'Though there was this time recently. A few of the lads went out on patrol in a chopper and saw some activity below them. They fired off a lume and there was a load of Iraqi farmers on the ground, all blokes, all giving each other a good seeing-to.'

He strolled off. As the light died, a strange rodent, a bit like a miniature kangaroo, hopped into view and stopped: it was a proper desert rat and it stood looking at me with disdain. I got the distinct impression it was wondering what the hell I was doing there. Then it bounced away, just as Mick strolled up with another lance corporal.

The 'pub' was an open-air space between the tents, about the size of a tennis court, with wooden tables and people shivering slightly in the cooling night air. This was the Oasis Bar – officially the junior ranks mess – and it was packed with men and women chatting away about the tribulations of the day as if they had just left the office back in London. Every now and then, distant gunfire would go off, a helicopter would clatter overhead or one of the unmanned drones would circle the camp, reminding me of where I was.

Since I was from *The Daily Mirror*, I was invited to buy a round by way of a peace offering; 16 cans of Heineken duty-free lager at a dollar apiece, and I was glad to oblige. Several times. I can't say I was scrupulous about the two-can rule and after a couple of hours I was feeling mildly light-headed. At some point, a hassled-looking Captain Eyton Parker turned up to have a word with me. Capt Parker, the press liaison officer, was a former Royal Artillery officer who had left and gone back to Civvy Street, but he had joined the TA and had been mobilised as the occupation dragged on. Back home, he ran a behaviour unit for schoolkids, perfect practice for dealing with unruly journalists like me.

'Ah, Chris,' he said. 'There you are.' He'd been searching all over the camp for me.

The squaddies all started shouting helpful things like 'He's a journalist, sir… where else would he be?' and 'He's been here all night, sir, he's really putting them away!'

'Tell you what, mate,' said Capt Parker. 'You finish your pint and

I'll drive you back to your digs so you can get some sleep. You look... tired. We'll take you out to look at a water treatment facility we've set up in the morning.'

I downed my can and excused myself to the other squaddies and Capt Parker – 'Call me Eyton,' he said – drove me to my tent where I was sparked out in about three minutes.

I was quickly made aware of the British Army's Rule Number One. You never sleep.

Rule Number Two is, if you do, you're woken three seconds later to go on a 16-hour venture to somewhere horrendous despite feeling like the living dead.

Suddenly, it was 5am and a clean-shaven, pristine and crisply-ironed Eyton Parker was coughing politely at the entrance to my tent to wake me up and show me the mess tent before we went off on my first relations-building exercise with the British Army. It was flagged up by a line of squaddies dumping their body armour and helmets at the door before cleaning their hands in a row of sinks placed outside. Inside, a hundred men and women, mainly from the ranks, were scoffing their first meal of the day, hurriedly, barely talking. Except for the uniforms, it was just like being in an office canteen. Within minutes, I was full of sausages, bacon and coffee and being whisked off to a small convoy of five Snatch wagons. As I watched the troops load weapons and ammunition, I made a quick call to *The Sun*'s Tom Newton-Dunn, a former *Mirror* man. Tom, who was already at Camp Dogwood, had spent time in Basra and must have visited this water works. It was worth ringing him to see what to expect.

He sounded fairly cheerful when he answered.

'Hughesy... hello mate! Heard you were in Basra. How's it going?'

'Not bad. What are you up to?'

'Can't say, I'm afraid. Hush-hush and all that.'

Petty point-scoring is all the rage with tabloid journalists, and there was no way Tom was going to tell me what he was working on, even though I'd be able to read all about it on the pooled wires a few hours later. I had to grin; I'd have been just the same.

'You twat,' I said. 'Listen, I'm going on this trip to look at some water facility in Umm Qasr. Sounds bloody boring. Is it?'

There was a silence and I could almost hear his brain switching into lying mode.

'Er… the water facility? Umm Qasr? Yes, mate… it's great. If you can't get a decent piece out of that you shouldn't be in this business.'

'You sure?'

'Yes, absolutely. Listen, mate, I've got to go… speak to you when we hand over.'

It was a fairly pointless lie and I laughed to myself. It wasn't that the water facility the British had mended was *actually* boring, it was vital. But when two of the world's largest economies invade a country with the ostensible aim of replacing the regime and saving the people from tyranny, they ought to ensure clean water remains available. Tony Blair might have thought it was dynamite news, but then he wasn't a journalist. It was the least the Iraqis could have expected, and 'Dog Bites Man' is never a story.

I put the sat phone away and was bundled into one of the Snatch wagons. Weapons loaded, we sped out of the camp, with me hunched up next to the legs of the soldier on 'top cover' – standing up, head and shoulders out of a hatch, scanning the streets for enemy shooters on rooftops or at the side of the road. The situation in Basra was reasonably peaceful – much safer than in the area around Camp Dogwood and further up in Baghdad – but vigilance was vital.

Umm Qasr is Iraq's only deep water port and lies on the western bank of the Khawr Abd Allah estuary leading into the Persian Gulf. It had taken several days for British Royal Marines from 40 Commando to take the town in Gulf War II and now it was a beachhead for humanitarian aid into the country. The water facility was basically a treatment plant with a huge tank full of water.

As I looked around under the gaze of the soldiers and some curious locals, an old man pushed to the front, his face sunned to the texture of a walnut, a pair of glasses held together by Sellotape and balanced on his large nose. He started shouting and complaining. Our Iraqi translator told me the old man was moaning that the water facility wasn't good enough and that the regeneration was not happening quickly enough.

The officer leading the visit, a Captain Mick O'Driscoll, tried to placate the man but it wasn't helping.

'We need help now,' he was shouting. 'We need electricity and medicines for our families.'

He had a point. Slowly, we backed away, smiling and trying to keep the atmosphere calm, conscious that some unseen younger man might be lining us up with an AK47 from a rooftop, until we were back in the wagons and on our way again. I felt for courageous men like Capt O'Driscoll and those under his command; the politicians had landed them with an impossible job. While they were risking their lives and sanity like this, Blair was striding the world stage, appearing on TV and boasting about our achievements, and it was mostly lies. The Iraqis were living in squalor and the Coalition's failure to fill the void left by Saddam was a great recruiting sergeant for the insurgents.

Next we visited Safwan Hill, a 1,000 ft high carbuncle that shot straight out of the flat desert and served as a communications base protected by a small number of squaddies. After a brief cup of tea, O'Driscoll and his men loaded up the wagons with boxes of water for the local kids. It was a regular trip: children started flocking to the Land Rovers as soon as they arrived at the bottom of the hill. The drivers trundled along slowly, the soldiers dropping bottles all along the road, O'Driscoll making sure every child had at least one. Some adults approached, and O'Driscoll stopped the vehicles and got out to hand over boxes of clothes. These had been collected by the troops on their own initiative, a kind gesture I felt was appreciated by the Iraqis. I couldn't get the phrase 'Lions led by Donkeys' out of my head, and the Donkeys were at Westminster.

Back in Basra, we approached the air base by a back road – it's important to vary your route to make ambushes harder to plan – which took us through a particularly poor area. A small group of youths hurled stones as we passed.

Ducking, one squaddie turned to me and said, 'Don't think we'll drop any water off for this lot today.'

Eyton Parker had arranged a packed schedule for me in Basra, knowing full well it was not going to get into the paper but wanting to keep me occupied anyway. There was very little else to do on the camp and, since I was there on a peace-keeping mission of my own, I said 'Yes' to everything. They were nothing but helpful. Over the next few days, Eyton displayed the patience of several saints as he tracked me down all over the base to show me new sections of the British re-generation effort that other hacks had ignored as they covered the war (and which I would ignore, too). I was shown how sappers were using the latest technology to clear away unexploded ordnance from residential areas, taken to meet local leaders who were working with the Brits and generally treated very well.

But I was glad when the week drew to a close. We'd got on well, and I'd enjoyed building bridges with the military (not literally), but Camp Dogwood – renamed 'Camp Incoming' by waggish NCOs – was calling.

* * * * *

My fellow 'embeds' had arrived in Basra for the deployment north to what the tabloids were now dubbing, in typically restrained terms, 'The Triangle of Death'. Many of them were radio and TV types, but on the print side of things there was David Harrisson from the *Sunday Telegraph* and *Daily Mail* photographer Mike Dunlea. We were all called down to the briefing room for a talk by a senior intelligence officer, who was uncomfortably forthcoming about Dogwood. He entered the room carrying a map of the country and treated us to an excellent explanation of which tribes were which, what threats were posed by whom and why the Black Watch and their colleagues were doing such a valuable job in interdicting the Fallujan insurgents. They had been involved in a large number of firefights and attacks on the camp were happening every day. But he explained how this had freed up the US Marines who had originally created Dogwood, allowing them to go into Fallujah as part of Operation Die Motherf*cker or whatever mad name they were calling their latest jaunt.

It made compelling listening and good reading, too: my copy made spreads in various papers, even though it was week three of the deployment and previous news teams had already cleaned up most of the coverage.

We flew up to Baghdad in an RAF Hercules C-130, which took off as close to vertically as possible to gain height quickly and avoid any surface-to-air missiles which might be sent our way. The Hercules is a big, bulbous monster of an aircraft, with none of the obvious comforts of a commercial flight. All of the insulation you see in a commercial flight is absent and the hard floor and ceiling are covered in harnesses to take cargo – a fire engine was strapped down next to me. It was an uneventful flight and another of those hairy landings and then a lot of waiting around at Baghdad airport before we could get our ride down to Dogwood. Bored, I had a look around the American PX shop. It was packed with military gear – webbing, knives, canteens and scarves of all kinds. Most of them seem to be labelled 'Special Ops', which would have been tremendously helpful if you got kidnapped.

I bought a miner's head torch for the evenings – absolutely essential if you need to go to the loo at night – and spent the next few minutes trying to cut the Special Ops label off the elastic strap. An American Marine Sergeant came bounding over to us, reading out our names and ordering us to form a line as a Blackhawk swooped down from the air and hovered down onto the tarmac.

'Sirs,' he shouted. 'Please shout out when I read your name from the manifest.'

I confirmed my name, and followed everyone else, running bent double towards the chopper, hurling my bags into the cabin at the back and then trying – and failing, again – to strap myself in. I was hanging on for grim death as the craft lurched into the air, pulled to the right and screamed away over Baghdad's rooftops, so low we had to hop up to clear telephone wires. David and Mike were as wide-eyed as I was: this was an even wilder ride than the one I'd had after the gun-running trip to Kirkuk earlier that year. Once clear of Baghdad, the pilot hugged the terrain, speeding past the farms and villages on the city's outskirts at 200mph and a height of 50–100 feet before heading out into the bland, empty desert.

After another 30 minutes of this terror, the Blackhawk banked hard to the left ahead of a group of armoured vehicles and sand berms, flared upwards and slammed into the ground, swathing the whole area in a cloud of grey sand. Almost immediately, the Darth Vader gunners were out of the cab, yelling and hustling us and our bags towards a giant man-made dune. As soon as we were clear, the chopper was off again, zipping south before any watching rebels had time to try to shoot it down on the way back. Ahead, a group of British soldiers was waving to us to run towards them, quickly. We clambered over the dune and there was Camp Dogwood: a remote clump of former factory buildings in the middle of nowhere. Clusters of tanks and armoured cars were dotted about, and I could see squaddies going about their business, cooking their evening meals or cleaning their weapons.

It was freezing; I felt colder than I had ever been, even though it was still just about daylight.

An officer, Captain Stuart McCauley, introduced himself to us and showed us to our quarters.

'It's a little sparse, I'm afraid,' he said, 'but you'll have to make do.'

He wasn't wrong. I was billeted with eight others in a small stone hut. There was no door, just a gauze fly net, and the beds were crammed side-by-side so tightly that the only way to get into bed was by climbing in from the end. It was to be the most uncomfortable seven nights' sleep I've ever had.

There were bags lying everywhere so I decided to leave the outgoing mob to pack first. Nick Allen, chief reporter at The Press Association, came along chewing a cheese cracker. 'Hello mate,' he said. 'Welcome to Camp Shithole.'

We shook hands. Nick and I had worked together at CentCom in Qatar in 2003 and it was good to see him again.

'This is the 'press tent',' he said, waving to a sand-bagged enclosure about 15 feet by 15 feet with a dozen satellite dishes poking out of the back. 'And this is our scoff.' Outside the tent were boxes of ration packs. Unlike the American MREs, these had to be cooked on a Hexi stove using fire-lighters. I didn't mind this, personally, because I only had to stand a few days of it, but I thought it was disgraceful that the Government couldn't supply its soldiers with decent food.

Sky and ITN were there, and the BBC Developing World Editor David Loyn, who greeted me with a friendly handshake as I stood looking at the press tent, a few tables, a sand floor and dust everywhere, with the usual generator banging away constantly outside, assaulting your eardrums.

Robbo, a Geordie Black Watch sergeant, bounded over. He wasn't exactly shy.

'Howay, man,' he said. 'Yous from the *Deely Mirrah*, aye? Cracking paper, that, like. Interview us, then. About the war, like.'

I hadn't even opened my mouth, before he was off again. In fact, I didn't get a word in edgeways. He must have read my mind or something, because he didn't even need any questions. He just delivered a rapid-fire string of answers.

'Go on then... ask us what it's like to be in a battle. Well, it's unbelievable at first, man. See a punter on the roof, give him a burst, then onto the next one, like. What about them bastaad roadside bombs, eh? Ya nah, IEDS, like? They're bad. You can't even see the bloody enemy, like. What was it like in Basra, eh? Well, at least in Basra you could see the punters coming at you. These punters are miles away, firing from behind bushes and rocks and that. Cowards, that's what th'are. You ever been shot at mate? Aye. Always thought it'd be a bit weird fighting out here, like, but that's what we do isn't it, canny lad? I'm in the Black Watch, there's a few of us here, like. Bollocks to all the rest, the infantry is where it's at, man – all muddy and covered in shite, get in amongst the punters, givin' 'em a doin'. Getting stuck in to the war, man, killing fucking rebels... terrorists, that's what th'are. That's what it's all aboot, man.'

He paused for breath. 'Come on, man... give us that ration pack and I'll stick a brew on for yous. You look bloody freezing, like.'

I'd fished three fleeces out of my bags, and a thermal T-shirt. With those, and gloves and a hat on, I was still shivering. Robbo had on a T-shirt and trousers. That's Geordies for you.

His Warrior crew, all skinheaded and mean-looking, were standing around, grinning. They'd obviously seen him in action before.

He'd crushed up the firelighters, lit a fire and got the water brewing up.

'Sugar, man? No? OK, mate. What's your name? Chris is it? OK, mate, here's your brew... see you later.'

And in a flash he had disappeared around the corner to assault someone else's eardrums.

David Harrisson and I had set about installing our satellite phones and dishes and chargers for every mobile device imaginable. The press tent soon became a messy spaghetti of wires and leads, which annoyed the TV guys. Most of them are decent, but one or two are utter prima donnas. They viewed us – and probably the Army – as mere irritants, obstacles in their way. A favourite trick among the more aggressive elements of the press is to fire a flashgun off in front of their cameras: it does something to the lenses and *really* winds them up.

That night David, Mike and I stayed up chatting in the dark outside until it became so unbelievably cold we had to call it a night. I crawled fully clothed into my bed, after stepping on various heads and feet as people screamed abuse at me, and lay flat on my back not daring to move. While Robbo had been interviewing himself for me, the best beds had been bagged – I'd been left with the one next to the door, the one with the excellent ventilation and air conditioning.

Two hours later, still awake, I realised I had forgotten to go to the toilet before I went to bed. I clambered to my feet, woke everyone up, and rummaged around for my body armour, helmet and head-torch, which was next to useless as the Army had given me a red filter to fit over the lens to prevent any enemy observers seeing it.

Outside, it was like I had stepped out into the Arctic, not an Arabian desert. It was bone-achingly cold, minus something awful degrees C, and I stood there, shaking madly, teeth chattering uncontrollably and peeing into a 'desert rose' – a tube made from water bottles stuck together and then rammed into the ground, so that the urine sinks away and doesn't affect camp hygiene. As I looked down, trying to make sure I wasn't missing the opening, a red dot slid across my legs and right on to the end of my... well, I'm sure you can fill in the blanks. I looked up and, in the darkness, I could just make out one of the sentries aiming at me from 30 yards away. He looked as though he was laughing, but I couldn't be sure. I hurriedly zipped myself back up and washed my hands with the bottle of liquid soap lying nearby – squaddies wash their hands all the time so that illnesses don't spread quickly through the ranks.

Two hundred yards away, I could just about make out the shapes of the Warriors sitting next to the berms protecting the camp. Over there, hundreds of Scotsmen were lying under canvas, filthy dirty and shivering in the bitter cold, only able to sleep because they were exhausted by the pressures of patrolling this vicious bandit country. Even further away, outside in the desert, scores of Welshmen from the Queen's Dragoon Guards were holed up in mini-camps from where they were conducting reconnaissance missions against the attackers. These were brave, brave men doing a job I couldn't possibly do, and my respect for them was growing all the time.

As I looked out into the near blackness I remembered briefly the Bedouin fire I had seen back in 2001, as I drove into Iraq just weeks after 9-11. Was that family still alive and wandering the western desert? I hoped so. There had to be some kind of constant that was not affected by this sodding war.

I turned and headed back to the tent. I weighted down the flap at the entrance with bricks, then bumped and cursed my way back into my sleeping bag, dozing amid the cacophony of snoring and muttering from my colleagues.

We were all woken at 5am by the sound of two officers talking loudly outside. I was already fully dressed so I got up and out.

'Good morning,' said one of them. 'You didn't hear anything in the night, then?'

'Not really,' I said. 'Why?'

He grinned and indicated a blackened crater a hundred yards or so away from the tent. A rocket had landed there during the night, and we'd all slept through it. They walked off, and I stared at the hole.

In between the room where we slept and the press tent was a little 10ft by 10ft area we called the 'patio', a dirt-floored, wind-blasted cooking area, sandbagged to eye-level and strewn with old ration-wrappers and other detritus. It was a source of constant irritation to the officers, who kept begging us to try and keep it tidy. A BBC cameraman called Duncan was already making tea and he passed me a huge box of rations. Shivering, I selected hamburger and beans and threw the foil-wrapped mess into a pan of water. I was starving: two minutes later, I was shovelling this lukewarm slop into my mouth like Gordon Ramsay had cooked it.

A few hundred yards away, Warrior tanks in platoons of four, with roughly 25 men aboard, were racing across the desert, churning up billowing clouds of reddish-grey sand which made it look like a sand storm was on the way. They were practising storming towards a makeshift bridge that was being built, dismantled and rebuilt by a group of engineers nearby. Clearly something was being planned.

'What's going on?' I asked a nearby officer, wiping bean juice out of my stubble.

'Big operation coming up,' he said. 'Put it this way, there won't be a bayonet left in camp when it happens… even you lot will be coming.

232

Maybe tonight.' He glanced at the satellite phone in my hand and waved his finger, as if to say *Don't even think about telling anyone.*

I walked off into the desert, putting on that damned body armour, and called the office.

It's always the same when you speak to the news desk. Whoever answers is all chirpy and friendly at first, in case it's a reader with a story. As soon as they realise it's just a reporter, they drop any pretence of being human. And if it's a reporter who they think is sunning himself in the Middle East, swinging the lead and pretending it's dangerous, they go all scoffing and sarcastic.

'Good morning, *Mirror* news desk, how may I help?'

'It's Chris.'

'Ah fucking hell, it's Hughesy. What's happening? Where are you?'

'I'm just checking in from Iraq, where, as you know, I'm embedded.'

'Ah, I see. Embedded, eh? Playing soldiers, are we? Camping out, like in the boy scouts? Got anything for morning conference?'

'Well, no. But I will have later.'

'What the fuck is it, then?'

'Not allowed to say.'

'Well that's a fat lot of fucking good, isn't it?'

'I'll be able to tell you later, once it's happened.'

'Oooh, fucking hell, you secret fucking squirrel, you. Alright, just give us a call.'

'Well, I won't be able to tell you via the phone.'

'Why not?'

'In case someone's intercepting the calls… I'll have to wire it.'

'Bloody hell… whatever.'

Crash.

Ah, well.

That afternoon we were called in to watch a briefing by a Lieutenant Colonel James Cowan who guided his senior officers through a detailed battle plan of a raid on a nearby village, planned for the early hours the next day. It was a pro-Saddam place, dubbed 'Millionaire's Row' by the intelligence officers who'd been building up files on it. It was thought to be housing some of the insurgents who were rocketing Camp Dogwood from up to eight miles away. The operation was code-named *Tobruk* – if the Americans had been planning it, doubtless they would have called it *Hell On Earth*, or *Endless Fury*, or some other adolescent, video game title. There was an intense atmosphere as Col Cowan addressed his men, who would in turn brief their subordinates. Using a huge map, he explained that an assault force of Warriors would pile out of Dogwood under the cover of night and stand guard as engineers threw a bridge over a tributary of the Euphrates which stood in the way of the target village. Once the bridge was secured, the entire force of almost 50 Warriors, Snatch vehicles and troop carriers would cross slowly over the bridge and then accelerate at full speed into the village several miles on. They would secure the main track going through it and dismount men who would launch a lightning assault on each target house, using the 'hard knock' approach and seizing a number of suspected 'players'. This meant driving over the garden wall, smashing down the door and storming into the house throwing flash-bang stun grenades into each room. They were obviously taking this seriously.

'We are here to keep the peace,' said Cowan. 'It would be good if we can catch these people in their beds, with not a single shot fired. We need the element of surprise. This could well be one of the biggest operations we do out here, chaps.'

In the distance, a *boom* sounded… then another, closer still.

Cowan didn't flinch. The booms were drawing nearer and, through the open window, we could see squaddies outside diving to the ground.

A loud *Take cover!* was shouted, as another rocket smashed into the ground inside the perimeter and exploded a hundred yards away.

But Cowan just coughed and looked irritated. 'The members of the press may sit down if they choose,' he said. 'But I am not allowing these bastards to interfere with my damned briefing. The rest of you lads will remain standing.'

It was all so ineffably British; none of us sat down. The shame would have been too much.

Eventually, the attack ended, as did the briefing. The junior officers went off to conduct their sub-briefings and we went to the press tent, David Harrisson and I already working on the line that this was the biggest British assault since the invasion, and payback time for the Black Watch losing men to roadside bombs.

Later, a Sergeant allocated journalists to various Warriors. My crew – call sign Brave Two Zero, believe it or not – would be first in and last out. I walked over to meet them. They were headed by a Lieutenant 'Bad-ass' Baddeley (so-called by the junior soldiers because his vehicle had been so badly shot up in Basra) and his irascible Sergeant, Alex Wilson. The inside of the Warrior was literally dripping in pornography, albeit of a very high standard.

Obviously, I find photographs of naked ladies dreadfully demeaning to women, but I couldn't help glancing at one or two of the images.

'What do you reckon, sir?' asked an 18-year-old Glaswegian, a salacious grin on his face. 'How do you rate our collection?'

I surveyed the impressive display.

'Well, I'd have to give it 7 out of 10,' I said. 'For the artistic photography, of course.'

'Oh, but of course,' said the squaddie, his grin widening. 'And would there be a young lady who might perhaps take sir's particular fancy?'

I thought for a moment or two before indicating that my preference was for the brunette next to the SA80 rifle which was leaning against the door, the muzzle positioned to cause maximum offence. He nodded the nod of an approving connoisseur. 'Aye,' he said, reflectively. 'She's got a cracking jack-and-danny on her. Genuine pornography star that one, sir. Seen her getting it off three guys in one of her best productions. Very good performer. *Excellent* performer, in fact.'

There then ensued a lively debate on which of the girls pictured on the Warrior walls was likely to provide the best 'blow job'. It was ended by Sgt Wilson, who detailed the extremely individual approach to the act of delivering oral sex of the blonde Jenna Jameson. 'Jenna's the girl,' he said. 'And I'll have nae more argument on the subject.'

It seemed like a good moment to bid them *adieu*. I went for a quick evening meal and turned in at about 9pm. After what felt like ten seconds sleep, the 18-year-old Scotsman came to the press tent and tapped my foot to wake me. It was pitch black, very early morning, and we were on the move.

I grabbed my bag, my small digital camera and a note book and threw my body armour and helmet on.

'Bloody hell,' I shuddered. 'It's cold.'

'Cold?' muttered the squaddie. 'It's bloody Baltic.'

As we approached the Warriors, it seemed as though the whole camp was there. Soldiers were cleaning their guns and piling ladders onto the vehicles so they could storm the upper floors of the target houses.

'Morning Mr Hughes,' said Sgt Wilson with a cheery grin. 'Are ye ready to go to war with the devils in skirts?'

This was what terrified First World War Germans had called The Black Watch when they saw these bagpipe-playing, kilted nutcases steaming into their front lines screaming and waving bloodied bayonets. I clambered aboard and took my place next to the cage – an iron mesh box which stops the revolving turret next to you from taking your arm off as it swivels under hydraulic power. With everyone inside, we sat in the near-dark, the only light a small red bulb on one side which cast a dim glow over the young soldiers and their paper ladies. We waited, engine idling, for about an hour, and I felt my nerves building. The insurgents had weapons that could penetrate even this armour and the thought of crossing that bridge was nagging away at me; a few months earlier, a Warrior crew had drowned when their vehicle had toppled off a bridge into a river. I had no idea how to get out of this thing if that happened. Then the driver increased the revs and we lurched forward, slowly trundling towards the start point for the attack. The 'go' signal came over the radio net and Sgt Wilson let out a blood-curdling scream. 'Let the devils in skirts get into 'em lads!' he yelled. 'Come on, the devils in skirts!' Then he switched on a Tannoy which belted out the stirring sound of the Black Watch favourite *Twa Recruiting Sergeants* and then *Scotland The Brave*.

At that instant, the driver gunned the engine and we screamed at 40mph towards the village, without stopping. We belted through the Iraqi countryside for an age before coming to a halt. The turret was swinging left to right and I could hear the bangs of the stun grenades as 'hard knock' teams battered their way into houses outside. Our Warrior was tasked with guarding the far end of the village. Sgt Wilson shouted at the two 'dismounts' to get ready and, pressing the switch that opened the rear door, ordered them out.

A dim, bluey-grey light flooded in as the pair leapt to the ground and took up firing positions. It was dawn, and I could see we were in a leafy, one-road village, the houses set back 100ft off the main drag. All along the half-mile road, stun grenades were still going off and I could see men and boys in their teens, handcuffed, being run along the road to waiting detainment vehicles.

I climbed out, gingerly, keeping my head down. Nearby, a group of balaclava-wearing Iraqi Special Forces men stood, waiting for orders. They looked like hard bastards. One of them nodded a hello. 'Very bad place, mister,' he said. 'Very bad place.'

They weren't needed. In four hours, about 100 men were arrested and not a shot fired. It was a classic example of how to take prisoners in an urban environment with the minimum of fuss, and it was a very impressive operation. I wondered how the US Marines would have handled it. Back at Dogwood, I filed my story – it made a spread under the headline 'Early Ba'ath' – and moved aside to let someone else use the satellite link. I felt drained and tired, the adrenalin of the day ebbing away, and I stood outside, leaning on some sandbags and staring into the nothingness of the desert. I'd grown to love the emptiness, the lack of man-made angles and the solitude. I was getting all quietly deep when one of the officers, Major Charlie Mayo, wandered over to me.

'I say, Chris,' he said, plummily. 'I understand you're something of an angler? Coarse, I suppose?'

I don't know if I was being paranoid about my northern roots, but I thought I detected something of a sneer. Coarse fishing is at the poor man's end of the fishing spectrum, blokes sat by the sides of drizzly canals hoping to catch a perch or carp, and this ex-public schoolboy was clearly making some sort of point.

'Well,' I said, 'I've done a bit of coarse fishing but mostly these days I fish for trout with a fly.'

He raised his eyebrows, suddenly impressed. 'Fly, eh? A gentleman angler, no less. You must come down to the estate I use… excellent trout fishing.'

'Thanks,' I said. 'Actually, Robbo and I were thinking of meeting up and doing a bit down in Wiltshire.'

He snorted at the mention of the Geordie sergeant. I got the idea he didn't think it was on to mix with the ranks. Then a slow grin came over his face. 'Do you know,' he said, 'I really think you ought to have joined the Army yourself when you were younger.' He paused, then delivered the punchline. 'Lance Corporal Hughes has rather a ring to it.'

'Fuck off, mate,' I said, rising to the bait like a particularly stupid trout on one of my own badly-tied flies. 'I'm probably better educated than you. I just never really fancied the idea of wearing a uniform and spending too much time getting covered in muck with other men, thanks.'

He laughed and then walked away, still chuckling; his wind-up had worked a treat.

(I hadn't warmed to him but he turned out to be a good guy. Another journalist, for reasons best known to himself, later told senior officers back in London that I had stolen a Land Rover and tried to take pictures of Iraqi detainees in the camp. The MoD called Dogwood with instructions that I was to be sent home forthwith if this was true. My plummy officer mate vouched for me, saying the whole thing was ridiculous, and the matter was dropped. I was innocent, by the way.)

We spent the next couple of days and nights out on patrol, sleeping under the stars.

Even colder, even more tired, all my energy gone, I couldn't wait to get home.

2005

Democracy

It's a funny old game, democracy.

George Bush and Tony Blair are mad on the stuff, always banging on about taking it to foreign countries and giving it to them, like medicine, whether they want it or not.

This is the same George Bush, of course, who got himself elected by the grace of a few hanging chads (whatever they are) and dodgy recounts, and who's currently so unpopular that he'd struggle to win a game of solitaire. And it's the same Tony Blair who was returned as Prime Minister in 2005 with less than a quarter of those eligible to vote actually voting for him, and who can't get education reforms through the House of Commons because even his own MPs hate him.

Actually, nearly everyone in the country hates him, and you can say the same for Bush in the States. And absolutely everyone hates them both in the Middle East (or the Muslim part of it, at least).

But with heroic disregard for their own unpopularity – or tremendous hubris, take your pick – these two great men vowed in early 2005 to bring democracy to Iraq.

Would this great crusade – I use the word advisedly – work? From what I'd seen of Iraq, I had my doubts, as did millions of others.

In advanced, first world countries like Britain and the USA, where the executive can be held to account by the courts, where people know they'll get another crack at voting these idiots out in a few years' time, and there's a proper system of law and order to keep everyone quiet until then, democracy works. I don't mean it works as in, your views get heard by the politicians and they do as we, the people, say. I'm not that stupid. But it works as the least-worst method of controlling the people and doing stuff on a just-about nationally-agreed basis.

Iraq is very different.

Firstly, there's the question of whether democracy is truly exportable and whether, just because it works reasonably well for people like us, it will work for Iraqis. What if they're really happy with autocracy? What if they like tribal rule? What if they like theocratic rule by hard-core mullahs? From my decadent western perspective, I might think they're mad, and I might be quite unable to understand why our one-person, one-vote-if-you-want system of government, imperfect as it is, isn't the only serious game in town. But to a large number of Iraqis, maybe that sounds mad.

Secondly, even if they like the idea in theory, what about the practice? The tribal antipathies and religious hatreds out there make even our Catholic-Protestant conflicts in Northern Ireland look small-time. If we can't get our own Irish nationalists and unionists to (genuinely) put down their guns and work together in parliament, when we've spent billions trying to make it happen, what hope do we have thousands of miles away? With elections on the way, we were about to find out. All the predictions were that the majority Shia population and the Kurds might take part, since they had the most to gain, and the minority Sunnis would not.

Even if we could get a decent number of them to take part, what about the terrorists? Many males over the age of 12 have an AK47, some have an RPG launcher and none of them wants to be told what to do or how to behave by Blair and Bush. A reasonable percentage of them are prepared to kill people, in brutal and bloody ways, to stop it happening.

Of course, it's all a bit like the old Irish joke, where someone asks an old fella how to get to Limerick and he says, *Well, I wouldn't start from here.*

Having overthrown Saddam and seen the country nosedive into murderous chaos, Bush and Blair had no alternative but to play the democracy card.

I hoped they could pull it off. But I wasn't betting much on it.

The timetable involved three dates: January 30, 2005, when the Iraqi people would choose temporary representatives for the newly-formed Transitional National Assembly; October 15, when they would ratify the constitution of Iraq; and December 15, when a general election was scheduled to elect a permanent Iraqi National Assembly.

Tabloids like wars (from a news point of view) because they offer black and white issues in vivid colour: it's us against them, with a backdrop of red-gold explosions, body counts and hardware. They don't normally like foreign elections, for the same reasons. Where's the drama? Where's the colour? What's it matter to us? But we couldn't ignore these ones.

Early in January, I began quietly lobbying the Ministry of Defence to get an embed as far north as possible, on the basis that any trouble was likely to happen in the Sunni heartlands. At the same time, I was trying, pathetically, to throw other journalists off the scent. I bumped into *The Sun*'s Tom Newton-Dunn at a Ministry of Defence press conference.

'You going to the elections, mate?' I said, half-heartedly.

'Nah, not bothering,' said Tom. 'The office doesn't give a stuff. It's not like it's going to make the paper. You?'

'Don't think we'll bother either,' I replied. 'News desk doesn't seem to be all that arsed about it.'

Of course, when the embed came through – for Camp Abu Naji, from where we'd cover the elections in Al Amarah – and *Daily Mirror* photographer James Vellacott and I arrived at RAF Brize Norton for our military flight to Basra, there was Newton-Dunn. We both pretended it was all down to a last minute change of mind by our offices.

Nothing's ever simple in Iraq, and the local bureaucrats were developing an impressive love of red-tape. If we wanted to cover the elections, we were going to need press passes. But these couldn't be handed out in Basra, oh, no. Instead, we were herded onto a British Special Forces Hercules C-130 troop carrier to Baghdad airport, and changed to a Blackhawk for a 10-minute hop across the city to the Green Zone, just to pick up those bloody passes. I couldn't help reflecting on the madness of this as I queued for hours, the atmosphere piano-wire tense, with the booming sound of distant bombs and the crack-crack of closer small arms fire filling the near-silence. This had been a totally unnecessary journey which could easily have cost us our lives and might still do that on the way back. (The point was made for me a few days later, just as the polls were closing, when the same

Hercules flight was brought down by a missile attack, killing 10 servicemen including SAS troopers.)

The tension was broken, slightly, when a particularly loud explosion close by shook the building and covered us in dust. There were a couple of old buffers from British TV ahead of us in the line. One turned to the other. 'I say, old boy,' he said, in the plummiest voice I've ever heard. 'That was an incy bit fruity.'

We cracked up.

Passes approved and collected, it was back onto the Blackhawks and then onto the Hercules. We stopped at Balad, a joint Special Forces camp from where British SAS and SBS were operating in tandem with US Delta Force and various other outfits, and picked up a pair of suntanned and bearded Brits in jeans, trainers and T-shirts. They sat as far away from us as possible as we headed back to Basra before a final flight to Camp Abu Naji – the most northerly British base for regular troops in what was at that point the most embattled region of UK-controlled Iraq. We belly-flopped lazily onto a dusty landing strip just outside Al Amarah and were run into an armoured convoy of Warriors for the short trip to the camp, a well-rocketed cluster of tents, razor wire and mud-berms buzzed over constantly by spooky drones looking for attackers.

That night, I celebrated my 42nd birthday with a few of the other journalists. We'd all secreted whisky and other spirits in our baggage, despite the stern warnings of the Regimental Sergeant Major, and we glugged them down in a quiet corner of the camp, one eye through the wire in case of attack, me trying to forget the onset of middle-age, my colleagues constantly trying to remind me of it. I'd like to describe it as a happy celebration full of cheerful joshing and witty reminiscence, but it all ended in an ugly row, as it does so often when you put a gang of raging egotists and a couple of pints of Scotch together in the desert. Eventually, some time in the middle of the night, we were all ordered to shut the f*** up and get to f***ing bed by a stern military voice. The Army got their own back by waking us up about two seconds after we had all nodded off and then making us wait for hours before moving out. I don't blame them: there was a real war raging somewhere out there, and they didn't need to be introduced to petty little squabbles between *The Mirror*, *The Sun* and the broadsheets.

As the sun started to come up in the pale blue-grey sky we set off, loaded in to the back of our appointed Snatch wagons, driving towards Al Amarah to watch Iraq respond to the invitation to become democratic, or at least a little bit democratic. To be honest, I expected very little, and with fairly good reason. The local enthusiasm for Iraq's first free elections was being somewhat muted by rebel posters springing up all over the towns and cities, showing a corpse and the words, 'You vote – you die.' Each voter's thumb was to be marked with indelible ink to stop multiple voting; it would also make it easier for these homicidal flyposters to spot the voters.

To combat this, the whole country was being 'locked down'. Car movements were banned, there was a total curfew in every city at night, and around each polling station, three rings of armour and automatic weapons were being installed. The Coalition would create the outer ring, the Iraqi Army the middle one and the Iraqi Police Service would patrol the area around the booth itself. The skies would be buzzing with assault helicopters, unmanned Predator drones and F18 jets to keep the rebel heads down and allow Iraq to go to the polls.

We parked up in our appointed spot as the sun was just poking over the telephone wires and bathing everything in a pinkish-orange glow.

I got out of the Land Rover. There was silence, apart from the low murmur of nearby squaddies and the rasping sound of a plastic bag blowing along the street in the cool, slightly humid breeze. I looked at my watch: it was 7.10am local time, and I had a strange feeling, as though I was about to witness history being made. Despite my habitual cynicism about the West's involvement in Iraq, I wondered whether I was wrong about all of this? Maybe this really was the dawn of a new era?

I squinted down the main drag, south of the town, straining to see if anyone was coming.

And… nothing. The streets were completely empty.

I looked at the other journalists, all peering expectantly down the same highway. Some were on tip-toes, now, craning their necks. Photographers were staring through their long-lenses, even the soldiers were looking around for voters.

Suddenly, one of the snappers put his cameras down on the rail of his Snatch wagon. 'Oh, fuck this,' he said. 'No cunt's turned up. Why did we bother? What a bag of bollocks.' We burst out laughing. Tens of thousands of people, from George Bush down, had put a million hours into planning this one day: forests of ballot papers had been printed in Switzerland, the military had spent tens of millions of pounds on securing the entire country and the entire world was focused on the election, and it had all been boiled down, in one pithy, Fleet Street phrase, to 'a bag of bollocks'. The chuckling was just petering out when there was a cry from a nearby Lance Corporal, staring though binoculars.

'Sir,' he yelled. 'Oh, my God! There's thousands of them. Thousands of them, sir. Tens of thousands.'

He was right: it was like a scene from *Zulu*. A myriad little black dots had appeared on the hillside half a mile away, hordes of people braving the gunmen to vote for the first time. They got closer and closer, marching determinedly, women in black-robed groups, heads covered, the men in robes or trousers and T-shirts stomping along, heads down, hardly speaking and apparently deep in thought. I watched them walking through our ranks, a never-ending stream of people, and it really did move me. Most had come from the south east of Al Amarah, through the marshes towards the Iranian border. Many had walked 20 miles or more, setting off in the night; briefly, I thought of our spoilt-rotten political process back home, where people bragged that they couldn't be bothered to vote. I grabbed a man, and spoke to him through an interpreter. He was Sami Ana, a 30-year-old who had walked 15 miles from the south. 'This is a wonderful day for us,' he said. 'The reason nobody is talking is that we are all thinking about what it all means. I am tired and I am hungry but this will be worth the long wait. I swear if I had one leg I would have made the journey still.'

James and I decided to head down to the polling station in the town, a frightening and potentially dangerous move. We would be leaving the relative safety of the Army line behind; they would be maintaining the outer cordon as per their agreement with the locals. Al Amarah was certain to contain some insurgents, so we would be relying on the Iraqi Army and the Iraqi Police Service to keep us out of harm's way. Given that the IPS was well-known for harbouring insurgents, that wasn't massively reassuring. We'd been given headsets and radios to take with us. 'If you get into serious trouble, press this button,' a young officer had told me. 'We'll come steaming in and try to get you out. But only press it if it's a serious emergency. We're not supposed to be in there.'

Nervously, we walked away past the growing queue of Iraqis, the British troops watching us through binoculars as we passed the Iraqi Army cordon and then walked around a corner through the Iraqi Police Service Cordon. I fingered the button on the radio all the way; I wondered what constituted an emergency.

Arriving at the polling station was like walking into a church: the men and women were solemnly casting their votes before shuffling out of the tiny room and back into the now-blinding sun. We felt tremendously privileged – among the few non-Iraqis allowed there – but also, oddly, as though we were intruding. James grabbed a few atmospheric photos and I interviewed a couple of men briefly, and we left, hurrying back to the protection of the Land Rovers. It all went amazingly quietly, apart from a couple of incidents. A man was shot by some Iraqi Army guards after a pick-up load of men roared past a check point, and a grenade was thrown near a school. As that exploded, our platoon dashed across town to see what was happening, screaming to a halt five minutes later, the troops 'bomb bursting' out of their wagons and taking up defensive firing positions.

Nervously, I followed one of the officers as he strolled down the middle of the road. 'No need to run, Chris,' he said. 'It doesn't appear right for a British officer to run in this area. It looks like we're not in control – OK, old chap? Just walk along with me and we'll see what all this is about.'

I would have laughed at his almost clichéd urbanity if I hadn't been so impressed and, simultaneously, scared.

It turned out to be nothing – the grenade had been chucked against a wall, almost certainly by a rebel trying to get rid of it before going to a checkpoint, as you might drop a can of ale from your pocket before being searched by the bouncers outside a nightclub. The rebel was long gone and the grenade had caused no real damage. A few locals stood around, and I watched as the British troops approached them politely and explained what they were doing before bidding them good day. It was all very different from the American approach.

As we drove back, we passed Rupert Hamer, a good friend of mine from *The Sunday Mirror*. Rupert was standing on the side of the street interviewing some squaddies. 'I say,' said the officer I was with. 'Isn't that one of your chaps? Looks like he's lost.'

I grinned. Rupert was obviously trying to squirrel away some exclusive that would hold for the following Sunday, a near-thankless task in a war of daily deadlines. I made a mental note to try and fill him with whisky that night and nick the tale off him. (I tried my damnedest but he kept schtum, and produced a great exclusive spread in the following week's *Sunday Mirror* detailing how the IPC were colluding with terrorists to tip them off about British Army patrols).

As soon as we'd got what we needed in Al Amarah we were whisked back to Abu Naji for a Sea King flight to the Queen's Dragoon Guards base close to the Iranian border. The MoD idea was that we'd cover a rural polling station too, to give balance to our pieces. We were up and away almost as soon as we sat down, and roaring east on another high-speed, low-level Alton Towers ride: a single .50 cal gunner pointed his weapon at the ground as the pilot swerved left and right, pitching his machine at seemingly impossible angles and throwing us all over the creaking cabin. James, held in by one strap, was loving every minute, hanging half out of the helicopter and taking arty aerial photos. I imagined the conversation with the insurance company's investigators, back at Canary Wharf: 'Well, he just sort of fell out – one minute he was there, and the next he was gone.' But luckily the strap held.

Suddenly, we banked hard, coming down in a fast descent to land a hundred yards from a group of bombed out buildings; I have no idea what this place had done to deserve the kicking it had received, but it must have been one of Saddam's military facilities before the war.

A tough-looking Welsh Sergeant came over as we got out of the chopper.

'Welcome to our humble abode, chaps,' he said. 'We're a bit pushed, so dump your gear in the tent over there and we'll whizz you into town for a look at what's happening.'

I looked around me. I'd been looking forward to this trip, because we were now just south of the point Julian Andrews and I had been trying to reach on our ludicrous day trip to find those caves, when we'd narrowly escaped being car-jacked back in 2003. I'd hoped I'd finally see those caves but, looking around me, I couldn't see anything even resembling one. I couldn't see much of anything, in fact, except shell holes, bomb craters, rubble and a few old armoured personnel carriers, slowly falling apart in the sun, and hundreds of square miles of flat, burnt marshland beyond the usual razor wire fence.

We sped into town, did a few quick pictures in the polling stations and tried to hide our disappointment at the lack of drama. With the butterfly attention spans of tabloid hacks, that sensation of feeling moved at the solemnity of the whole affair had all-but evaporated, and we wanted to file our words and pictures and move on. It was getting late by now, and all the dashing about on helicopters was getting us closer to our deadlines. But the three-hour time difference was a blessing and, as long as I got cracking, I could get my stuff over in time. Back at the camp, I hammered out a thousand words on my laptop – quite good words they were too, if I say so myself – and pressed 'send'. Nothing. Nightmare. The office needed the copy and the satellite link was dead. I had to call the copytakers. These people are a hangover from the days before laptops and email, when we all had to ring in and dictate our stories, taking care to speak slowly and precisely to avoid errors. This is important. A colleague of mine once dictated a story describing a woman as a 'mother of three'; he was disconcerted, to say the least, to see this description appear in the newspaper the next day as 'murderer of three'. I looked at my watch: 45 minutes to deadline. Plenty of time. I collected my thoughts and dialled, reminding myself to keep calm.

The woman I got through to wasn't exactly delighted to speak to me.

'I was just about to finish for the day,' she said. 'I suppose I'll have to stick around, now.' Theatrical sigh. I suppose you will, I thought, but then you could be out here in this dusty shithole surrounded by nutters who want to kill you. 'OK,' she said. 'What's your story about? Iraq, is it? That's not very interesting, is it? I've just taken one about Posh Spice. Now that was interesting.'

'Right,' I said. 'Whatever. Er. OK. Ready? Right.' I gathered myself, and starting dictating. 'They came in their tens of thousands yesterday…'

'Sorry love,' she said. 'I can't hear a word you're saying. Did you say something about people in tents and sandals?'

'No. They came in their tens of thousands...'

'Sorry, love. Who did? Have I missed something?'

'The Iraqis did.'

'Well, don't you want to say that first?'

'Well, that'll become clear later.'

'Sorry, love, I can't hear you. It's a very bad line. You must be in a dreadful area.' (Then, to her colleague, 'I can't hear a word he's saying, he must be in a shit area.')

'It is a shit, area, yes. Can we get on with the copy?' Shouting by now, just to try and make myself heard.

We carried on like this for three quarters of an hour, me painstakingly spelling every name three times and hoping and praying that she wasn't mangling my copy too badly.

Eventually we waded through it and she had the good grace to pass the words on to the news desk while I returned to my shit area. It can't be easy being on their end of conversations like this: the only calls you're going to get are from reporters who are boiling with frustration because their computer has just gone on the blink.

Ten minutes later, the desk rang.

'That's great stuff, Chris, thanks. It's a quiet news day back here so Richard will be pleased with that.'

'Great,' I said. 'It was actually quite amazing this morning. All those people.'

'Yeh? Whatever. Hey, listen. Did you fly up from Basra in a Special Forces Hercules?'

'Yes. Why?'

'It was shot down late last night. Missile strike. Ten dead. Can you get us anything on it?'

'I'll give it a go.'

Click.

The answer, actually, was no. I was only 100 miles away from the smoking remains of the chopper but I might as well have been 100,000 miles away. They had more chance of getting information in London than I did, out here in this desolate nowhere with a dodgy laptop and a knackered satellite phone. Still, I rang the MoD and got what details they could give me – ridiculous really, the office is only a couple of miles from Whitehall, as the crow flies, and a call from there would have cost about 10p.

And that was that.

We'd seen Iraq wake up to its brave new dawn. As had been widely predicted, the two parties supported by the majority Shia community won a majority of seats and the Kurds were also strongly represented. Parties representing the Sunni Arab community effectively boycotted the elections. It had all passed off relatively peacefully. There were 44 reported deaths around polling stations in at least nine separate attacks on election day, which was way better than it might have been (although others surely died on their way to and from voting and the actual death toll was certainly higher). Voter turnout ranged from 89% in Kurdish areas to 2% in the Sunni region of Anbar, home to the rebel towns of Fallujah and Ramadi, whose low turnout was predictable. With a total of some 8.4 million votes cast, a 58% turnout, the Iraqi Electoral Commission hailed the day as a success, as did George Bush and Tony Blair.

Off the record, British officers back in Basra were less optimistic, predicting an escalation in sectarian violence during the summer, and they were right. Thankfully, I spent most of the rest of the year sitting at my desk in Canary Wharf and drinking beer in Fulham, where the insurgency was slightly lower key. I did go back for the October ratification of the constitution, but it was an uneventful week, mostly spent in the back of a Chinook as the Army carried out 'Eagle VCPs' – aerial car checkpoints, where they would swoop down and offload 40 soldiers to intercept suspicious vehicles. I'd had high hopes for this trip but it produced very little in the paper. The most exciting moment came when I woke one night to find my good friend Christian Fraser, then BBC Radio Five Live's man on the front line, rolling around on the floor shouting his head off.

I peered down and saw him wedged between two bunks, almost completely strait-jacketed inside his flack jacket and wriggling like mad. I couldn't work out whether he was trying to get into it or out of it.

'What the bloody hell are you doing?' I said.

'It's all going off Hughesy,' he said. 'The alarms, mate... we're being rocketed! It's going off! I think you're supposed to get on the floor. Or something. Fuck it… I think I'm stuck.'

He was obviously dreaming. 'Fraser, you daft sod,' I said. 'It's not going off at all… it's all quiet. There was a couple of those flaming drones taking off, that's all.'

Eventually, he calmed down and, with the help of a few other reporters, I managed to get him back out of his Kevlar and back into bed.

When something like this happens, you have to tread very carefully around the guy; he's going to be embarrassed enough, so the last thing he needs is people taking the mickey. You need to leave it alone for a while. We waited until around ten seconds after he woke up before giving it to him with both barrels. Poor guy, he had no memory of what had happened at all.

My plan, once I got back, was to try to get out to Fallujah for the December elections proper. The Americans claimed the place was 'peaceful' now. I wanted to see that for myself, and I wanted to see how the city had changed since the 2003 incident.

* * * * *

December came, and I managed to get myself a place in Fallujah with the Yanks and a few other British hacks. After the now familiar spiral dive to Baghdad airport, we were flown out to the rebel city in the west, in another careering, swooping, speeding Blackhawk.

We landed on a dusty landing zone by the side of the huge Marine camp from where members of the Regimental Combat Team were dispatched on daily patrols, forming a ring of M16s and armour around Fallujah along with the Iraqi Army and Police.

The place was besieged, a modern-day Stalingrad with dust for snow: no-one went in or came out unless they had the right credentials.

A Major strode over to us as the Blackhawk lifted off.

'OK, listen up,' he said. 'In a short while, we're gonna load up into these armoured personnel carriers and go into Fallujah to our camp there. You will need your body armour and helmets on. If we come under attack, do not move. Stay low at all times. Leave it to us.'

I looked at the gaggle of Marines who would be accompanying us. They looked filthy, worn out and vacant with tiredness. They also looked about 12 years old.

'This trip will take us along the most dangerous roads in the world,' said the Major. 'Fallujah is Guerrilla Central, the most dangerous city on earth, and the camp we are headed for is rocketed every day and every night. Your lives are in danger if you do not follow instructions.'

He walked away, barking orders at his soldiers and we stood around, waiting. An hour or so later we were in the armoured vehicles and trundling through the desert on the half hour ride to the outskirts of the city. As it came into view, my jaw fell open. The place had changed out of all recognition since I'd last seen it. Houses and shops and many of the mosques for which it was famed had been smashed to bits. Half of its 350,000 inhabitants were dead or gone: where before it had been alive with people, now it was a ghost town, but a ghost town filled with the constant, percussive sound of small arms fire and occasional explosions. I saw no-one but a few women and old men hanging around a raggedy-looking market-place. They looked only briefly at our convoy before looking away and hurrying along, head down, about their business.

I couldn't get my bearings. As we roared down the main drag, passing empty side streets full of burnt-out cars, I thought I recognised the place where I'd seen those young men shot dead on that awful day, but I couldn't be sure.

Hearts and minds, George Bush had said. Hearts and minds? It was nothing but a sick joke.

A mile into the city, we turned off the road and into a maze of concrete blast walls that led to the heart of the camp, a steel and concrete fortress for a hard-core unit of the Regimental Combat Team. Inside, we got out and hurried to a former gym, our dormitory for the next couple of nights. As we stowed our bags next to the bunks, a couple of officers came in and started briefing us to within an inch of our lives about how much work had been done to reconstruct Fallujah.

'Yes,' I wanted to say. 'But it didn't need reconstructing till you lot got here.'

'One final thing,' said one of them. 'You're in a lot of danger here. The toilet facilities are 20 metres outside and in sniper range from the apartment buildings across the way. We've had them take shots at people so if you want to leave this building please sign out, keep your head down and run. Sign back in where you return.'

There was an uncomfortable silence and then people started working on their pre-election pieces. I wandered off for a smoke in an uncovered area outside – though out of the view of the gunmen in the flats – and bumped into a US Marine who was loitering there.

He offered me a light for my cigarette. 'This your first time in Aye-Rak?' he asked.

'No, I've been here a dozen or so times,' I said.

'OK,' he said. 'First time in Fallujah?'

'No, I was here in 2003.'

'Uh-huh. Ever been shot at?'

'I don't know,' I said. 'Maybe. I've had bullets come very near but I can't say whether they were aiming at me.'

'Blown up?'

'No,' I said.

He grinned. 'Well, that's not a whole bunch of fun.'

'Where you from?' I asked.

'Bakersfield,' he said. 'In California. Hope I get back there one day.'

He looked suddenly very scared and very young.

Nearby, another young Marine climbed a ladder for a stint doing roof-cover. Below him, a beautiful, black girl soldier struggled to pass up a huge .50 calibre machine gun on a tripod. He hauled it from her and disappeared over the ledge and out of sight.

'Be careful, Tony,' shouted the girl. 'I don't want you to get hurt. Be careful while you're up there.'

There was no answer.

She turned and saw me watching and her expression of concern slipped into a glare.

I smiled. 'Hi,' I said.

'Whatever,' she snapped, before disappearing back inside.

I looked at the kid from Bakersfield. 'Sorry about that, man,' he said. 'I don't think she meant to be rude. Lot of pressure out here. Lot of pressure.'

Nearby, another exhausted Marine sat on the ground, his head in his hands, not talking to anyone.

They were gung-ho, some of them, and their leaders – from Bush down to the senior officers on the ground here – were making plenty of mistakes. But these were just young soldiers who were going out on patrol and killing people, every day. They were being killed, too. The horrors they must have witnessed seemed to be taking their toll.

We went inside for more briefings about the elections, again with the rattle of small arms fire in the background. It intensified after dark, and came closer, but I managed, somehow, to get to sleep. In the morning, I opted to be one of the first out into Fallujah to visit two of the city's polling stations.

We pulled out in a convoy of Humvees, and I saw Fallujah out of the back. The streets seemed a little busier than they had the previous day but the atmosphere was very tense. At the voting halls, the same security arrangements were in place as had been the case further east in the spring: Coalition troops manning the outer ring, with the Iraqi Army and then the Iraqi Police Service inside. I left my Humvee and walked the 400 yards down to the door, past the hostile queue of Fallujans, my guts churning with fear and adrenalin. I was told to remove my body armour and leave my mobile phone at the entrance. Inside, I spoke to three men in their early twenties.

'Do you remember the shooting of the students?' I asked.

'Yes, yes,' they answered.

'Did that make you angry? Did it make the city rise up?'

Again, they nodded their heads.

'Have you been involved in the uprising?'

A stupid question, in retrospect. They looked sheepish and shook their heads slowly. That was the end of that conversation.

In the corner of the room a group of Iraqi men was glaring at me. It felt like a good time to leave.

At the second station, the Iraqi police were wearing balaclavas, as this area of Fallujah was believed to be particularly dangerous. Here, the insurgents were more forthcoming. A fat, scruffily-dressed man approached me, prodding me in the chest threateningly.

'George Bush, Tony Blair very bad,' he said. 'Saddam good.'

Then he pointed his thumb at his own chest, indicating he was talking about himself. He then raised his right hand level with his shoulder, miming the motion of aiming a rocket-propelled grenade then said, 'American, British, Shia… booom, booom.'

He paused and looked me up and down. 'Give me your watch,' he said, smiling menacingly.

I backed away, shaking my head, and got out, leaving him behind, cackling.

I hurried back to the relative safety of the US troops, the irony – that I had come to despise what they were doing but still sought their protection – once again not lost on me. A couple of hours after we'd arrived, we were out of there, the scowls and gestures of a subjugated, but defiant, people sending us on our way.

Had the elections been a success?

Well, locally, even in the Sunni heartlands, almost 45 per cent of those registered to vote had turned up; they were terrified of being marginalised by a Shia-led government.

Maybe there is some small hope that, one day, Iraq will embrace democracy. Maybe this was the first step on a long road.

But at what cost, and how long will it take?

2006

In The Green Zone

I've been to Iraq a dozen or so times now, and I've watched it slide from a reasonably safe, ordered country into a murderous bearpit of savage infighting and bestial cruelty.

I'm not saying it was wrong to oust Saddam Hussein. Plenty of people died in his torture chambers, and I witnessed the grief of some of their relatives when the mass grave was uncovered near Abu Ghraib.

But the way in which the White House – and, to a lesser extent, Downing Street – has allowed the country to slip into chaos and horror is evidence of an almost criminal incompetence of the highest kind.

I don't know what I'd have done differently. I'm sure it's very hard to plan for creating a new civil society from the ashes of a ruling junta which you have just smashed. But then, it's not my job to rebuild societies because I don't go around destroying the juntas in the first place. With the power to invade Iraq and remove its leaders came the responsibility to ensure basic standards of law and order prevailed – to make sure, for God's sake, that there was plenty of clean water available, and a regular electricity supply.

In that, George Bush and Tony Blair have failed, completely. Worse still are their regular assertions that all is well, and that the end, however far away and however uncertain, is justifying these appalling means.

How many people must die – at the rate of thousands a month – before they apologise and admit their errors? How many minibuses of workers, schoolchildren and funeral mourners must be machine-gunned in broad daylight? How many men, women and children have to be tortured to death with power drills, or shot in the street, or kidnapped and strangled?

During my time in Iraq, I've gradually begun to side with the Iraqi people. Not the killers, or the car-jackers, or the looters, but the ordinary Iraqis, who just want life to return to some kind of normality. That's the thing about actually being there: you see things as they see them. Until you've actually seen how they're forced to live under the fist of their American occupiers, you can't understand. Until you've had to step back sharply to avoid a 30 tonne armoured vehicle which suddenly appears and roars down your narrow street, and you've seen the look of fear on the faces of mothers rushing to gather up their children, and you've choked alongside them on the dust and the diesel fumes, you can't understand it. Until you've had to brake and swerve to a halt in your car, and watch a column of sand-coloured tanks and trucks, topped by unsmiling men aiming machine guns in every direction, cut straight through the traffic, you can't understand it. Until you've seen wide-eyed Iraqi men manhandled by screaming Marines, threatened, sworn at and punched to the ground, and watched frightened women pushed aside, children knocked to the ground, and seen wrecked shops, houses and even mosques, you can't understand it.

The Americans have been heavily criticised for the way they have behaved in Iraq and, from what I have seen, many of them have deserved every last cough and spit of the invective poured on them, and more besides.

Of course, there are plenty of Americans in Iraq, military and otherwise, who are decent men and women doing their best to help the Iraqis rebuild their country. But for all George Bush's talk of winning 'hearts and minds', a significant number of US soldiers on the ground seem little more than gum-chewing grunts with nothing but scorn for the people they have conquered.

The major incidents have made headlines around the world – the massacres in Fallujah and Haditha, the Abu Ghraib disgrace, the rape of a young girl and the murder of her family in the summer of 2006. But dreadful as these (we hope) isolated happenings are, it's the humdrummery, the banal, everyday abuse and the casual contempt that too many American soldiers show the Iraqi population that is truly unforgivable.

That contempt is perhaps best illustrated in Baghdad's Green Zone, a little US oasis of relative calm and safety in the seething, boiling mess of the city. It's a monument to the colossal arrogance and narrow-mindedness of the American military, and nowhere shows this better than the PX, the army shop. On my last trip to Iraq, after the elections late last year, I wandered in to this humming, air-conditioned grotto and found, amidst all the war ephemera and American snacks, a selection of t-shirts for the grunts to buy.

'We went to Iraq and we kicked ass', read the slogan on one.

'Who's Your Bagh-daddy?' asked another.

I ask you: what kind of mental incompetent would want to buy that sort of trash? Who would *sell* it? What are they so proud of? Don't they get it? Yes, they'd 'kicked ass', if kicking ass means using superior technology to destroy enemy tanks before you yourself are in any danger, or shooting up God-knows-how-many families in their cars just for daring to drive towards your positions, or hunkering down inside armoured vehicles and concrete barricades while abandoning the people you've 'liberated' to the psychopaths. Way to go, guys! You sure showed them Aye-Rakis!

The Green Zone is crawling with wannabes, REMF soldiers and civilians who buy the kit, get the stamp in their passport and never really see any danger. They'll sit drinking cold beers and eating in the Chinese restaurant or the Pizza Hut, their meal only interrupted by the whump-whump of Blackhawks bringing in the dead and injured grunts from the killing zones around the city. A little work on their thousand yard stare and their war stories, and back home they can pass themselves off as heroes.

Billions of dollars in contracts is being funnelled through this place while outside people are living in terrible fear and squalor.

The aggressive ill-treatment of the few Iraqis allowed inside the Green Zone – mainly menial workers and translators – is sickening, too. On the day I arrived and went to check in at the Al Rasheed hotel, I watched an American soldier approach a local woman. His weapon pointed at her, his face puce with anger, he screamed, 'You! Fucking *you*! You, in the heels and the skirt! Fucking drop the mobile phone on the ground and walk here! Walk to me! Fucking *walk* to me! *You fucking walk to me!*'

He was utterly out of his depth, and almost out of control, and he was holding a Minimi gun, which fires 700 rounds a minute and can cut a man in half.

The woman looked terrified and bewildered, and she started to cry.

Her crime? Using that mobile. It was one of the ways insurgents used to set bombs off, so I was not without sympathy for the soldier's reaction. But the nearest sign forbidding the use of phones *was in English*. Is it just me, or is that the most bone-headedly stupid thing you've ever heard?

I'd come full circle here. Years earlier, I'd met Tariq Aziz at the conference centre opposite the Al Rasheed, and I'd stayed in the hotel before the war. Then, this woman would have been terrified of the Mukhabarat. Now it was the Marines.

I've not been back to Iraq since then. The story has moved on, to Afghanistan, where British soldiers are fighting and dying in the hills. I've been out there – where the professionalism of our troops is still highly impressive – and to Beirut, when Israel invaded in the late summer of 2006.

I'm still not an expert on the Middle East. But then, who is?

My mind goes back to graffiti scrawled by an American soldier inside the toilets at Camp Fallujah: *Fighting for freedom is like fucking for virginity*.

I think we're in for a very long haul.

Postscript

I've not seen Nibras since he told me about the death of his daughter. A few weeks after that, his Thuraya satellite phone stopped working and I have been unable to contact him. I hope he's still alive, and that we'll meet again one day.

I'd not seen Adil since Julian and I left Baghdad after the attempted car-jacking a couple of years ago. As I wrote this book, I needed to check a few facts and tally up stories. I tried to contact him via friends working in the Green Zone – where he'd last been seen – but no-one knew where he was or what had happened to him. From being a familiar sight to Western journalists, he'd seemingly disappeared. As security in Baghdad deteriorated ever further, I began to fear the worst.

Then, a few weeks ago, I got this email:

> *Hi brother !!!!!!!!!!!!*
> *it's me Adil ,how r u ' Iam good my family is allright Iam still working as supervisor of a group of mechanics!!!!! hope one day I could see you ' how is Jolian are you still in contact with him !! where are you right now are you still in Daily Merror, Tell me ? Are you still following Iraq news !! it's bad !!haaa it's not as you left it ' we are knoking the door of the civil war ' but there is still a hope to avoid it wiht united covernment !! please be in touch !!!*

It was great to hear from him. And interesting, too, to see his spin-free assessment of the situation in his country. George Bush and Tony Blair may deny it, but Iraq *is* very close to civil war now. That's the truth, from the man on the street in Baghdad, the Iraqi Everyman. Adil is a man who walks every day from his humble home to his humble job, through streets often stained with those tell-tale remnants of suicide bombings, the chewing gum gobbets of flesh. He lives with the sound of gunfire ringing in his ears, and he lives and breathes the stench of anarchy.

But as with many people I have met there, despite the hell that their lives have become, Adil still clings to the hope that Iraq has a better future.

I hope he's right.